# MYSTICAL KISS
# OF GOD

"I know that Cosme's healing work was instrumental in accelerating the healing of my ankle, the post-traumatic stress disorder and the myriad of post-transplant symptoms.... In the year that has passed since this experience, I realize that it has sustained me, healed me, brought peace into my soul, and restored what I thought was an absolute loss of hope. I am so grateful to Cosme for sharing the gift of his healing hands and his love with me. "

—Christine Fischer

When Cosme massaged me, ... he saw the six-inch scar on my belly, and I told him that I had my gallbladder removed when I was only seventeen.... Cosme spent the next thirty minutes pushing and prodding at my stomach. He let me know that there was still a hole where the gallbladder once was and that he needed to move things around, that were frozen in place from the shock of the surgery.... When he was finished, I stood up, looked at my stomach and saw that it had changed. My belly had shrunk by at least one inch. I had my gallbladder out some fifteen years earlier, suffered IBS, and after this massage it was gone. Two years later there is still no sign of discomfort or pain in my belly. I've never felt better!...

Cosme did not "save" anyone, but he did help John to save himself. Cosme helped John to get over a twenty-year addiction to a very powerful and readily available drug. John and I work in Hollywood and "anything goes" in Hollywood! Now we have the energy, self-awareness and power to realize that even in Hollywood, with all its party atmosphere, and "go, go, go at any cost," we have the ability to live our own lives in our own way.

—Mary (anon.)

Thank you. I feel better than I have for years, physically, and I am filled with resolution, confidence, and I am so close to my spiritual self again, at last.

—Toni Lynd

Throughout history and in every culture on earth, there have been individuals endowed with the special gift of healing and spiritual insights. This is always the hero's journey of great challenges and even greater accomplishments illustrated in this recounting of Reverend Cosme's teachings and compassionate healing practices to which he has dedicated himself for over forty years. His still unfolding odyssey is abundant with insights and inspiration to all who will be touched by this book.

—Dr Kenneth R. Pelletier, Clinical Professor of Medicine, Author, *The Best Alternative Medicine: What Works? What Does Not?*

Cosme brings to us a practical mysticism for today. He has entered the ancient wisdom, through direct experience, to retrieve the essence which he offers to us simply, openly, and freely. Anyone on a spiritual path might well pay close attention to the information in this book ... it leads to wisdom!

—Stan Padilla, Native American Artist, Educator and Cultural Activist

He talked to me and got to know me, before proceeding to the actual healing.... [H]e was able to "see" and report energy imbalances, to analyze specific health problems, and to give me specific remedies to correct everything that was "out of alignment," in all realms. He "read" my hands, my feet, and my body with prophetic insight and accuracy.

—Ava Goldman

Cosme [was] ... recommended ... to me for my younger daughter who has suffered from acute asthma since birth. Nicole's first healing from Cosme brought excellent results... As to this date, approximately one year later, Nicole has had freedom from asthma for the first time in her life.

—Jane Steinberg

Cosme is like a master gardener and you are the garden. He evaluates you and then cultivates and plants special items in your life for you to harvest. Essentially, he helps you garden your life.

—Michelle Shafer

To make a long story short, with a combination of Cosme's healing work, fasting and prayer, my cyst shrank dramatically. After seven days I called my doctor (who had been worried about my condition) and requested another sonogram. I told him I thought the cyst was gone, but if medical evidence showed otherwise, I would go ahead with the exploratory surgery. The sonogram showed the cyst had literally disappeared. The doctor was amazed and I was convinced that I could take part in my health and healing in a more active manner.

—BettyKay Basso

# THE MYSTICAL KISS OF GOD

*The Stories and Teachings of an Hawai'ian Healer*

COSME CASTANIETO

Disclaimer: Any health and healing examples or suggestions given in this book should never be substituted for the advice and recommendations given by your medical doctor.

Published by Castanieto Enterprises, Nevada City, CA

ISBN -10: 0-9794126-0-9
ISBN -13: 978-0-9794126-0-8

Library of Congress Copyright TX6-559-721 2007

Cover photo: Iguazu Falls in South America,
    by Cherylann Castanieto
Author photo: Suzy Bayne

Second printing 2007

Printed in the United States of America

10   9   8   7   6   5   4   3   2   1

# Dedication

To God, who created
this whole universe...
with Love

including we the humans...
the animals, the rocks, the birds, the
plants and trees, the bees and the beautiful
butterflies and flowers
All of us who are here on Earth together,
helping each other and co-creating with
LOVE
and our mystical connection
to each other

and to the masters
prophets, angels and nature spirits
who have given us guidelines and blessings
for living a healthy, wholesome and happy life
here on earth.

Cosme Castanieto

# Table of Contents

# Foreword

Cosme Castanieto is truly a most extraordinary human being, healer, and friend. He was born and raised in Hawai'i of Filipino descent, and comes from a family lineage of spiritual healers. Extensively trained and initiated by some of the most famous healers in the Philippines, he rediscovered the healing knowledge of his ancestors. But always in search of broadening and deepening his gifts, Cosme continued his quest for knowledge and learning, which has taken him to many places in the world. Cosme, also known as "the happy Hawai'ian," has had a busy schedule of healings, lectures and classes for more than forty years.

*The Mystical Kiss of God* is the story of this spiritual healer. The story unfolds to share Cosme's early influences in Hawai'i, his mystical visions and guidance, and his training, both on the inner and outer levels. There are many stories of outstanding healings. Cosme's secrets of longevity and rejuvenation, and co-creating with God, give us the same opportunity to have the same incredible health, youth and energy that Cosme radiates.

Through Cosme's eyes, we are given an inside view of how a spiritual healer sees and feels. We learn why so many prayers are not answered and how we can change that. He compassionately addresses alcohol and drug addiction and gives new hope and insight for those who are following this path. He describes in great detail how he sees the body's energy with his spiritual gifts. Myriad practical and inspirational teachings and discussions of healing case histories give us valuable information for helping ourselves and others. There are many exercises and practices for accelerating our own spiritual intuition and evolution, which can help us reach our highest potential.

Cosme was ordained as a minister and is the co-founder of Universal Cosara Temples. Being a certified massage therapist and having extensive training in many healing modalities, Cosme is gifted in reading the body. After he reads the body, he works on the body with a unique type of massage, energy and body work set to music. His highly developed spiritual energy comes through his hands and emanates from his whole being. Cosme scans the whole body, with all his senses, both ordinary and extrasensory, and then identifies the imbalances and blockages. He uses a combination of music, massage and body alignment, observing and adjusting the energy flows all through the healing session. The patient's cells and organs are infused with healing energy and the person is brought back into balance. The even flow of energy that is created during the treatment, circulates in the body and energy field, accelerating the healing process.

Cosme says, "Everything has to be done with love. You are the kings and queens of your castle, and the parts of the body are the servants. You are also the music director of your body. Each organ is an instrument in the orchestra. We have the ability to co-create with God because our souls are a part of God. We can re-create and rejuvenate our body! We can re-create our life!"

Cosme believes that the soul of the person and God need to be united in the heart. Cosme says, "Often, they're not, and the person's life and health is messed up." After helping a person unify their soul and God within the heart, Cosme often sees miraculous results in the person's health and life. When this union takes place, Cosme calls it "the kiss of God." After this union the person begins to feel, speak and emanate love, beauty, authority, truth, illumination, light and warmth. This sacred union is a kind of spiritually activated electrical circuit that illuminates when the positive and negative poles come together.

I met Cosme twenty-eight years ago at a spiritual gathering at Mother Mary's Garden in Grass Valley, California. He doesn't look much older now than he did then. Of all the people at this spiritual gathering, Cosme attracted my attention the most. His radiant smile and hearty laugh had a musical quality ... like little bells ringing. I guessed by his tan face and black hair that he might be from some other culture. With him were two women, who carried a kind and serene energy. I found out later that these two women were healers who worked with him ... Bea and Clara.

Ida and Sam Partridge were hosting the event and they were proudly inviting the guests to visit the interiors of the room-sized pyramids that they had just finished constructing. These meditation pyramids were proportioned like the Egyptian pyramids at Gizah. Their exteriors were covered with glistening quartz crystals.

Cosme invited me to step into one of them and offered to do a prayer and blessing for my baby daughter and me. When he started to pray, I heard an accent which I couldn't place, and I felt the most amazing warmth of love and peace flowing through me. My baby fell asleep. We stepped out from this energized chamber back into the sunlight and began to talk.

"Where are you from?" I asked. He told me he was born in Hawai'i and spoke Pidgin English. He laughed that tinkling-bell laugh again. His face was clear, and his eyes were bright, deep, and wise—and there was the ever-present smile—as open and trusting as a young child.

We talked about his healing work. He had been in Vietnam during the war, as a photographer. While he was there, Jesus and Mother Mary appeared to him in visions. There had been ancestral lines of healers on both sides of Cosme's family which stopped when his parents were unable to continue it. But it was apparent that God had entrusted Cosme with a special gift. Because of the break in the lineage, Cosme had to rediscover it himself. He had to find and create his own training. As a result of this quest he has turned out to be a totally unique, one-of-a-kind healer and spiritual teacher. The word Cosme likes is "universal."

Before long the three healers came to visit us on a cold and windy day. We set up a makeshift clinic in one of our bedrooms. I made phone calls to let friends and neighbors know that they were doing healings. The news traveled by "word of mouth" too, and soon our living room was filled with people. Whether there was a need for physical healing or not, everyone got a great "tune up" and left feeling open, clear, and filled with light.

The people who had illnesses and physical problems all came out feeling much better. Some were completely healed. What impressed me the most was the change in the faces and postures. Grey, colorless, or drawn faces came out looking pink, radiant and youthful-looking. The sparkle of life and hope was back in their eyes. There was a lightness in their step. They stood up straighter and wore a smile on their face. Because I was the hostess, I was able to observe this with the many people who came and went during all the visits.

Before long, Cosme and Clara purchased a beautiful healing center a few miles outside of Nevada City, California, with a small group of their spiritual friends. We were so happy to have them settle in our community, just three miles down the road. People could now visit "Cosara" for healings, spiritual teachings and training in the healing arts. Everyone on the property cared for the land and practiced healing. During those early years Cosme developed the "Spiritual Process." This is a guided healing and clearing journey through one's own inner space, a process which takes from one-to-two days to complete. Cosme and several other people began to "take people through the process." So now "Cosara" had people coming for the process as well as for healings. There were many overnight guests in tents and there were always a lot of people around, including those who had traveled long distances to find healing and transformation.

Memorable healings took place. I can remember Cosme holding hands in a circle with a group of us, leading us in prayer and affirmations. We all saw him turn into a golden Buddha! The energy was transcendent and powerful. This was fascinating because Cosme's orientation is Christian, and Jesus is his healing master. But again, Cosme respects all religions and is a universal being!

Cosme traveled often, "going on the road for God." I would eagerly await Cosme's arrival home from so many different trips. He did healing in many places and would further his knowledge and skills—to the North Pole, to the Philippines, to Brazil, to Hawai'i, and to many places around North America. I was eager to hear about the trips and the fascinating healers and mystics that he had met, and I was always ready to get a tune-up (healing treatment) from Cosme too. Regular healings over the years helped me to recover from and eventually heal from severe immune deficiency. I recall two different occasions when Cosme saved my life. On one critical night he stayed awake all night, praying out loud for me, with his hands placed on my body. He was told by his guidance that if he prayed for me all night, that I would make it. Dawn came and I was still there. Finally he could go home and get a little sleep.

There were many healing sessions throughout the years when I experienced a feeling of bliss, as if I was in the presence of angels. I'm sure I was! There were times when I felt like I was floating a few inches off the table. Before leaving I said, "Thank you." But Cosme would always say, "Don't thank us, Thank God!"

Time flies by, and twenty-eight years have elapsed. Clara has gone over to "the other side." Cosme's nineteen-year-old son, Orion, is a joy and blessing in Cosme's life. Cherylann, Cosme's lovely wife, is a brilliant healer herself. She specializes in nutritional counseling, iridology, hypnotherapy and color therapy. Cosme's and Cherylann's work is very complimentary. Many people who come to Cosme for healings also have nutritional consultations with Cherylann. I have seen both Cosme's and Cherylann's healing work grow and blossom, as they never end their quest for raising up their healing work to higher and higher frequencies.

Our families have been close friends for a long time now. We've shared many meals and helped each other out in a number of ways. I can remember many mornings coming down to "Cosara" to "work out" with Cosme on the exercise machine. Often he had photographs spread out, all over the floor, that he was preparing for a client's wedding or graduation album. Often he would tell me that he was up all night ... or had just two or three hours of sleep. Just a little sleep is all he needs, and he is cheerful with no coffee in the morning, just orange juice.

Our families took a trip to Hawai'i together one time and stayed with Cosme's relatives. We also traveled together, years ago, to Topeka, Kansas to a cross-cultural gathering of spiritual teachers and healers from all the major religions. Cosme and my husband Paul, both ministers, were among the presenters. These memories are precious.

Recently Cosme and Cherylann have taken frequent trips to Brazil to visit the healing *casa* of John of God. This world famous healer has many thousands of people coming to him, as many miraculous healings have occurred. John of God, the channel for the divine healings, has recognized both Cosme and Cherylann as gifted healers. He asked Cosme to sit next to him and assist with his prayer and energy. He gifted Cherylann with one of the Casa's crystal light therapy beds and asked her to take it home and treat people with it. Nobody had told John of God that Cherylann had studied and practiced both color, light and crystal therapy for many years. But the saints, doctors and angels, in the heavens who work through John of God recognized her expertise and sensitivity and honored her in this way.

Cosme "walks his talk," and lives his life according to spiritual guidance. I have seen this all through the years. He is the epitome of cheerfulness, love, optimism and inspiration. He will also make people giggle and laugh, as the aloha spirit and sense of play are a part of his Hawai'ian nature. Cosme is always called the Hawai'ian "clown" or the happy Hawai'ian by his friends. He still has his Hawai'ian local-boy accent and big hearty laugh. "You may take Cosme out of Hawai'i, but you can't take the Hawai'ian out of Cosme." Even when talking about serious matters of health and spirituality, Cosme often cracks jokes. His spiritual and practical advice is important to pay attention to, as it is often most accurate. He is a man whose priority in life is to serve God and help people. His prayers are powerful. His healing work, too, is powerful and life changing, as spirit uses him as a vehicle of inspiration, healing and blessing.

This book, entitled *The Mystical Kiss of God*, holds a treasure-trove of inspiration about living a healthy, happy, spiritual life. There are exercises for calming emotional upsets, re-charging the bodies energies, developing strong intuition, communicating clearly, protecting ourselves from negativity, changing the vibration of our food, opening our hearts, making prayers that are answered, and opening up our spiritual energy, just to name a few. Cosme does talk about God a lot, but his understanding of God is not a man with a white beard sitting on a throne in heaven. He talks about his understanding of God in such a way that it is Christian, but also universal. A Buddhist might say, "Ah, this is what we call "mind" or "emptiness."

Cosme also shares a vast knowledge of healing and self-healing methods and links these teachings to living life according to spiritual law. He differentiates man-made laws from God's laws, which are ageless and universal. Having demonstrated youthfulness and rejuvenation himself, he can speak with authority about the fountain of youth. He shares his secrets about how we can rejuvenate ourselves, so that we can be youthful and healthy all the way into our elder years.

There is a quote from Max Freedom Long, who studied the Hawai'ian Kahunas (healers, mystics, holy people) early in the twentieth century. One kahuna finally shared with him the secret of the Kahunas: "Think only good, good, good, and then you will be filled with light. Then you will have power and you can use it." When I heard this quote, I thought, well, that's Cosme. He does think only good, good, good, and he is filled with light ... and he is *always* helping people with joy and a smile.

Nancy Clemens
friend and editor
Nevada City, California
July, 2005

# Introduction

*The Mystical Kiss of God*

In the book of Genesis, in the Bible, God said, "Let there be light." God is like the sun rays that are shining down upon us on this earth. When the soul comes into the body at the birth of a child, that light determines what the child's life lessons are going to be. The soul of that child is the God-light that can illuminate and bless that life. It can help that child learn to be a co-creator with God, as part of God lives within the heart of that child—that God-light that gave the spark of life to the child.

When that God-light abides in a person's heart, it is in its natural home. But for so many people the soul, or God-light, becomes misplaced in the body, due to stress, trauma and conflict, which is abundant on our planet at this time.

The God-light needs to be brought back into the heart. In my healing sessions and "spiritual process" I often help a person unify their heart and God's light. There is a polarity energy here that ignites like electricity, when the heart and the God-light come together. The lights turn on. This powerful current is running through the negative and positive poles. This is the mystical kiss of God!

When God's light is abiding in its natural home, in a person's heart, they will speak with love, beauty and truth. Authority, warmth and light will emanate from them. When that light shines, and God is working through them, that warm, shining light will magnetize people to them who need help. People who are far away in the dark and the cold will find their way to the fireplace of God's warmth and light and love. They will come for comfort, guidance, understanding, compassion and healing. They will have love and peace as a result, not war, not conflict.

This inner God-light can be multi-dimensional as it plays out in our lives. For some souls there may be one main lesson that they are here to learn in this life. For others there may be many. Some will be fairly easy lessons, and others will be difficult or complicated. Some souls come to pay a debt and some come to do service. Some souls are here to do both.

In life everything is the Alpha and the Omega. . .the beginning and the end, the yin and the yang, the feminine and the masculine. This cycle is part of nature. We live with these polarities on a dualistic planet. Dualism unifies when we bring in a third element to create a triangle ... the light of God. Every organ and every cell has a positive and negative polarity, a yin and a yang, a front and back and side to side.

When a healer works, he or she will ignite and balance that negative and positive polarity in each cell and organ, with the light and the love of God that is coming through them. The cells become illuminated and that light begins the healing process. In the case of a very great healer like John of God in Brazil, or the late Katherine Kuhlman, that illumination may bring about instantaneous and miraculous healing!

John of God in Brazil gives people triangles made out of wood as a meditation focus and for a blessing for their home. This is sacred geometry. It has so many meanings or aspects, throughout all cultures and traditions. It goes back to the very beginning. It could be seen as the Father, Son and Holy Spirit. So many sacred things are triangles. Our own body is anchored in the earth, and our crown or spirit connects us to the sky. The third part of our body's triangle is the powerful energy of the kiss of God that takes place in the heart. The light that ignites the negative and positive poles is the third part of the triangle.

When we arrive as a newborn to this world, we are at the beginning of this cycle. New growth is our next step in this evolution. You see, the heart is like this, as I see it. We have no real control over it, as God controls our heart. God beats our heart. It is marvelous how we breathe without thinking about it. What makes us breathe, if not God? Our life is really a miracle. We do very little to control our breath or our heartbeat. There is a great mystery about this spark of life that ignites our heart and our breath. When they cease, our body can no longer live here. No one can analyze or dissect this spark of life. It remains a mystery!

Our heart lives in the temple of our body. Out of it comes the music. I always tell people, "You are the music director of your own body. All your organs and body parts are like instruments in the orchestra. Your direction, through your spirit, is what keeps the music in harmony and sounding beautiful." I also say to people, "Your body is like a sacred temple or a castle. It is your home while you are here on earth. You must take good care of it so that you can have a full life ... and the time to complete your life's lessons, and the chance to be creative and of service. I also say, "You are the Kings and Queens of that castle. Take good care of it. Learn to make it operate at its full potential. Learn the secrets of its energy centers (the chakras) and learn to clear them, harmonize them, and light them up. You will then have a living rainbow activated and radiating in your body. You may even find the spiritual pot of gold at the end of the rainbow. Love and nurture your body, and learn the secrets of youth and rejuvenation, so that it will last for a long time. You will then have energy and health and a clear, creative mind right into your old age.

When people abuse their bodies, they may not realize that they are abusing a sacred gift and opportunity that God gave to them. It is precious beyond our human understanding. When people say they don't believe in God, I say, "Well, stop your heart. Stop your breath." A person can't do it for very long.

These things I am talking about in this book do not belong to any one religion. These are universal truths. All cultures and religions have their teachers and healers to help people and teach them to live life according to spiritual law. No matter what culture or tradition we come from, we all have a heartbeat and we all have a breath. Just as the sun shines upon all of us equally all over this Earth, God's love and light also shines equally upon all the peoples of this Earth.

*Knowing God*

I often refer to "God," so it is important for people to know what I mean when I say "God." Some people have trouble with this word, or this concept. Well, you can call God. . . The Creator, The Higher Power, Allah, Jehovah, The Great White Spirit, the Great Mystery or some other name. One way or another, life doesn't work very well if we do not connect with this divine force which I call God.

God is vibrating with unconditional love! God is light! God is omnipotent! You can express things about God, but God is so infinite, that it is impossible to really decipher what God really is. It is really beyond any definition—or gender—as God is here, God is there and God is everywhere. God created the whole universe with unconditional love. We have a tendency to not be able to understand our true value or to know that we have God inside of us. In the Bible it tells us that we are made in God's image and likeness. We are co-creators and many times, unfortunately, we don't realize it. It doesn't matter what religion we follow. It is the same for all people of all religions. God is within all of us.

Peoples of the world do things differently. They have different cultures and different religions. No matter what a person follows, they need to take the next step in their life. Things that Jesus did, we can do also. We all have this potential. People of all religions can do these great things. Jesus said that we could do even greater things than he did. Jesus is pointing out to us that we have God and the power and grace of God within us. When we open up all the way and become illuminated with love and light, we have access to the gifts of the spirit, which are the gifts of God's love. Miracles can happen through this illuminated love!

I feel that we are co-creators with God. In this way we can change things. We don't have to take any of the sicknesses into our own body. We can intend, with God's help to keep sickness out of our body. We can create any positive condition in this way. Because we are a co-creator with God and have that sacred energy inside of us, we need to be careful with the words we think with and the words we say. We actually manifest with these spoken or unspoken words. What we create with our thoughts and words, we become. We manifest the things that we think about the most. It is not healthy to be entertaining negative thoughts or fearful visualizations, as eventually we are likely to manifest them. Our minds, hearts and words have a tremendous creative power.

God goes through every part of our muscle, bone, nerve and everything. There is a beacon of light within us and that beacon is the God within us. We have our soul with us. When both our soul and God work together, we can create anything together. We can create something good for ourselves and other people. We can also create something bad that can hurt ourselves or other people, when the ego gets ahead of God. We create so many things in our bodies. Sometimes conditions are environmentally caused, but often we create our own sicknesses and blockages by being out of balance.

Where did we come from originally? We need to remember where we originally came from. I remember a good friend would say, "It's like all of us have come from the sun of God, from the heart sun of God." We go out from the one sun like the sun's rays and experience many things in life. A lot of times later on in life, we can look back at life and say, "Where do we come from?" And who will remember where they came from? We come from God's love, God's truth and God's way.

What is in the small is also in the large. Whatever is in the large is also in the small. God is the large, but God is also within the small, within ourselves. It is like the two sides of the coin. . .the positive and the negative. . .heads and tails. So whatever you do, there will always be people who will be against you and there will always be people who will be for you. We all need to learn to deal with negativity in a positive way. See what you can learn from the negative things in life. When can you see that someone's hurtful behavior is about them, not about you, even when it is directed at you? How do you adjust and get positive energy to manifest again and work with you?

There are people who say that they channel God or other high spiritual beings, from the other side or other dimension. Why not go for the highest level and communicate with God and the angels? Some people think it's great that they're getting advice from regular people that have gone to the other side ... like aunties and uncles. Why not go for the best information and guidance? Maybe these relatives messed up their lives here on earth. Maybe they're not in a position to give good advice. Some people choose a lower form of life. It may be a part of their growth and what their life lesson is about. Sooner or later they will face their own creations and learn from them. I can look at a person's heart and look ahead, twenty years, and see into their future life. I can see what kind of ill health they will have from what they are creating in the present. People don't actually realize that they are co-creators with God. They forget that, or don't know it, and in the end they pay for it. They go to a doctor and say, "Fix me." But the answer is not there. A doctor can take out a tumor or do by-pass surgery, but he may not be able to put all the pieces back together again, in a person who has not taken care of themselves.

There are many physical churches and temples in the world with all kinds of different looking architecture. But there is also a church inside of us. Both of them can be enhanced. Both of them can be loved. Both of them can be looked at. By doing this, there is more protection for a person. We can listen to certain things from our family or when we go to church. We can listen to the minister, priest or rabbi talking about certain things. We get information from outside of ourselves to take into our bodies. But we also need to work with the energy inside, the God that is within us. We need to learn to listen from the inside. It is already all in there.

One of the reasons that I wanted to write this book is to help people clear all this up and have a good life. People need to begin to understand the spiritual basics. Life may be difficult, but life can also be simple. Because so many people are missing the basic things, they tend to complicate their life and make it much more difficult. It's like saying, "Here's a piece of custard pie." I love the custard pie that they make in Hawai'i. Say, for instance, that the pie represents God. People have a tendency to dissect God in half and then in quarters and then into eighths, sixteenths and thirty-seconds. They're trying to find God. Basically the more they dissect God, the less they know of God. I suggest eating the whole pie.

Eating the whole pie and filling yourself with God's love brings an illuminated state and a deep sense of serenity. That peaceful, loving state helps us to feel at one with everything and to have a loving attitude towards everyone and everything. Life becomes happier and healthier and more simple. Old bad habits and associations fade away, and we are more likely to want to be kind and helpful. This peace is so deep that even the wild animals can become tame around a person filled with God. St. Francis of Assisi is famous for walking up to a vicious wolf who had killed many men. He was filled with God's light and he had no fear. The wolf laid down at his feet and made peace with the nearby town which agreed to put food out for the wolf for the rest of his life. The wolf made an agreement with Francis that he would never harm another person again. There are many stories of saints from all religions who were so filled with God that they were completely connected to nature and the creation. They could pacify wild animals and storms and create peace wherever they went. We, too, as co-creators with God, can receive that love and peace and walk in harmony as peacemakers on this earth.

*Understanding Illness: Sickness as a Way to Know God*

Sometimes sickness or injuries actually teach people. A lot of times I hear people tell me that they got sick, and by being sick they really found out what is most important in their life. It's God. If they weren't sick or injured, they might not have come to know that. My doctor friend who is famous for his books about health, healing and longevity interviewed many people who had been ill. He would ask, "How did you actually get to where you are now?" Many patients said, "Well, I got very, very sick, but when I came out from it, it turned out to be a gift from God." I feel that life is such that when we break a bone, it hurts a lot. When the bone knits back together, it doesn't always fit just perfectly, but it will have a lot of calcium build-up and be really strong. The bone may be even stronger than it was before.

This is what adversity has done for me in my early life. It has made my life stronger and better. And so, this is why I am successful. By being stronger I am a better channel for God. I am better able to help people get well, so that they can work again and take care of their families. I give thanks to God. This is my gift. God's blessing comes through me to bless people with healing. We don't appreciate many things in life if we've never been through sickness.

Emotions can affect a person tremendously and create sickness too. When I scan the body and look with my third eye, I see things that most other people don't see. Emotional problems usually appear in the back of the brains. The emotions from childhood until now are all there. The back of the head can appear dark to me. It can look twisted. It can look grey. It can be a blackish burgundy color. These colors have come to represent, to me, the need to work a lot of things out in this life. It shows a lot of hardships to work through. And it short-circuits the back of the brain. Then as the nerve goes down from the brain, it goes down the spine and down to the shoulders and creates tension and pain. That emotional energy can affect a person tremendously. People are not generally aware that the back of their brains are all plugged up with unclear emotional energy.

People need to remember to come back and become whole again. From the little pieces to the very large, the puzzle has to be put back together again, like the pieces of pie becoming a whole circle. This is how life is. People need to understand that they are here on Earth to learn. Life has a purpose for all of us. I see it as a schooling for all of us. Besides schooling from real schools, kindergarten through high school, there is schooling in our relationship with Mother Earth. There is schooling in our relationship with other people. There is a schooling with our relationship to the stars, the galaxies and other parts of the universe. People have a tendency not to think about that or even realize it. Most people think of things on a very small scale. But as a co-creator with God we can create and manifest on larger and larger scales. We are the ones who determine our own limits. We are all in the school of this human life together.

# 1

# How I Work As a Healer ... and a Spiritual Mechanic

*Body Scanning in Healing*

Originally I had a healing partner named Clara. She was a gifted healer, and for a number of years we worked together as a team. She did her scanning by running her hands a few inches above the person's body. She could feel the hot and the cold spots and how strongly and quickly the energy was moving in the person's body. She drew her hands from the feet, up the spine to the top of the head. . .all the time scanning with her hand just a few inches above the body. Her hands would always be above the body, and sometimes she scanned the body a number of times. She could see how the spiritual energy was moving. She got a lot of information this way. She could feel the blockages. Just by this scanning, the healing energy in her hands began to release the blockages.

To open the healing, I have to get into the real stuff, at the core of the person. I call it the engine. I listen to how it hums and how it all works together, or how it doesn't work together. I like to see myself as directed by God to be a spiritual mechanic or spiritual angel. I use the sense of smell. I can feel a person without going into their body or interfering with their free will. I am just looking, because my clients ask me to look, by making an appointment with me.

*I Would Do the Massage and Body Work*

After Clara was done with this part, I would come in and do the physical part, the massage and body work. I worked with unblocking the blockages and getting the energy moving smoothly throughout the whole body. Where there were cold spots, it showed that there was no energy running through. Where there were hot spots, there were dense blockages in that area — or the heat could mean inflammation, as well. And when there is a tremendous amount of energy built up, there is a lot of pain. The area needs to be unblocked before the pain is relieved.

### Laying on of Hands Wasn't Enough

When we first started healing as a team, laying on of hands gave us about thirteen percent healings. So the margin of improving someone's health was too small. I had to question myself, asking if laying on of hands was good enough for solving more complex health problems. It wasn't enough. It didn't solve the problem yet. So I had to go into the physical, spiritual, mental and emotional bodies of a person to find the source of the problem which caused the sickness or pain.

### Looking Deep into the Soul

When I look at people, I look first at the outside to see if they are male or female. I go beyond looking at the clothing and the shape of their face. I go beyond their race and religion. I go deep into the soul. I look at them from the inside of the body out. That kind of looking tells me the truth, because the aura can change according to people's moods and emotions.

### I Ask God to Tell Me About People

When I see a person that I have never met before, I want to know the truth about that person, so that I can truly help them. I talk to God, inside of myself. I say, "God, show me the truth about this man or show me the truth about this woman." In a matter of seconds the truth comes out. You can't hide anything from God. You can try to hide it or forget about it, but the truth is always there.

*Using a Spiritual X-Ray or Catscan to Diagnose*

When I look at people, I can see different things in them. If they try to hide something on one level, I can go to another level to look. It's like an x-ray or catscan, or a nuclear test that has no toxic radiation. When I read a person, they know I am telling the truth because I know more about them than they do. I go beyond that and tell them what the problem is that I see inside of them. If they have a problem, I also see where it is coming from. They know it is true. Once I do the reading, then they really open up even more when I do a healing on them. They surrender even more to God. They know that they were not taken advantage of or misguided.

*Learning to Heal Alone*

I had a partner for a long time, but my partner went her own way. I was all alone. So I said to God, "God, I need some help." I kept saying this for one month. I realized that I had to do the healing work alone now, and I needed to learn some of the parts of the healing work that my partner did when we were together. She specialized in reading the body, praying and singing. I needed to develop even more senses and broaden my work now. Reading people's bodies would have to become a new specialty. So after my partner moved on, I began to use my sense of smell. I learned to scan and read the body. I began to smell, taste, feel and hear organs. I learned to hear the body and the movement that was taking place inside. I was seeing with my third eye. So when I talked to the person and told them what I had seen, the person would say I was right. They would say, "That's absolutely right. That's what I've been telling my doctor was wrong with me, and my doctor thinks that I should see a psychiatrist. The problem's not really in my head at all." So I have been through this kind of a story many times, and we have gotten to the bottom of some serious and mysterious health problems.

*Discovering the Need to Align the Subtle Bodies: The Auric Field*

When I talk about these bodies, I am talking about what a lot of people call the "human aura." I see it more as a spiritual body or bodies, made of light and colors. The physical body is what we all know. It has all the organs, the blood, the lymph system, the nervous system. That is self-explanatory.

## The Bodies

In the early days of my healing work I wasn't getting a complete success rate until I started working with all the bodies. I had one guy who had an amputated leg. We were able to find energy still going through the area where his leg would have been. That energy was still there, energetically, and we could feel it in our scanning. It was very interesting and showed that the spiritual part of the body was still there, like a phantom of the leg that had been there before.

## Reconnecting All the Bodies

Sometimes the lower, middle and upper parts of the body are not working together or are not energetically harmonized. This condition may be caused from surgery or it can be caused by hurtful experiences. When all the bodies are not connected together, they need to be reconnected. What I do is reconnect all the bodies. It's like, "Hey, Nancy meet Tom. Tom meet Nancy. Long time no see huh?" It's like that. People forget that the other parts of the body can be disconnected and this causes the body to shut down. Sickness, pain or emotional distress are a result of these disconnections.

## The Emotional Body

The emotional body plays a very important part. Disturbing emotions can drag you down. You can lose your energy instantaneously, in a matter of split seconds. I've seen it happen to too many people. Many people let their emotions run uncontrolled for years and years, because of uncertainty, habits, and fear of facing their problems. Sometimes you can control your emotions, and other times you don't. You can actually learn to excel at controlling your emotions. You will have a lot of energy and vitality if you do.

The emotional body is an energetic body that surrounds and penetrates the physical body. Sometimes I can see the emotional body like two hula-hoops spinning around in circles. When the emotional body has gone out of whack, it's an uncontrollable, chaotic spinning. It doesn't go around smoothly. It's wobbly. When it's wobbly like this, it makes more work for the body, and throws the other subtle energy bodies out of place when this happens. The emotional body is also made up of lights. Colored lights appear in the solar plexus area. These sometimes can be dark lights or they can be bright lights. The solar plexus area can be spinning or be almost still. These colors and activities that I observe help me determine what causes the problem there. So the emotional body can appear inwardly or outwardly.

The condition of the emotional body and how it gets that way is simple. It depends entirely on how a person thinks. The left side of the brain is the logical, intellectual side. The right side of the brain is the spiritual, intuitive, and creative side of the brain. The rear part of the brain is our emotions and memory banks from childhood until now.

### Stuffed Emotions: The Pathway to Illness

When a person can't relate to or solve a problem in the brain, they put it into storage. They put it into the solar plexus area, and the liver and gall bladder area. That becomes an organ dysfunction or "garbage disposal," as I would call it. People tend to get all plugged up there, and the longer it stays there, the person gets more sluggish and more irritable. They become angry, even if they don't show it outwardly. It could be repressed anger and could take the form of resentment or passive hostility.

People can also become fearful from having all these repressed emotions stuck there. It causes an imbalance. If it stays in the solar plexus for a long time, it can kick up to the thyroid and cause problems there. It can actually become extreme.

After the thyroid has had problems for some time, it gets tired of getting all the garbage in there, so it is kicked into the heart area. The heart begins to really overwork, which causes a lot of ailments in the heart and the rest of the physical body. It becomes a pathway and chain-reaction of dysfunction.

## Emotional Disturbance in the Solar Plexus

What happens is that people in America, particularly, tend to get very emotional. The solar plexus area is like a system of electrical wires, which is the nervous system. The nervous system gets twisted with stress and causes all kinds of ailments. It basically gets burned out, and adrenal and nervous exhaustion are often one of the physical results as well as nervous exhaustion. You know, if you have a piece of rope, and you have one person hold one end and you hold the other end, and it begins to twist, it gets tangled into a big knot. And that's what happens to people's abdomens when they're under stress. They have big knots of tangled energy. When the nervous system shuts down, you can't nourish the organs. The organs weaken and begin to shut down. The lymphatic system begins to have blockages in it too. All kinds of physical ailments can result from stress. So the truth is, we need to correct our spiritual body and keep our emotions calm and clear.

## Depression

If a person is emotionally depressed, the physical blockage goes from the liver, gall bladder, and solar plexus area, down to the kidneys. The person starts to get lower back problems. Then the kidneys and adrenals begin to get really sluggish. They begin to work real slow, and the fluid moves really slowly in that area and doesn't do a very fast job of filtering the blood or cleansing the lymphatic system.

### The Appearance of a Chaotic Emotional Body

These bodies are not in balance when they seem scattered and out of alignment with each other. The emotional body can react like a hula-hoop. It begins to move around the body. It can be like a typhoon or hurricane coming through. It's also like a plant or a flower. When the wind comes along, it sways along with the wind changes. It sways in different directions. An outside force can actually interfere with the bodies, just as inner emotional forces can. When inner and outer forces collide, it's like a hurricane coming through. It becomes like a war zone inside of yourself. You know, when you can't figure out how to deal with a disturbing situation, there's a push-pull reaction. When an outside force, such as a difficult person or situation comes along, it makes for a lot more difficulty. Then there can be the possibility of two sets of emotional storms interacting with each other.

### How Disturbed Emotions Can Throw Out the Lower Back

So when emotional upset or chaos is taking place, the sacrum or tailbone area begins to pull off center and then the lower back can go out of place. It can also cause a real pain in the butt. The old expression that someone is "a pain in the butt," comes from upset emotions going to the buttocks area. It's similar to when the wind blows very, very strongly and comes up from the ground. It's not grounded any more.

### Shallow Breathing and Depression

At the same time that it does that, the emotions affect the breathing apparatus. The breathing becomes very, very shallow. Medical researchers have found that most people who are depressed are breathing shallowly. They don't take a deep breath. All these systems are interconnected. So, as a healer, I have to open up the blockages and let the light shine through again. So this is my experience as a healer and a seer.

*Smell and Colors Give Me Information*

When I first put the person up on the massage table, I ask them if they have any questions while I am reading the bodies. After the reading, I ask if I have missed something, and if so, what did I miss? I have them lie on their stomach with their clothes on but socks off. Then I will sniff, because we come from the animal kingdom and can develop our sense of smell, like a dog. I can smell the fragrance that comes from the physical body and also the fragrance of the soul. I can smell fragrances from each of the physical organs. Depending on the type of perfume a woman wears, I will learn about her personality. When I am smelling all these things, the energy is flying back and forth, like light waves. When I begin to smell, I go beyond physical smell. When I smell the body, I can see the colors that are connected to the smells. The colors give me more information. This has nothing to do with whether the person is clean or not. These are smells and fragrances that the average person would never detect. It is a kind of extrasensory gift. I am a spiritual detective in a way, finding many extrasensory clues that help me to understand a person's health and problems. I need to have information from several of my ways of seeing to know for sure that the problem is there. I can't play with people's lives. I need to be accurate.

*Seeing a Medical Doctor First*

Doctors have the training with blood tests and so many ways of screening the body. I prefer that people see their doctor before they come to see me. If I am telling the truth and I read the body correctly, the person won't doubt me if it matches up with what the doctor's tests or exam has shown. If I tell someone something incorrect, they wouldn't believe me, but when I read it correctly they believe me, because they can feel the truth.

Today a lot of people are going through mental depression and take a lot of drugs. They take antidepressants, like Prozac and other similar drugs. There's nothing better than having your own body do the healing, because it has the capacity to do so! If your body has problems, then there are often natural ways of healing it. Broken bones or appendicitis surely need the help of medical doctors and a hospital, but there are many conditions that respond well to natural healing.

## Medical Doctors and Spiritual Healers

If you're a real scientific person, you probably will consult a medical doctor with your health problems. Some people are from a country that has hardly anything in the way of health care, especially for poor people. Going to healers is the road they often take, and it works for them much of the time. What's so nice about this is that in a foreign country these people get to the root cause and then understand why they have certain effects. The medical field usually deals with the pain and the symptoms and relieving them. It doesn't deal with the real cause or root of the problem. Usually there is a spiritual or emotional root. That is one of the real differences between the world of Western doctors and spiritual healers. So, I feel that medical doctors would have a higher rate of success in healing people if they suggested adding a spiritual healer to the healing team.

Going to the root of the problem is different than relieving symptoms. Giving a medical exam, listening to the heartbeat, and what the patient has to say gives a lot of clues to what the problems are. Communication is very important. Both methods of healing are important. When a person has a spiritual healer and a medical doctor that can work in harmony, it can solve a lot of problems.

## Using the Bible as a Blessing

It is an interesting thing for people to know how connected they are to God in the healing process. I get the reading first from opening up the Bible and using the Bible as a guide. The theme of what that person is going through at the moment is revealed by where the Bible opens up. I just let it open where it wants to, after making a silent prayer for guidance for the person. It opens to a place, and then you ask God to show you how close the person is to God, and then the Bible reading gives you a kind of read-out.

### The Massage

After I scan and read the body, I give the person a good massage. I use olive oil, as it is the only oil that regenerates the physical and spiritual body simultaneously. It is the only oil that I know of that does that. I use a touch of pure essential oil of lemon grass, because it makes the body wake up, like a spark plug. When I work on a person, I don't smell the scent of the lemon grass oil at all anymore, as my sense of smell is focused on all the other diagnostic smells.

So when I massage a person, it's like God massaging the person. It is a spiritual ecstatic experience. It feels like at least five people working on the person simultaneously. What I am doing is similar to making a basket. You know, you go in and out, weaving a basket. This is what I am doing with the physical, mental, emotional and spiritual bodies. I am going in and out of the body and I "have a ball" doing this. It is just like being on a ski lift, going up and down the slope and really enjoying it, but it's on a spiritual level.

### Looking Inside the Body to Determine Problems

I have a kind of gift of psychic smell—maybe a psychic aroma detector. I can smell different kinds of sicknesses and emotions. It helps me in my healing work to know what's going on with someone. When I smell certain wealthy people, I can smell the desire of luxurious, material things. They may have a certain smell when they die. At the end, the desire for luxury dies. You can't take it with you. The body cries because the real essence is not there any more, as it's going to God. The essence of the person is with God first, not in the physical plane, not with the habit of wanting luxurious things.

There have been a few times that the smells were really bad, to the point that I almost needed to vomit. They were cases where the colon area was completely blocked, or if the body was dying. There are times when I look in the person's eyes and listen to the power box of the person's voice. I can sometimes tell how long it will be before the person is going to die, and how much strength and life force is left in their body. That is fast and easy for me. You see, I like to look inside the body with a kind of spiritual x-ray vision. It gives me more of the truth than just looking at the signs on the outside of the body ... the eyes, the face, the feet, the skin color, the liveliness of the eyes, and so forth. Looking inside is fun for me. The body can be a like a big, shiny Cadillac car that looks really good on the outside, but then, when you open the hood, there may be a faulty engine inside or no engine. I prefer looking at the engine because the only way the Cadillac can go up the hill is with an engine. So the engine and the insides of the body are more important than looking at the aura. The aura can change according to the person's moods, so I prefer to go into the main core of the body, or the engine. I'm doing this with my third eye and all my other senses ... even the hair on my skin acts as antennae.

You know, we all come from the same place, whether we know it or not ... and that's from our creator, God. Part of my gift comes from feeling one with God, with all of the trees and the animals. Being in relationship with everything, from a place of love, helps open these gifts. People do have their free will to make their own choices in life. When I work with God, I do not interfere with a person's individuality or personality. I have learned to have harmonious energy with all that is around me. As I read a person, I am in contact with every part of who they are, because they are also a part of God. I don't go into a person's body in a merging way. I just look to see how I can help them.

### Reading the Body and the Body's Music

Many people feel that palm-readers are charlatans. I don't read hands and feet in the same way they do. I am not a fortune teller, but I am a servant of God. Part of my body-reading is doing a detailed reading from looking at every little line, skin texture, shape etc. of the feet. Besides smell, I can read all of it. It tells me things and it talks to me. Each line has significance, and a lot of times it tells me about the person's health because the bottom of the feet have the reflex points that relate to each part of the body. Again, it is the macrocosm and microcosm. So what I am doing is checking the body out by using more than four different methods. I am cross-checking the accuracy and making sure that they all match the information I am getting.

I can scan and look into the body and see how the heart and lungs are, and then have a look at how the arteries are. A strong, healthy person has a bright, white light around them. Looking at how strong or how weak that white light is can tell me a lot about the person. If there's a bright white light around the jaw area, it indicates a healthy person. If a person is weak, sick or old, that light energy in the jaw area grows dim. When someone grinds their teeth during their sleep, the energy field around the jaw starts to dim. The jaw area is connected to the brain, so one thing that may not seem important, like grinding teeth, may be very important, as it affects the brain. The average person who thinks that they're "open" may only be three-to-six percent open, on the average. I can see how much life force is in a person. We all have the capability to read the body, the way I do. It's just our own feeling of limitation that tells us that we can't do it.

### The Music of the Body and the Dancing Massage

After I scan the whole body, I pray over the person. Then I use olive oil and give a massage treatment. I use certain music for the person and then I dance with it, as I am giving the massage. I'm dancing with God, the music, and the person's body, all at the same time. It's a kind of massage that goes with the rhythm and melody of the body's music. We are the music director. Each one of the organs has its own note and emotion that it is related to. Then, when we listen and play all of them together, we have an orchestra.

Some instruments in the body's orchestra may be out of tune, so I have to get them in tune. I co-ordinate all the music so that it's playing together as a harmonious family. Instead of playing a couple of different tunes at the same time, it becomes one tune.

There are many times that the right food for the person is not being fed to the body. The person may have had surgery twenty years before, but the body is still in shock. In that case I have to "defrost" the body. So it's interesting. For me, I'm continuously learning and experiencing new things about healing. There are things that I see over and over again, but, you know, each person's vibration is different. In this way, I learn from everyone.

## *My Little One-to-Ten Scale*

We could set up a scale from one to ten that represents how "in tune" you are with God's vibration. A ten would be a perfect attunement with God. When I see a person that is a number three, the person is off by seven points. From there you can get a general idea how "off" the person's body is—how connected or disconnected they are. This is simple mathematics, and God works with me with these very simple methods, because I am a very simple-minded person. I don't have an intricate, complex mind like other people do. A lot of times I look at a person and I seem to be looking down at the maze of their life. They may not know which way to turn. I look at the person and look down on this maze and see how very simple it is to find their way out. It is the human being that makes it so difficult. People tend to make things ten thousand times harder than they should be. If you keep things simple, you don't have trouble with your boyfriend or girlfriend or your partner. Keeping things with a lower nature out of your life, like unsavory TV shows or movies, helps to keep life so much more harmonious.

## *Spiritually Directed Body Work*

During a massage I may be working on the neck one moment, and then the next moment I may be working on a thigh, ankle, foot or stomach. I move by the direction of the Holy Spirit. I see how the energy moves from left to right in the head, and if it crosses over going down to the foot. You can work on the right foot, and then watch the energy cross over to the left part of the brain. It's a kind of criss-cross. I am also reconnecting that part too. I work diagonally, vertically and horizontally to reintegrate all the bodies. At times I may seem to be massaging in the same way, but the spiritual vibration is very different for each individual. The energy comes out of my hands in a unique spiritual way to give the person what they need at the time. The spirit directs me completely, and that's how I know where I'm going next. I am obedient to the spirit and I never forget that I am just a vehicle for God's love. Massage and healing work is not done well if it is just done by some formula or inflexible routine. For me, it is different each time, depending on what the person needs at that particular moment in their life. When I am doing this work, I feel like I'm working on a thousand different levels simultaneously.

## Different Ways to Get Help

Doctors, therapists and psychiatrists are all good, but none of them address the subtle energy issues that I can see. The work I do covers all the areas and sees the person's body more as a multi-dimensional cube, rather than a two-dimensional square. I feel that the major difference between me and most other doctors and therapists is that I am a vehicle for God's love and healing. So, when a person starts to take responsibility for their life, then they are not defensive about the suggestions I make for them. They realize that I am tuning into a higher power for my information. And, I always ask God to correct me if I am wrong and to help me to make myself better.

## The Vibration in My Hands and Body

When I put my hands on a person, my hands vibrate with the healing energy in a very strong way ... because I am very, very relaxed. Then my hands are receptive and open to God's healing energy to come through me. The patient really wants God's healing energy to touch and heal them—to relieve their sickness, their pain, and their emotional distress. If I hold my hands over the person's, and my hands don't vibrate and move, it tells me that the person has blockages that need to be opened up. They may be frustrated or angry, you know, all this stuff that people carry around like heavy baggage. When my hands don't move and vibrate, I may have to use God's spiritual "Draino," and push it through the body and flush them out. It comes in, through me, like a lightning explosion. My breathing changes and I can feel so much energy coming instantly through my body. The body of the person I'm working on may vibrate and shake from head to toe, and front to back. This can happen with the healing energy, because it is coming in at such an accelerated rate. It is really strong, as it goes through me to the person. I am just a channel. This energy clears the blockages. I could almost relate it to the spin cycle of a washing machine. Everything in the washer spins around the sides with the centrifugal force, keeping the center clear. It just pushes it out with the force of the Holy Spirit! I call this clear area, the center point. You can get a piece of rope, and if you have something on the end and spin it around, it is going to kick it off. Basically, this is one way I work with people to get the negativity kicked out of the body, real fast. And, I have a blast! I love being able to give God's healing blessing.

### The More You Relax, the More God's Energy Can Flow Through You

When I am through working with all the people that come for healing, I relax. I might be driving home or flying home, and I am actually communicating with God. It's like a personal talk back and forth. The talk is not in words, but in the heart and mind. I get certain information such as when to do the next healing session for someone or when to go back home, and many insights. There may be something that I want to do for myself personally. I check the weather and I check on my body's energy level. Even when the physical part of me is tired, the spiritual part can still be strong. Then God can work through me a whole lot better. Tiredness removes obstacles, the personality, and reveals the density in you. Tiredness can make you so relaxed and soft inside. One very important truth is that the more you relax, the more God's energy can flow through you. When you are all up-tight and contracted, God's energy just does not flow through you very well.

Part of the purpose of the massage work I do in my healings is to help people relax enough so that God's energy can flow through them. Many times when I am working with people, I have my eyes closed. I am very, very relaxed, almost sleeping. This is why I am able to handle so many people. The deep state of relaxation is very important to being expanded intuitively and being able to be in communion and attunement with God.

## Connecting and Disconnecting

Then there is the issue of seeing the energy field, or aura, of individuals. Say for instance, I am walking around the county fair, with hundreds of people everywhere, a whole crowd. When I work with one person after another, I am totally focused on them and involved with helping them. But then I drop the energy, and disconnect from them once they leave the room. I make a separation, but God doesn't. God continues to work with them. Then the next person comes in. I work with them, and again I'm completely focused. Once they are done, they are out. I refocus step by step. I have trained myself, so that I will not go into or merge with other people's energy. I want them to have their own privacy. I have no right to enter their energy field. So when I am out in public, I am completely shut off, as far as reading people goes. I am in a spiritual energy but not a reading energy. I enjoy the beauty of nature and people that are near me. I trained myself to be able to open up and then shut down. The only way I would open up, in my off time, would be if God turned my head or got my attention in some way. If God said, "Go ahead, help that person," then I would do it. My intention is to be obedient to God.

One of my friends can read people, right off the bat. But me, I personally set up my system so that the person has their privacy. When someone asks me for help, or comes to me for a healing session, then I focus on them, and the abilities that God has given me activate. When I'm out in public, I purposely do not have that energy turned on. It is completely shut off. It is almost like everyone is talking at the same time and I don't hear anything. Many intuitive people get an overload when they don't turn their gifts off in a crowd. They even tend to gain weight from picking up other people's energy all the time. I have learned from other healers things that work and things that don't.

*Keeping the Frequency High ... I Don't Pick up Sickness*

What I do have is God's light shining through me. I just let it spark and I let it shine. I walk along and I have my protection from this light. I give good energy to people who need help. Not too many people can just shut it off like I can. Often I have seen healers picking up other people's emotions and aches and pains. I could see that it weighed them down and made their life difficult. That is why it was so important for me to train myself not to take on these burdens.

A lot of spiritual people do their massages and healing work and pick up the pains and feelings from the person they are working on. Usually, when I get through with a healing, I wash my hands as a ritual to cleanse the other person's energy from mine. It is actually a ritual of separation. At times when I am working, the energy is so high that it doesn't bother me or hurt the other person either. In fact, it is healing and helpful. The higher the energy that can come through, the better the healing. When the energy is high, I can work with twenty people and the energy doesn't dwindle down from person to person. With such a high-frequency spiritual light, I can work with twenty-five people a day. One time in three-and-a-half days I worked with between seventy and eighty people. I didn't know if it was night or day. I didn't know if it was raining or shining outside. You know, I am in a special world with God and with the particular person that I am helping. When I do that, I don't have any outside interference.

## Empathy

When you can feel exactly what another person is feeling, that is called empathy. I can feel exactly what the person is feeling, but I stay out of them. I don't jump into them to find that out. I can feel it from the outside and even from a distance. I don't merge with them because their problem is not my problem. I'm willing to help them, and I do that by trying to be in the best attunement with God that I can. When I'm in tune with God, I can find the different problems and sicknesses of people very easily.

### After Balancing All the Bodies

After the massage and healing is completed, all the bodies are balanced: physical, mental, emotional and spiritual. The body comes together again as a harmonious whole or a finely woven basket. Then I say, "Okay, go take a walk and take yourself out on a little road test." People walk around and go, "Wow, I feel just fantastic!"

### The Connection to God Is Changeable

Some people come to me many times, over a span of years. They may be connected to God at one time more than another. They may be different again the next time I see them. They may be having a hard time and not feeling close to God. They may be feeling depressed but trying to cover it up. But to me, it will show up as a challenge the person is having at the moment. Sometimes depression makes people slip back into unhealthy habits. The same old habit that didn't work before can come out again. The person may wear the same old shoes again that don't fit. This gets very uncomfortable.

### Talk to God If You Get Depressed

When people get depressed, they slip back into old, unhealthy habits and they forget to inspire themselves. They may feel sad or hopeless. They may be disappointed, disillusioned or heartbroken. At this point it is important to have a really good heart-to-heart talk with God. It is important to ask God to show us the next step and to give us help and inspiration to start over again.

We all have free will. We can all choose to walk with God or fall back into old, bad habits. Sometimes when people are going through a dark night of the soul, it is actually an opportunity to learn and grow. It is also important for people to ask God to be with them during these dark times.

### Gaining Experience, Gaining Gifts

There was one occasion when I had five carloads of people that came in to do the spiritual process. The more I was saying, "Oh, no" inside, the more people showed up. This was a semi-emergency that I had to deal with. So I said, "Okay, God, I will make a deal with you. God, you know I will handle all the people you want me to handle this month. I don't care. Make me work for eighteen or twenty-four hours a day. I will do it. But I would appreciate it if next month I could have a rest."

So I had to work with all the different people. I didn't know it at the time, but there was a reason for it. I would gain valuable experience and new spiritual gifts.

### The Visionary Gift

One person came in who was able to see very clearly with their third eye. So when I worked with this person, I was able to see through the body with a kind of x-ray vision. I saw certain things. Very shortly after that, she described to me what she saw about herself. What I saw and what she saw was exactly the same, and both of our visions were accurate.

### Talking to People in Their Own Language

Sometimes it is very hard for people to face the truth. So when I'm helping people, God speaks through me in such a way that they are able to understand. If the person is a mechanic, then I talk to them on a mechanic level. If the person is a housewife, then I will talk to her with plates, spoons, knives, forks and kids, for example. I relate what I am talking about with their own language, symbols and interests, so that they can understand me clearly. If the person is a cowboy, I will talk to them in their own language, kind of rough and tough, you know.

### A Trip to a Famous Hospital in Kansas

One time around 1980, I went to a very prestigious hospital and clinic in Topeka, Kansas, as a guest of some doctors there. The doctors and researchers wanted to tell me the patient's history. Then they wanted to see if I could pick up any additional intuitive information that would be helpful for curing the person. I said,

"No, I don't want to know the history. I just want to go in blind and see what I can find, without any preconditioning or information."

## We Were Asked Not to Touch the Patients

My healing partner and I were asked not to touch or do any "laying on of hands" with any of the patients. So we met and observed patients. We used the nurse and the doctor, as proxies, for the healing of one particular patient. We focused our healing energies on the patient ... and that patient's energy system. The next day, there was a change in the whole vibration of the patient and the patient had returned to normal.

But, the doctors and nurses surprised us by not asking us one single question about how it was done, but they asked us to come back and help again. They said, "Do whatever you want to do when you come back." Since we were not allowed to touch the patients, we shot them with healing energy. I held the hands of the doctor and my healing partner held the hands of the nurse. We had the patient sitting between the doctor and the nurse. So the healing energy hit the patient from both directions, without us ever touching the patient. Healing energy works! It can travel to someone through someone else's body. It moves through matter. The doctor and the nurse felt the energy going through them. They couldn't deny it or explain it either. It's a good way to do a healing if you can't touch the person for some reason.

## We Asked God to Heal Them

That is what happened in Kansas. I cried when we left because they didn't even seem interested in asking us how we did it. It was very, very simple. When people don't know how to do something, they usually make things a lot more complicated than they need to be. We simply asked God to come through us to heal these people, especially that one patient who was sitting in between the doctor and the nurse. The higher I felt the light, the higher I felt the love. You see, the heart comes up vibrationally, with music. The heart comes up vibrationally with color and with light. The heart comes up vibrationally with love. You know, I can even smell the heart, with my psychic senses.

## Psychic Taste

Another person came in and had a sense of taste. So I worked with this person and started tasting certain psychic tastes. This person had a gift of tasting certain tastes in their own mouth that helped in diagnosing sicknesses and conditions in other people. In a short time it seemed his gift was transferred to me. The man with the gift of taste would describe a taste to me and suddenly I could taste it and describe it back to him.

## Spiritual Music in the Body

Another thing I want to share is about hearing certain music, in the spiritual dimension, when I scan a person's body. During this period of time a woman was visiting who had the gift of hearing clairaudiently. She would describe to me what she would hear. This is a kind of psychic hearing of music or things that most other people can't hear. Now this is a gift, and not the phenomena of hearing voices, the way psychotic people hear things — although some psychotic people may have some clairaudience but in a chaotic and disturbed mind. People need to be grounded, emotionally stable, and living close to God before they open up these spiritual and psychic gifts. So when I was working with this woman, she would be hearing music and messages clairaudiently, and I would be experiencing and hearing exactly what she heard, at the same time.

## Gaining Validation and Confidence

By these other gifted people showing up here, and sharing their hearing, seeing, tasting and smelling with me, God gave me validation that my readings were accurate, as these other people had gotten the same information that I got. God had given me all of these gifts, and he wanted to take any doubt away from me about my accuracy in scanning and reading the body. He sent in these helpers, who specialized in certain areas, to help confirm my own "reading" ability.

Having so many people to work on, all at once, turned out to be like an intensive, advanced class which strengthened my confidence. After that, from that time on, I had no more war within myself. I had no more doubts. Then, when I began to work with people, I told them what I saw. This experience with the other gifted people helped me to know that I had been given confirmation about reading things accurately.

### Further Training by Validation with Gifted Clients

One person was able to smell psychic smells, or smells that most people couldn't smell. I was able to smell exactly what they were smelling at the same time, so I found out that my smelling gift was accurate. Another person who had their third eye open was reporting seeing certain things clairvoyantly. Just before they would say something about what they were seeing, I would have a vision of the same thing. This showed me what they were going through in the spiritual process. I was seeing exactly the same thing that they were seeing. It was also a validating experience for me to know that what I was seeing with my third eye was accurate. Another person was really gifted with taste. I was able to taste it before she ever spoke about tasting certain things, like certain foods. Even if she was talking about eating foods I had never even eaten, I could taste the foods she was talking about. All this was really interesting because, as I was helping these people, I was helping myself at the same time. It was a higher level of my training and also a validation that the information I was receiving was correct. This was one of the ways I was able to open other faculties of my bodies and use God's gift of extrasensory smell, taste, physical and spiritual seeing, and feeling. The combinations of these gifts gave me the ability to read and really help people.

Once I got through March, working with all these people, I had a break and could go down to San Francisco. While there, I saw a movie called "Competition." As I was listening to this woman playing the piano, I noticed I was able to listen to more than a thousand different levels simultaneously. The month of March had given me an opportunity to become a better channel. I could see through people to see what was really going on with them.

In the "spiritual process," we also treat the yin and the yang in people. The right side of the body is positive or yang, and the left side of the body is negative or yin. We need to have our yin and yang in balance, both from side to side and head to foot. The body has to be in balance in order to feed energy to the organs correctly. I know people who "channel" who are only about ten percent accurate. This is another reason why I wanted to be a better channel of God's love. It is a good thing. I am glad that I am able to help and be of service to others.

Some spiritual processes have similarities. There are some things that are the same about them, but each one is very unique. The spiritual process is a journey inside yourself to find out the truth about yourself, rather than being dependent on other people's opinions of you. The process teaches you how to communicate with the God within, so the truth can come out. The enrichment which opens up inside shows outside. You develop more confidence in yourself as you have greater accuracy in seeing your own truth.

### More Validation by Healing Large Numbers

One time I was up in Coeur D'Alene, Idaho, and Spokane, Washington. There were certain days that I worked with a hundred people. I usually had someone take notes, when I was reading a person's body. Both of the ladies that facilitated for me, in these locations, knew people there and called them. After everyone left, both of them came up to me and said that on every single person I read, that I was one hundred percent accurate. These ladies knew all these people. Hearing of the accuracy of these readings bolstered my confidence too. I knew that God was working through me to bless and heal the people. The more confidence you have and the more you open up to God's flow, the stronger the readings and healings become.

If a person doubts God, then that doubt puts a filter into the brains or into the body, which ends up short-circuiting the system. Then there's not enough energy coming through the body to nourish the body, or open a strong sense of intuition. Doubt tends to shut a lot of systems down. It also seriously interferes with creative manifestation. Love, faith, hope, gratitude and confidence open the body's systems and energy, creating a strong connection to God and spirit and to healing and positive manifestation.

### Times of Doubt and Lost Faith

There are times in life when a person may be having a lot of negative experiences. They may still be praying to God, but they think God isn't answering their prayers or has abandoned them. Because bad or painful things keep happening, in spite of their prayers for God's help, they might lose faith. Sometimes a person may say, "I've been asking for God's help, presence and light in my life, and yet bad things just keep happening over and over again. It doesn't seem like God's there for me."

Sometimes we need to look around and see what's going on, so that we can get more information about what's happening to our body, mind, or life. Then we need to go inside and talk to God again. And then we can go from here to the greater God, who lives upstairs, and see what happens when we make this communication.

Then we also have people who are healers, who work with God's light, who we can communicate with. We can ask them for insight and help. If we trust them, often they can help us. They may be able to fill in the gap, or they may help us to see a wrong turn that we've made or are still making. They may help us see our "blind spots." It's a little like going through a maze. Each thing we go through is a learning stage.

### More Body Scanning

When the spiritual body can't feed the physical body, the physical body begins to die. It just doesn't have enough light to run on. The body really runs on light the same way a car runs on gasoline. So it is like not having enough gas in the car. The person gets into a lower vibration and the person begins to deceive people. They may also be deceiving themselves. The lying becomes a habit, and it is very detrimental to themselves and the people around them, as well.

So going up the spine tells me many different things. There are times that the butt area, the neck and chest are all out of alignment, as if they're on different planes. When the body gets warped like this, it tends to get sick. When I tell a person what I see, I tell them that it is something that they created or that someone else created for them. It could mean power by association or keeping the wrong company. I also see how the energy moves on the back of the neck and the color of the energy of the brains. I also look at the nervous system and the circulatory system and touch in with many details, if they're relevant to the person's present or future health. There are times when I hear the sound of metal scraping against concrete or sidewalk. That sound in a person's body usually tells me that the person has cancer.

## A Body, Mind and Spirit Approach in Scanning

If a medical doctor wanted to work with me, I would say "Bring in a patient that you and I have never seen before, who has some kind of an ailment. Now you go first and see what's wrong with the person." The M.D. would do their exam and tests first, and then I would work with the patient and do it my way. The doctor may be limited to the physical body. My work deals with the person's body, mind and spirit. I will go into a great deal of detail. I am also listening to the music of the person's body, and I am doing my whole exam with God. When I'm reading, it tells what is happening genetically with the person, too. It shows me whether they have thyroid problems, stomach problems, lower back or abdominal problems, and so forth. It tells me if the electricity of the body is short-circuiting itself and whether the body is working together or separately, or if one energy goes one way and one goes the other way. If the body is not working as a family, it has its own ego in each foot, and it can cause the body to trip or short-circuit. Sometimes the body looks yellow, and that often means that the liver is congested or ill. If the person looks green, it can be toxic intestines. The big toe, and how it curves, shows me the emotional content in the back of the brains.

It tells me how the pituitary gland is functioning, and how much endocrine chemistry is coming in, and whether it is working either in balance or imbalance. The throat or neck area shows me how a person short-circuits themselves. Just by examining the foot, I am shown everything about the body.

Then I go up the back of the calf and I look at the back of the knees. This will tell me how the energy is moving. It will tell me if the person thinks too much, or if they have a knee problem, or if the muscle is off. It shows me if there will be future problems with the knees. It shows it to me because it is pre-set. There is a sound to it. There is a physical attitude that it shows. If you move the knee this way, the muscle may pull to an angle that will cause problems in the knee's future. It shows up for me automatically. The knees represent understanding about life. If a person doesn't understand life, then the person's knees look really "off" to me. Sometimes knee problems come from an excess of stress and strain from physical activity. Now football players' injuries are on a whole different level. That's more of a mechanical problem. They often have to have sport microsurgery. That is one of the hazards of the game.

I was talking to someone who was telling me that the bones and muscles are in threes. I think it could be true, as three is a very important number. After reading the feet, knees and legs, I go up and check out the butt area. I can go in and see how the tailbone and sacrum area are doing. I check how it goes up and down and then side to side. The root chakra is right there, so I can see the vitality of it, if it is bright or dark. I can see if it is kind of plugged up, like a pipe that's needing the roto-rooter. From there I will go up the spine, and it will tell me if there is a problem in the prostrate area or lower back. I can sense if the blood is healthy. The energy will shake and vibrate, when you look at it on a spiritual level. As you go up towards the solar plexus area, sometimes the energy shakes there, as it enters the chakra. If it goes in like a big dynamite explosion, it shows that there is a blockage in the path. It indicates very heavy emotional problems or a big upset. Sometimes a person can look bloated or pregnant in the butt or solar plexus area due to emotional holding or blockage. All the parts of the whole body are in a conversation with each other. It is really interesting.

After I have checked out the whole back side of a person, I ask them to turn over and I do the scan on the front of the body. If someone is a very emotional person, they will be very easy for me to read. If a person is very cold and guarded, it is harder for me to read them. They are shielding themselves and holding everything in. So there is another layer of armor to penetrate when I read someone like that. This is often the case with a very skeptical person, someone who is afraid to reveal themselves to anyone, or who has difficulty with the concept of a God. The truth about the person will come out just the same.

## Crooks and Crooked Energy

You and I could be walking down the street and see a regular guy walking along. But if we checked him out spiritually, we might find out that he has crooked energy running through his body and that he conducts a crooked life that matches his energy. This shows that his own behavior has warped energy and that the bad behavior warps the energy. You may wonder what comes first ... the warped energy or the warped behavior. It is the bad behavior that warps the energy. That is what comes first. The soul always knows when you're off in yourself, because the soul is part of God. When I check people's energy on the massage table, and it runs crooked instead of straight, it tells me that the person is dishonest. You know how they call people that are crooks?—"crooked." This is literally true of their energy. So what happens here is that the energy runs crooked in some way when I read people who are crooks. If the person is not a crook but just dishonest, the crooked energy may not be as severe.

## The Stomach That Spoke to Me

I remember one woman who came to me with a stomach problem. Her stomach spoke to me saying, "I am tired of eating potatoes." I asked the woman what she had been eating and she answered, "Potatoes." I told her what her stomach had told me. She said that she had just been to India and didn't have much money left to buy food and potatoes were cheap. The body speaks to me. It is always so interesting and I am always learning something new.

With an alcoholic or drug user there is a characteristic smell. The liver starts to fall apart, big time. I see the pores of the skin begin to open wide and I also see the brain looking warped, lopsided, and short of oxygen. I see the muscles and the nervous system begin to get hardened, small and thin. Part of the body looks grey and black, and if there's anger or rage, there will be a lot of red that shows up.

### A Story of the Ashram with Red Brains

One time in Nevada City a group of people came from an Ashram for a healing. I was wondering why they all had the same red color in their brains. It had always indicated anger to me, when I had seen it in the past. The anger must be connected to the Guru, or the leader of the group, I thought. I heard, through other people, that the Guru who was in charge of this group had a lot of anger towards me, as he thought that I was stealing his students away from him. So I sent a message back to him that I was not here to steal his people but only to help them to heal themselves of headaches, lower back problems, stomach problems and so forth. I also said that if they were more balanced and relieved of pain that they would do better in their meditation. So what a surprise I had when here comes the Guru, or leader of the Ashram, to see me. He had a big red mark in his brains, just as I thought. It was the same as all his students, except the area of red in his brains was larger. I worked with him and corrected the problem that he had. Afterwards he confessed that he didn't really want to be a guru anymore. Six months later I saw him again. He told me that he had quit his life as a guru. He had decided that what he needed to experience was love.

### Group Energy and Group Themes

This man's group had this characteristic red mark, but any spiritual or religious group will have something that shows up that they all have in common. Each group is together because they are learning a lesson in common or are working out certain things as a group. Once I went to a Zen Buddhist group, and every single person that I worked with there had similar problems and themes in their life. All of them were very sympathetic and compassionate people, but they all had depression, sadness and lower back problems.

As I travel to many places around this earth, I see the same things about locations. Certain types of people are attracted to living in a certain location that has a certain energy field and certain qualities that appeal to them or help them in their growth. As I see things, it is like pieces of a jigsaw puzzle that begin to slide together. When people have a strong guidance to move to a drastically different location, it may indicate that they are ready to shift vibrations and explore new aspects of themselves.

Here in the Sierra foothills of California, in Nevada City, we live on top of both gold and quartz crystal. Both have a high spiritual frequency. Many people who are healers or spiritual seekers are attracted to this area and make it their home. There are also many spiritual groups and retreat centers in this area. This is a demonstration of how the earth supports certain qualities and energies that people are striving to develop and open. Not only do we have these minerals, but we have beautiful mountains, a sacred river and many lakes nearby. There are pine and cedar forests all around us. It is an excellent location for spiritual retreats and workshops, as nature joins in and enhances the process.

*Exorcising Negative Entities*

Sometimes a spirit will come out of the person to attack me. Once it sees that I'm not afraid of it, it will go back into the person and hide. They may have never guessed that they have a spirit possession. I will surely get it out of the person before they leave the healing session. Sometimes I see slimy worms on people's faces, coming out of the nose, the ears, eyes and mouth. Now, that makes me feel very uncomfortable. This can show up when a person is very, very intelligent but really lacking the God-spirit and light inside. Possessions by bad spirits and entities are at times the cause of serious physical health problems or mental illness. At times these entities are passed down through the generations in a family.

There is also another way to pick them up that most people won't want to hear about. And that is sex. When a person has sex with another person who has an entity attachment, it can jump into the other person and start bothering their life. So I want to warn everyone, that besides the dangers of sexually transmitted diseases or unwanted pregnancy, there is the additional danger of picking up someone's entities. Some of the entities have appeared to me as crocodiles, snakes, monsters or human beings.

There is the strongest danger when you are having sex with someone who is a drug or alcohol abuser, or someone who is angry and violent. But there are other cases where the person will seem nice, charming and charismatic. You may get pleasure from the sexual experience, but it could be dangerous to you in invisible subtle ways. This is an even greater reason not to be involved in casual sex. You don't know the person. When there is God's love blessing the union, and the people know each other well, and are committed, then there is a sacred spiritual experience that can happen for the couple.

Taking an entity out of a person is easy at times and at other times difficult. I have enough spiritual muscle to do the job with God's help. All that is shown to me. It may sound like a psychedelic light show, but I have to admit how I see is not how the average person sees. People wonder how I get this information. It may sound like nonsense to them. The Bible talks repeatedly about casting out demons and bad spirits. This tradition of exorcism exists in Hinduism, Tibetan Buddhism, and many other religions too. Many native tribes believe in spirit possession and have their experts to help with this type of problem. So it's hard to tell other people how I get this information. I have a unique way of seeing things, and God has given me this gift.

### Picking up Other People's Energy

Sometimes, for instance, someone in your family is really sick and that sick energy sticks to you. If your body does not release it, then you carry that negative energy around with you. You feel bad or tired or get sick too.

We all need to understand what belongs to us and what belongs to others. We're talking about problems, moods, sickness and energy. We can't take other people's problems into our body. If we do that, then we begin to die.

### The "Protection" Exercise

Sometimes you feel stagnant or stuck, and other people's energy seems to stick to us. Other people's negative emotions can be attached to us and can make us feel heavy and dull. There is a wonderful exercise that can be used once a day or more to give us a strong light of spiritual protection. It helps all of our chakras to open and beam more brightly, and it helps to strengthen and open our auric field. The more we practice this exercise, the stronger our spiritual protection will be.

If possible, stand outside in the sunshine, or, if you cannot go outside, visualize standing in the sunshine. Stand straight and tall and ground yourself into Mother Earth. Then visualize bringing the rays of the sun, which is above you, down to the sacrum or root chakra. While pulling the sun rays down through the body, inhale. Then visualize and imagine the sun's rays radiating out from all sides of you ... front and back, sides, top and bottom ... all the way around you ... and then out 21 miles from you, while you exhale. If you can't do this at first, just imagine sending the light rays out for five miles in all directions. Gradually visualize, imagine and sense them going into infinity. For much stronger protection do this same exercise but pull the energy all the way down to the feet. When you exhale bring the energy up into an eggshell of golden light around you.

### A Protection for Sleeping

Before going to sleep, pray for your protection during sleep and pull creamy colored moon beams down and let them merge into your body and also surround your body. You will sleep well.

*Lessons from the Gypsies, and Other Healers*

I've seen other healers take on other people's energy. I've seen it with the gypsies, the American Indians and the Philippino healers. I learned a big lesson from many of them: We don't need to take on the sickness of others. I've watched and learned from all the other healers I have met in my life. Many healers take the sickness of their patients into their own body. They may vomit afterwards or do some ritual to take it out of themselves, or they may be sick for a while. But I claim that it is not necessary to take the sickness into the body, in the first place. You cannot do healing work this way and stay healthy yourself.

I have learned from these healer's mistakes. They may do things this way because it has been a custom or tradition with their own people. It may be the way they were taught. It may come from their own culture or their own beliefs and religion. But they usually die at an early age.

*Observing Inaccurate Information in Some Healers*

Doing healing work for forty years, I have encountered many things in life. I have watched other channels, healers and ministers. I found out that many times information that they brought through was inaccurate or not the complete truth. I saw that professional and gifted people could be unclear due to emotions, due to the way they think or the way they were brought up as children. Something in the past conditioned them to think in a certain way. Their personality influences their spiritual gifts. When the energy within the body is not clear, they can't pull through the right information for themselves and other people. Being completely clear is very important for getting clear and correct information and guidance to help people.

*Experiences with Other Healers*

I have watched many types of healers work, from evangelists, American Indians, Filipino healers, and spiritualists. I saw how they dealt with people and how the healing affected the people. Religion and cultural customs have certain ways of influencing how they work. We can speed up the process of effectiveness in healing by working directly with God. It is not good to work with lower spirits using black magic. We don't want to work this way. We will only work with God's help and healing.

I have a technique that I use. In a way, I suppose you might say that it is a bit like white magic, but I pray for God's help to come through in giving us information. White magic or using the blessings of God and the angels has no harmful effect, and does not come back on us in a harmful way.

### Katherine Kuhlman ... the Famous Faith Healer

For example, a long time ago I went to see the famous faith healer, Katherine Kuhlman, at Shriners Auditorium in Los Angeles, California. There was a huge crowd there to see her, as usual. When she held out her hands to send healing energy, I could see a white transparent spiral. When it came towards me, it hit my third eye. I was slain in the spirit. In other words, I just fell down. The power was so great that it knocked me to the floor. You see other people falling down, and there are people there especially to catch people. But until it happened to me, I didn't know if it was for real or not. The power can be so great that you couldn't help but fall down. Being slain in the spirit is caused by very, very strong light energy that comes from God. Katherine Kuhlman was an instrument of God's healing. The Holy Spirit would come down, come through her body, and then flow out of her to help and heal people. The purpose of falling down like that, or being slain in the spirit, is that your whole body is in a state of surrender. When you are surrendered, and really relaxed, healing energy can flow through your body so much better.

### Two Types of Surrender

There are two types of surrender ... one is by water, usually done by baptism. Water is part of our earth and one of the elements.

The second type of surrender is by fire ... by the power of the Holy Spirit. Many people have described it as being like a transparent fire energy. When Katherine Kuhlman did her healing, the Holy Spirit would come through her hands, her body, her voice, and the live music to touch the people in the audiences. Many, many people had miraculous healings. The Holy Spirit does not burn you like regular fire does, but it is a fiery-like energy that can open up your channels and chakras. It is a spiritual blessing that quickens your spiritual abilities and your spiritual life. It comes down from the heavens. So the first type of surrender is by water—an earthly element—and the second comes from the heavens. When you surrender to the Holy Spirit fire, you surrender your emotions, your electrical system and your flesh. These two surrenders are where heaven and earth meet. Once a person witnesses this, then it is most likely that they will become a believer in God and the Holy Spirit.

You see, my work is different from the work of other healers. I wasn't meant to go into an auditorium like that, doing that kind of healing work. There are certain people who do it. There is also a certain kind of music that goes well with evangelical healing services. Katherine Kuhlman had a beautiful choir of over two hundred people. The music was so inspiring. They all wore pastel colors and it was really nice. She had a grand piano and some beautiful solo singers too. The energy with this music was so highly elevated. It was great! After she died, it took a few years before another person, similar to her, came out to the public Her gift was given to the next person that would share it with the world. This time it is a man and his name is Benny Hinn. He uses similar music and does the same things she did. He modified her style but kept the same style of healing.

In the Bible there is talk of Adam and Eve. They had two sons. One son had a gift. The other son came along to kill his brother in order to get the gift. It's like that. It's a gift that goes from generation to generation. It's passed on through the blood line. In the Philippines the Filipino healers have their gifts passed from one generation to another too. I believe that Benny Hinn is the real thing. He has a lot of personality. Some people don't like him. A person with a big ego might not be able to see him in a pure way. His spirit might have a certain vibration that attracts certain spirits and angels that can do healing work with people. He is just very, very strong and really proud of what he is doing. He has helped a lot of people. Not everyone can do the kind of work he does. I finally got his CD. I like it because it reminds me of going to see Katherine Kuhlman.

# 2

# My Early Life

## Early Life

I started getting closer to God when I went to City College of San Francisco. About 1964 I took classes for two years, preparing to take the test to be a draftsman. At that time I wanted to be an engineer, because it was a career that made good money. For the whole year I prepared to take the test. After taking all the classes, I flunked the test by three points. So I decided to have three occupations. The first choice was to be a chef. The second choice was merchandising, and the third choice was photography. I decided to accept challenges and make these goals. I feel that we all need to have goals and direction in life. We need to face reality, and look at things directly. Then we need to move towards our goals and wishes. So I figured if I had three wishes, it would be like having a ladder and climbing to the top of the roof of the house on this ladder. If your first choice doesn't work for you, then you take a few steps back down the ladder, and if your second choice doesn't work, you take a few steps further down the ladder. If you fall, you won't fall too hard because you are closer to the ground. We should choose things in life in threes. To me, the number three is a sacred number.

## Finding God in Nature

For me being in a place of natural beauty, in a rural area, makes me feel closer to God. I found God through nature when I was studying at the college in San Francisco. I took a photography course in composition and design. We had to find different things that looked alike. For example, one person took a picture of a flower with a little tail and then he took another picture of the rear end of an elephant. They had similarities in shape.

Another person took a picture of a service bell from a view looking down at the top of it. The similar picture was a picture of a woman's breast. It was a real challenging class.

I went out into nature and saw the beautiful things that God had put everywhere. I used my heart and my eyes with my camera and found God in all of nature.

## Seeing Good and Bad Spirits, as a Kid

When I was a young kid, I could see bad spirits and I could see good spirits. This was in Hawai'i. When I was four years old, my sister was getting ready for school and I was walking down the outside staircase with my sister. As I went down, I saw a really huge spirit. You know, it was a ghost that you could see right through. You could see a kind of whitish color.

One time we saw a spirit hanging from a tree with a rope around its neck. My sisters were all going to yell and scream, because they saw it too. They all ran into the house, really scared. When they told our Mom about it, they all got a spanking. What I did was look at the spirit directly with my physical eyes. I took two steps backwards but kept watching it. Right after that, it took off. That was a really early experience with seeing spirits. The tree was actually next to a bridge. People used to live under the bridge and later I found out that this guy had hung himself there, in a tree. So his spirit was flying around, caught in an astral vibration.

## The Bad Spirit that Gobbled up Our Chicken

Another time I was home and my Mom and Dad were sleeping in the back bedroom. We kids were up early in the morning and we were looking out of the window screen towards our chicken coop. A bush, in the yard, opened up and we saw a bad spirit coming out of it. She was purple-colored with dry wrinkled up skin, really ugly teeth and had a hood over her head. I watched her open up the door to our chicken coop. She picked up all of our chickens, one at a time, shoving them down her throat, and swallowing them whole.

So I told my Mom and Dad what happened to our chickens. They said, "Oh, someone must have come over and stole our chickens." They realized that all of the chickens were missing, but they didn't believe what I told them. My sisters don't remember this experience today, but I remember that they were there and that they saw it with me. They saw that ugly spirit swallowing our chickens—and then it just disappeared right into a hole. When I talk to my sisters, they don't remember it at all. But they do remember seeing a spirit and then going in the house to tell about it and getting a spanking. They remember that. I remember that I was four years old because my sister was a year older than I was. She was already in kindergarten and was five years old. That is how I know for sure that I was four years old.

### Two Things I Learned in High School

In high school in Hawai'i I had a teacher who taught English literature. One of her teachings was, "Be free, but not too free." She said, if you saw a beautiful woman and raped her, that was an example of being too free. So when it comes to the law, you could be put in jail if you are too free. So to be free is not to be too free. That teaching kept me in line throughout my whole life.

The second thing I learned was, if you want to get ahead in life, stick with smart people. I joined the biology club in high school and I did stick with all the smart people. Once I had a chance to be hypnotized by a black man. It was very, very positive for me, because it really made me focus better in life. As I went through life, I did stick with a lot of smart people. But I went ahead and found God and I stuck with God, first. I trust and depend on God. If things don't go right, I ask God, "Where did I go wrong?" But God always comes out right in the end, with the guidance he gives, even if it seems to be wrong guidance, at a certain point.

### Visions of Jesus, While at College

I experienced many things when I was alone. One time in Georgia I studied fashion photography. All the rooms were filled up at the school, so they had to put us up in a hotel in town. It was twenty-seven girls to every guy. I was standing in line and up front at the desk the guy said, "Who wants to be in a room alone?" There were ten or eleven people in front of me. I said, "I do." So I had a room to myself. It was a small room, but it was nice. I would be sleeping in that room and Jesus would appear to me. He took me on tours, in a visionary state, throughout the whole universe. Another time I took a speech class to improve my English. Early in the morning I said, "Okay God, I'm putting everything on automatic. Go get 'em." I went to class and the students and teacher listened to me talk and all of them said afterwards that it was the best speech they had ever heard in their whole life. Here is another instance where God worked through me.

Another time I had to give a lecture for an assistant teacher. The students said that it was the best lecture they had ever heard in their whole life. So there is more to it than words when you invite God to be in you and with you. There is a light energy. It is God working through you. So things happen. A lot of things happen like that, and it is a blessing. I keep it with me.

So when a person is looking for love—the love of another person, the love of animals, the love of nature, the love of a car, the love of a job, or the love of money—this may be what they think they are seeking. But they are really looking for the love of God, and may not even know it. That is the real hunger inside of people, and many people look in the wrong places and find substitutes for what their heart is really yearning for.

*Visions of the Hawai'ian King and His Warriors in the Sky*

Another early experience of seeing spirits in Hawai'i was seeing King Kamehameha and his warriors up in the sky wearing their red and yellow robes and high hats. I also saw a car looking in the window of the car. I looked above our car and I saw that it was floating up in the air like that. Someone was driving the car and I was looking out from that car and looking up at the sky. It happened when I was a little kid.

*Spirits of Royal Hawai'ians and the Mana of the Bones*

The old kings and queens of Hawai'i are still very, very much alive. Their spirits are very highly respected by the Kahunas (traditional Hawai'ian priests). There are burial grounds in Hawai'i where the Evi (bones) are thought to emit mana and power for all time. This is thought to be especially true of the bones of the royalty and Ali'i (warriors, nobility, and royal court) So Hawai'ians are especially sensitive about their burial grounds. They insist on having their burial grounds respected and left undisturbed. Today there are housing and shopping mall developers on the Islands who are not respecting burial grounds. The Hawai'ian people are distressed to have bull dozers digging up the bones of their relatives and ancestors. This must be stopped. None of us would want our grandma or ancestors dug up.

*A Strange Hawai'ian Custom from Long Ago*

Long ago poorer people in Hawai'i would do almost anything to give their children a greater opportunity to prosper and have a good life. They would often want their child to be adopted by the royal court. Mothers would come and bring their baby to a certain place near the King's palace to be noticed and picked up by someone from the royal court. If rats came along and ate the baby, it would supposedly show that the baby was not pure enough to be adopted by the royal family. If the baby survived with no mishap, the baby would be seen as pure enough to be adopted by the royal family.

*Strict Rules for Hawai'ian Healers*

The Hawai'ians had a really strict rule. If a person committed adultery or murdered someone, even unintentionally, the person was dropped over the edge of a cliff. Sometime in the past there may have been human sacrifices. But of course, that's not true today or for a very, very long time. There are still traditional Hawai'ian Kahuna healers on the Islands today who use spiritual healing gifts, herbal medicine, and rituals.

## *In My Family the Practice of Healing Had Stopped*

In my family we had an ancestral line of healers, but in my Mother's and Father's generation they stopped carrying on the healing traditions. We had healers on both sides of the family. When the tradition stops with one generation, it is difficult for the next generations to be taught. The family continues to produce the gift, but when the teaching stops, it leaves a gifted young person without family teachers and mentors.

## *Re-Discovering the Healing Gift Through the Spirit*

In my family it is the same. The healing gift has come down from one generation to another. My parents didn't really practice their gifts, so I had to rediscover the gift through the spirit. My work is very versatile. I work with medical doctors, Native Americans and Gurus from India. I work with everyday people of all kinds and all ages. I work with people with any and every type of condition. It is not my work to change people or their beliefs. For me, the example of the Christ is the force that I connect with.

In my case much of my teaching came directly from spirit. But I had to go searching for teaching and teachers, too. I went back to our family roots by going to the Philippines to meet and learn from the healers and psychic surgeons over there. I had to search for the teaching and I had to rediscover it all over again. On both my Mother's and Father's side of the family, the practice of healing had stopped with my parents. So in this lifetime I had to make up for lost time so that I would be able to help people who were sick, hurt, wounded, and experiencing pain and suffering. I had inherited the blood line and the gift, but I did not have the training. My parents couldn't educate me, as they weren't practicing healing. I had to start at the beginning. But I didn't mind finding it for myself. I am able to help a lot more people in this lifetime because of going out and searching for my healing training. Today I enjoy helping people to help themselves by giving them healing tools and reconnecting them to God in a stronger way. My main goal with people is to increase the love and light and happiness inside of them so it can shine out in all directions like a blazing sun.

In Hawai'i it is so easy to feel the presence of God, or Keakua, the Hawai'ian name for God. There are the mountains and the ocean that surrounds each of the islands. There are the beautiful rainbows and the thick mist that rises up from the mountains after the rain. The sun, the ocean and the flowers all play with each other, and the energy is very nourishing and very healing. The breezes come through softly and caress your aura, taking all the unwanted attachments off of you, so you feel so free, so clear and so happy. Also the heartbeat of the inner Earth comes out and, yes, it really has a nice rhythm, like a drum.

### The Hawai'ian Islands Still Have Their Healing Magic

Today Hawai'i has native Hawai'ian people, but it also has many other people who have come to live there. There has been intermarriage over the past two hundred years, and today most local people are mixtures of Hawai'ian, Chinese, Filipino, Japanese, Portuguese and European. There are many white people (Haoles) who have come to live on the Islands too. But the Islands continue to have their own magic in spite of the settlers who have brought mainland culture with them. The breezes, the beautiful ocean and beaches are so lovely. The sweet-smelling flowers and delicious tropical fruits are all so healing. The Aloha spirit of unconditional love is still very much alive in the Islands and is the trademark of happy Hawai'ian people. People here in California call me the Happy Hawai'ian. "You can take Cosme out of Hawai'i, but you can't take the Hawai'ian out of Cosme."

### The Hawai'ian People

I really like the way the Hawai'ian people (and the people who live in Hawai'i) live their lives. You can see all their Aloha (love) and peace and connectedness to family (Ohana). It is very important for them to love and take care of the land (Aina). Most people grow a garden and fruit trees. Hawai'ians really love their children (Keiki) and their food too. Everyone in Hawai'i loves to eat. I love to eat all the local food when I go to visit over there. My sister just flew in to visit us here and brought my favorite custard pie from Oahu.

*God Must Really Love Blue and Green*

When we look at planet Earth from outer space, we think God must have really liked blue and green a lot. The Earth looks green. The sky and the oceans look blue. When blue and green are mingled together, we get the color of aqua, which is a pale version of turquoise. When you see this beauty, you will feel the presence of God in nature. When I go to Hawai'i, I love to go to Hanama Bay on the Island of Oahu. The water in the bay is aqua and it is so beautiful. Boy, the body feels really good and at peace, when you are there. It is so very healing. It is one of my favorite places to go. I love to get there early before other people get there. Hawai'i is like paradise. The energy is so very much alive.

# THE VIETNAM WAR

## *Louisiana*

I remember when I left Hawai'i and went to Louisiana. I was stationed there in the Air Force. There were alligators and swamps there. When I returned to Hawai'i, I really appreciated it a lot more. I said, "I didn't realize that Hawai'i is so beautiful. Louisiana was good for eating though. There was really good fish and shrimp.

In Louisiana the energy was real heavy. I felt that a lot of witchcraft and racial prejudice was being practiced there, at the time. I was stationed in the Air Force there, at the time of the Vietnam War. At that time I was not as spiritually sensitive as I am now, so I didn't feel it as strongly then. As I grew spiritually, I got to be a lot more sensitive. One time I went there to visit one of my sergeant friends that I knew during the sixties. We planned to stay for a visit, but it ended up being briefer than we thought. We couldn't stand the vibration in Louisiana and had to leave. We had to drive all the way to Texas to get out of that energy. It sure was a difficult energy. My body got really, really, extremely sensitive. As I developed spiritually, I could feel more and more subtle levels of energy. It's so interesting to feel how different places make us feel.

## The Air Force

I was stationed at Shreveport, Louisiana, Air Force base for training, and then after that I went to Thailand. I loved it there because the people are very nice. When they greet you, they kind of sing, "How are you? I am fine. Thank you." There is such a singing vibration there. The girls loved me there because I look like a Thai man. Then I came back to the states and God said, "You are going to go to Vietnam to learn about humility, but you will come back alive." I said, "Okay."

## The Vietnam War

A week later I got my papers and went to Vietnam, and I was there for nine months. Jesus appeared to me while I was there and said, "Wait and be patient and I will show you the way." I said, "Okay." I had no doubt. I went out to help with the handicapped kids. A group of us military guys went to a place where the kids don't have any arms and legs, you know. They had no homes and had lost many limbs. It was in a rectangle-shaped building with a balcony. We played with the kids, just making them happy and making them laugh with some good light energy.

## Saigon, the Ice Cream Base

When I was in Vietnam, I was stationed in Saigon, which they call the ice cream base because it was the safest base in Vietnam. On the front lines you had the Korean fighter army. On the second line you had the U.S. Army. On the third line you had the Air Force and the military from Australia. On the sidelines we had the helicopter gunners, and then there were the jets. We had everything. So sometimes the missiles coming off our base would trigger the radar and the sirens, and we would have to take cover. If a real missle did hit our base, and it hit right between two barracks, it would actually wipe out both sides of the barracks. That's how powerful it was. There were two Vietkong up on our water tower one time before I got there. It took us a few days to get them off of it, you know. So I wondered what they were going to do up on the tower. There was shooting and I decided I didn't want to get in the way of gunfire. So when the siren went off, I put on my helmet and vest, grabbed my food bag and ran downstairs. If I couldn't get out of there, at least I was pretty well set up with food. I worked twelve hour shifts.

### I Knew I Would Come Back Alive

We had bombings close by, but not directly on us. I knew I would come back alive. Actually, the only real danger was the missiles.

It was really neat when I was in Thailand. I was exercising and lifting weights. I gained fifteen pounds. At that time my job was working with the quality control of the photography division. We had to carry big boxes of chemicals for the developing lab. The first three months I carried all these boxes with strength. In the next three months, back in Vietnam, I had to use a dolly as I had lost twenty pounds, and couldn't carry all that weight anymore. It was a good thing that I gained weight in Thailand, because I lost so much weight, right after that, in Vietnam. You know, we were really lucky to have an air-conditioned place to work in, because it was so hot over there. When it wasn't hot, it was rainy.

### The Karma of War

I was in Vietnam during the war. If you go to war because you want to kill people, you end up being karmically responsible for it. But if you go to war because you want to help free people, you have a different motivation. You intention is different and the responsibility of the war is more on the government than on you. There is a difference. Motivation is important. It is everything, really.

### Keeping a Sense of Humor ... Even About Vietnam

People often ask me if I was in Vietnam and I say, "Yes, I was in Saigon. I was behind fences." People asked why, and I would say joking, "Because I was too dangerous for the enemies. I was so dangerous that they had to keep me inside." But, I felt that I was serving my country so that we could have freedom here in the United States. But like I say, when it comes to politics, if the politicians don't tell the truth, I don't have to vote for them.

## My First Spiritual Reading in Vietnam

When I was in Vietnam, I would get together with high officers and airmen from Australia. They would show me pictures of their family members back home. They would say, "Tell me about my wife." or "Tell me about my girlfriend." My third eye would go into the picture to the person's third eye. I would barely touch into their third eye, before it would kick back to me from the picture and hit my third eye. Then I had the information so I could tell them exactly what I saw about their wife, girlfriend or relative. In both Vietnam and Thailand, guys would show me pictures of their girlfriends and wives. At that time I was young and I wasn't that confident. I wondered if I was giving them the right information, or if I was just playing a guessing game. But the guys always said, "Cosme, you're right about that." You can't play games with people if they are asking you serious questions about their loved ones. You need to get it right, you know. So that is what I used to do before, when I was still a young kid. I could never figure out how people read other people. I knew that I knew a lot more details about people than most readers. But in some ways I didn't know anything myself, really, because it was all coming from spirit.

One time I had a guy ask me to read his palm while I was mixing photographic chemicals. I said, "yes" and then, without looking at his hand, just started to give him his reading. He was shocked with the accuracy and told me I was right about everything. He was shocked.

## Seeing Visions in the Sand

Remember, I had a spiritual teacher that came in and showed me how he manifested things, on the sand. I saw the river appear. I saw a waterfall forging ahead. And so one of my assignments was to discover the purpose of these visions, which had appeared to me, in the sand.

### Hawai'ian Herbalist Infuses a Plant with a Healing Energy

I remember a woman in Hawai'i who grew herbs in her yard. One day another woman came to her house and wanted some herbs from this woman, to help a health problem. The woman had just given the last of a particular type of herb away to someone else. She didn't have any more of the kind the woman came for. So the Hawai'ian herbalist went to a different plant and prayed over it. Through this prayer she changed the vibration of the plant to be just what the woman needed to heal her health problem.

### A Story from Georgia

I will tell you a story about something that happened to me a long time ago. I went to Georgia to study fashion photography. I had found human love with a female friend—not sexual love, but love. I had found her in Georgia and then it came time for me to go home for Easter. When I got back to Georgia, she didn't want to have anything to do with me any more. It seemed that God had given me love and then taken it out of my life. For six days and six nights I heaved, I choked, I got real sick. I was on my knees. I didn't care anything about cars, school, nothing. It's almost like a person wants to commit suicide. I didn't actually want to commit suicide, but it is a feeling of wanting to do this. This emptiness and voidness is so very strong. I can see how some people in this state give in to suicide. What a shame, too, because all this pain does pass and life begins fresh again. I told one of my friends about what I had experienced so long ago. My friend was going through a similar experience. I said, "I know a little of what you're going through because I went through something similar a long time ago."

### The Apparition of the Geisha

After six days of this horrible state of body and mind, I heard a wind blowing through silk cloth, coming from the East. As the wind blew, it came towards me and entered my body. I took a deep breath and I could feel my inner chalice being filled up and coming back to life again. My whole being was filled and I was kneeling, facing towards the East. Then I saw a vision of a Japanese Geisha lady. Her long beautiful hair was up on the top of her head in a most ornamental and artistic hair style. She was very beautiful, feminine and shy.

"See, you are nothing without God's Love," she said to me. "See, you are nothing without God's love … and breath … the breath is light." So that is the nucleus of the individual. When God's love comes back into you, you realize that it was missing. You were depending too much on human love, which is fickle and uncertain, compared to the constant love of God. I will never forget the awful despair that came when I depended more on human love than God's love.

### Learning Through Years of Experience

When I came back to the United States, I met different people who taught me so many different things, at different times. I would be in a store, and meet and talk to people. One thing led to another. People taught me things and showed me the way. I was guided spiritually to work with people who helped me learn new things about healing. Over the years, each new person I worked with helped me to learn more about human nature and healing. It doesn't all happen over night. It takes many years to learn and gain experience and to develop love and compassion. You need to know what people are going through in life, in order to help them.

# 3

# Stories of Healing

## The Power of Visualization

One day a young kid, Daniel, came in to see me with a pulled and twisted ligament. He hurt himself the week before, and his friend brought him to me. He could hardly walk, and he had to hop in like a rabbit. He came in at ten o'clock in the morning. At three o'clock in the afternoon he was supposed to run a race at the track. It was a hundred yard dash and relay race. He was ready to be replaced by someone else, due to his injury. But he decided to come to see me, so I worked with him. I taught him how to send energy from the starting line to the finish line.

I taught him first to send energy from his heart up to his third eye (between the brows) and then project it to the finish line. He practiced that visualization. He did that, and when they called out, "On your mark, get set, go!", he kicked off, and he saw his energy from all of his subtle bodies already at the finish line. He ran right towards his projected energy. It was like a rubber band pulling him forward. So by doing this, you actually increase your energy, rather than lose energy, by the time you get to the finish line.

At the local high school race he was able to match the record for the hundred yard dash. Doing this kind of visualization really helped him excel in his athletics. In addition, the day he came to see me, he was able to run the relay race and his team came in first place. It wasn't until later that night when he came home that he thought about it and said, "Wow, all that happened, just as I visualized it earlier in the day with Cosme."

Visualization can be used this way for all athletics and for many other purposes to help us achieve our goals and heal our emotions and body.

## The Woman with the Troubles of Job

There are many ways that God works with people. I had one interesting experience. A Jewish woman said to me, "How can I believe in God? In Nazi Germany you needed papers to move around. I didn't have any papers. We were hiding. I was scared and dying. I was trying my best to survive. How can I believe in God? I had a son and I was getting my M.D." I think she said she was on call as a psychiatrist. She told her son to get off the telephone because she had some calls that she was expecting. Her son had problems with his girlfriend and was talking to her, trying to work things out. Shortly after that her son committed suicide. The woman said, "How can you believe in God when something like that happens?" And she continued to say, "I went to San Francisco, parked my car and got out. This guy came along with a gun and shot me. I fell down on the ground and he took my keys, jumped in my car and was going to run me over. So I began to get up to run away and he shot me again. How can I believe in God, when all these bad things have happened to me? He didn't help me."

I couldn't really work with her because she had her mind set rigidly in that way. She couldn't open up to believe in God. Many months later, I was in Berkeley. I was invited by my friend to go swimming at the pool at the Claremont Hotel. Someone came over and said, "Hi, Cosme." It was this same woman. She looked at me and said, "Everything's okay now, Cosme. Thank you." God worked with her in a way that she was able to soften and to understand and accept what had happened to her in her past. Somehow God had worked with her on the inside and somehow she had listened.

## A Woman Who Felt God Had No Mercy

A woman came in one time for a healing. She parked her car and sat there for forty-five minutes. She was supposed to be here at two o'clock; it was already two forty-five. So she finally came up to the door and came in. She wanted to get help, but she found every which way to tell me that she couldn't get help, because she had broken every commandment in the Bible. She had a great fear of being helped. And she didn't believe in God, because she thought that God has no mercy. She came in, but didn't have a healing. She would only let herself talk to me for a little while. She was really hard on herself and thought God had no forgiveness and no mercy. So, you know, a person has to learn certain lessons. I can do only so much. I can't help a person unless they want to be helped, or are at least open to being helped. And I am the type of person who would not look at a person just to see through them. I am a person who has caring and respect for them. So, I find I can only help people if they want help. And I do sometimes feel like a little angel with a magic wand, blessing people and helping them to fulfill their wishes. That's how I feel a lot of times; but of course, it is God working through me that does the miracles and the healings. After a healing is over and someone thanks me, I say "Don't thank me, thank God." They need to thank God in heaven and thank God within themselves. The God within is receiving the love from the ALL God who is everywhere. It's a kind of mirror: "as above, so below."

### People Who Enjoy Illegal Activity

It really affects me when I see from the third eye. Once I knew a woman who was selling drugs. I could see that intuitively. She wanted me to do a healing on her. She was selling drugs to kids and I don't like that at all. She was also doing drugs, herself. I could see how it had destroyed her body chemistry and her brains. What I found out was that she was wanted by the law and was running from the cops. If she drove her car, she could be pulled over, arrested and taken in. I've seen both men and women who were wanted by the law. I can read that with the third eye. Then later I find out from them, that it is the truth. Somehow it is a game that some people like to play. They don't want to be responsible for their actions and like to do illegal things. Someone has to come in and be responsible by taking charge and making sure that they are headed in the right direction.

*Pulling Off Negative Energies*

One time I was working with a young girl, who was in a very bad car accident. I saw that her nervous system was shot. There was energy coming from outside that was interfering with this child. Sure enough, when I spoke to her and her Mother, there was interference from someone else. I could see the energy coming in on her. It wasn't good energy. People want to know what causes these energies to come in on people. Sometimes I know and sometimes I don't. When I don't, I ask the question and the information will come to me. I ask, "Where does it come from? Is it male or female? Is it family or is it unrelated?" Sometimes I have to pull it off or out of the person. If it's from someone really hateful or a bad spirit, it could be so negative that it could cause the person to die. So this is something that has to be dealt with. Sometimes it's easy to pull out. Other times it is more difficult.

Then you can almost instantly see the result in the person's problems or ailments. They begin to get much healthier, and their disposition goes from confusion, irritability or depression to contented or happy. It is a wonderful thing to see. Western medical doctors know nothing about illnesses caused from invisible outside energies or negative thoughts and intentions from others.

*God Said, "Two Weeks"*

In one case that I remember, I wanted to go back and see this client again, but God said "No." Then I heard something inside my mind regarding "two weeks." I didn't know what that meant exactly. Two weeks later the person went over to the other side. I wanted to help the person, but God wouldn't let me go. That person also had this very strong luxury desire and had the psychic smell that goes with that. Very few other people can smell this kind of psychic smell. It has nothing to do with cleanliness. The person can be squeaky clean, yet I may be able to smell a psychic smell of some kind, which helps me understand their condition.

### *Taking the Pain out of Cancer*

A woman came to me once who had cancer of the bones, the breast and the lungs. She was very, very sensitive. I said, "Don't worry. My hands are soft like cotton. They come from God." I really worked on her, inside and out. I went into areas where she had felt pain before. But during the massage and healing work she did not feel one single bit of pain. It's different if you do it by yourself, without God's help. You could hurt a person in this delicate condition. It's different when you do it with God's help and guidance. The chances of hurting someone are very, very slim. She walked out very, very happy. So, when working with people, you work with all the muscles, all the organs. You re-align the spine. You work with opening up the lymphatic system to make it flow. You work with balancing the nervous system and the circulatory system. You balance the right and left hemispheres of the brain.

This is the human orchestra. Working on the spine reminds me of playing the piano. This is why I use my fingers a lot. People who do massage are not trained to use their fingers the way I use them. I do a lot of detail work with my fingers, because with the fingers you can play the music of the person's body. When you play the music of the person's body, it is like, "Wow, I am an instrument. I feel good. I feel this music." If you are familiar with your own inner music, you will love it even more.

### *The Touch of Love*

What I learned is, whether I am working with a young kid, a man, or a woman, they all want to be touched because they want to have love. At some point in their life they have missed the love that they wanted to have. When love is missing, there is an emptiness, a voidness in that part of the body.

So when I put my hands on or over the place that has the holes, it is the love of God that comes through and heals that part. The love of God will fill the holes and the void places that were lacking love. The wound, whether it is physical or spiritual, will heal really quickly, in most cases. Whatever the case, it could be physical pain or mental pain. The body becomes well again and the person feels whole.

Sometimes I lift the body up, in my visualization and prayer, to God in the heavens. I do this so that the body can be blessed by God. The body becomes like a holy altar. I am making an offering to God, of this person.

### The Death Angels

Occasionally, when I see that a person is ready to die, I can see three or more angels around them. If five angels come in, I say, "God, not now ... not in my house."

### Harsh Truths from God

There are times that people are told things that come out of my mouth, but it is God telling them these things. I am just the mouthpiece. At times they are told things that could be seen as critical—about ways they need to shape up in their life. They are told things that will help them make their life work in a healthy, wholesome way. God is doing it, through me. So it is a whole different kind of interaction. There is no meanness or cruelty in the criticism. It is meant to help them make healthy changes or to see through their blind spots.

### Don't Thank Me, Thank God

When people thank me at the end of their healing, I say, "Don't thank me, thank God. It is God that is in heaven, that you are thanking, but also the part of God that is in you, as well."

### Cleansing a House with Ginger

Once I was visiting a home where the previous owner had died of a brain tumor. I got a very interesting inner direction to go to that house, later, and to burn fresh ginger. I was told that this would purify the energy from the previous sickness that had lingered in this house.

When I went back to this house, I put the fresh ginger on a piece of hot, burning charcoal that was placed in a pan. I could also have put the fresh ginger on the end of a burning stick. What it does is smoke, but it will have a completely different reaction.

The reaction is that all of the atoms and molecules of the cancer energy that was in the house would be sucked up, like in a vacuum cleaner, and removed. I burned the ginger throughout the whole house. After I was finished, I took the ginger to a bigger place to have it burned. You have the choice of disposing of it by completely burning it outside, or burying it under the ground. In this case, I decided to burn it, outside, in a burn pile.

Usually I use frankincense, cedar or sage to clear a house or area of negative energy or sickness. But this inner direction that I received was just the opposite. I had to draw the energy into something, like a vacuum cleaner, rather than disperse the energy and drive it out or neutralize it. The particular condition will be what determines what our inner direction guides us to do.

## Dancing to Celebrate a Healing

There was a woman in Escondito who came to see me when I was working late one evening in the back room of an herb shop. She was eighty years old and I worked with her for about an hour. The music was still playing soft and sweet. She was so happy and felt so good. I was happy for her, so we danced around the massage table for another forty-five minutes like angels and butterflies. We were just having fun.

## Jolts of Energy After a Healing

There was another person in Watsonville one time. I worked with her and she felt so good afterward that she went home and cleaned her whole house both inside and outside, including her windows. A few days later she came back and said, "What happened?" All the work she did, and all the energy that she had, really shocked her.

## Best to Rest and Recharge

I prefer that people rest and recharge their body after a healing, as the effects of healing are continuing for days. But she did the opposite. She did all this work. The interesting part is that we couldn't recognize her at all afterwards. Her hair, her face, her body, and even her aura completely changed. It was amazing.

## Changes in Appearance After Healing

When I work with people, I see them lose five years right in front of my face, in many different instances. There have been three people in my life that have lost twenty years in an hour-and-a-half, right in front of my face. I was blinking my eyes and saying to myself, "Am I seeing things?" People do change in front of me, and they do look completely refreshed, and the color of their face gets healthy and bright. The lines and bags on the face fade away. The eyes look sparkling and bright. Everything in their aura changes to very beautiful colors. I've seen this happen many, many times. The body and soul feel at peace.

## The Before and After Polaroid Photo

Once an elderly woman came in to see me with a polaroid camera in her hand. She said, "Cosme, can you take a picture of me before and after?" I said, "Why?" She said, "I want to show my grandchildren how I looked before, and then after, a healing." Anyway, I took a picture of her both before and after. In the "after" shot you could see a violet light all over her, inside and outside the body. Her face looked like a young kid. She was so happy and radiant. I've seen so many wonderful miracles. Not everyone can get helped, but most people do. At least I know that what I give is one hundred percent.

## Advanced Cancer

Another time a woman came in with her boyfriend. She was about thirty-five years old, but she looked like she was ninety years old. She had done a lot of drinking, drugs and loose sex in the past. She had had a very active life, but now she was so sick that she had stopped doing all those things. She went to a doctor and the doctor couldn't help her. She was dying from cancer, and she was in deep, deep pain. After I worked with her, she was able to walk, and she was hungry for the first time in a long time.

Her boyfriend came up to me and said, "You know, I have taken her to all kinds of doctors. Nothing like this has ever happened before. Now I see my woman walking around, smiling and being able to eat again. Before, I had to carry her just about everywhere we went, because she was too exhausted to walk." Her cancer was very advanced and two weeks later she died. But she left this world without pain. God was able to help her in that way. She really got a blessing.

### Healing a Little Baby

My first experience that really got me into healing work took place in Oregon. A mother brought her one-month-old baby in to see me. The baby couldn't drink milk and was kind of grey looking. The eyes were crossed and one hand was locked in a tight fist. I asked God what was wrong, and I found out that this problem came from another life.

This child had gone into the bathroom and had gotten into the medicine cabinet in a previous life. It took something which was poisonous and the child died. Then almost immediately the child's spirit jumped into another body and was born again. So this being was still in shock, and the shock carried over into the new little baby body. Even though she was in a new body, the memory of being poisoned in the previous life was still affecting this baby.

So what we had to do was draw the poison out of the body from the head down to the foot and then out. After the body was cleared, we charged the baby up with God's energy. In the twenty minutes we were praying, the child had opened up spiritually. The face turned from grey to a healthy pink. The hand that was tightly closed opened up and was relaxed after the healing. The eyes were no longer crossed and the baby smiled. I told the mother, "Start feeding the baby with water first. Then feed the baby some milk tomorrow." Everything went just fine after the healing. God had touched this little baby.

The normal doctor would have no idea that a physical problem could come from a past life. I don't expect people to believe in past lives, just because I do. The more deeply I go spiritually, the more I see things from the past lives of people. People don't understand all the time, or even see it that way. It's okay. I find that there are times when certain problems can be solved on this plane, you know, in this lifetime, that had its roots in a past life.

### Traveling Back to Another Lifetime

Sometimes I need to spiritually travel back to another lifetime to clear up a problem. Once the problem is cleared up in the "root cellar," it is very smooth after that. Usually, when a baby is first born, I can already know ahead of time what the personality is going to be like, what the child needs to learn, the health conditions it will have, the destiny, and the possible careers that he or she can choose. I see the dangerous parts of their life, too, and when they are going to get married.

### A Forecast for My Niece

When my sister's daughter was born, I was able to tell my sister what her personality would be like and the exact year she would be getting married and how many kids she would have. It was very precise information.

### A Skeptical Mother and Sick Son

When I get ready to speak to people, I say, "God, I need some help." To give you an example: I went to Wichita, Kansas one time, years ago. I got a call from a person that wanted to bring their teenager to me for a healing. The parent then said that they didn't believe in this kind of work at all. I said, "That's okay, come on in, my friend. You will change your mind." So they came to see me.

The mother was really skeptical. She asked me, "What is your name? How much education have you had? Do you take drugs? Do you smoke?" She was detailed in her interview of me. So I worked with her son and found out that the problem was an entangled nervous system in his hip area and it came from his mother. After I got through with him, he asked his mother if she wanted to get up on the table. She said, "No." I needed to work with this boy a second time to get better results.

### The Video at Menninger's Would Be Convincing

I wanted the skeptical mother and her son to go to the Menninger Foundation and watch a video about different gurus hooked up to biofeedback machines. The video showed what they could do with their brain waves. It showed them perfectly synchronizing the two sides of the brain with a high amplitude of theta-state brain waves. This is very impressive and indicates high levels of intuition and creativity. It usually comes from a very disciplined and spiritual mind and an integrated body, mind and spirit. They also could demonstrate voluntary control of autonomic states. An example of this is to pierce the body with a large knitting needle and then control the blood flow with their mind. They could start the blood flow, stop the blood flow, and then start it up again, if they wanted to. They could also demonstrate almost instantaneous healing of wounds.

The Menninger Foundation did a lot of research on Gurus from India and Tibet, Native American medicine people and healers, and internationally known mystics. They knew they had something to learn from spiritually gifted people and they wanted scientific evidence to explain it.

### Would the Mother Be More Receptive?

I suggested that the mother and son have dinner and then come back to see me. I thought that I had planted certain seeds of energy into the son that would ripen and also make the Mother more receptive. I thought that by the time they got through having dinner, and seeing the video, that the mother might change her mind. The son might begin to talk to his mom and his energy might transfer to the mom to help change and uplift her vibration.

### When Things Seem Impossible, God Can Create Miracles

The Mother and son came back after dinner and I said to God silently, "God, help me with this boy and his mom." I took the mom around the corner and said, "I want to get you out of earshot and talk to you privately." I told her that I saw that she had had eleven relationships in her life and that she had gotten to the point of hating men. I told her that she was projecting this hatred and resentment of men onto her own kids, especially the son who had the sickness in his hip area. I told her that it was not fair to do this and that all her anger was affecting him.

### She Agreed with All That I Told Her

The Mother agreed that what I had told her was the truth. Then her son asked if she would get up on the table for a healing. She agreed. Then I was able to work with both her and son. So when there seems to be something that is impossible, God can perform miracles.

### Telling Heavy Truths in a Light, Joking Way

Usually when I talk to people, they are not offended by the way I talk to them. I speak in a very kind and direct way, but I also joke around to lighten up the energy. They have been hurt enough in life, so there is no sense in hurting a person any more. I will talk to them in a joking way and then give them the choices to make. You will find out that ninety percent of the time they will make the right choice. When it is very hard to speak, you need some help from God. You always get the truth that way. Because when you speak, it's like God talking personally to them.

### The Photography Job that Led to a Healing

Once I did a photography job for a woman and her children. I got to know her and heard about the problems that she was going through. You can see it in the photographs. Usually it shows up in the photograph, if you look at it carefully. Her husband died and she remarried. I got to know them as a couple and was once invited to visit their home. I was one of the very few men who was able to do a healing on her. I used oil on her and helped her heal her bodies. I speak in the plural about bodies, because she was hurt by so many different men in her past. To have a stranger like me come in, who she knew only as a photographer, took trust. That trust took her to the next level and created a tremendous amount of growth for her, in the sense of her feeling more safe. I have a high respect for women. I have four sisters. When you work for forty years, you see a lot of things happening. The sexual energy is a very sacred energy when it is used in the correct way. It is nature's way of keeping life going. It is the procreative energy that keeps children coming into families. It is a natural instinct and it is a joyful thing to experience in marriage.

### From 65 to 95 Percent Healing Success Rate

After learning to co-create with God, another healer found that when she did her healing, she said, "Hey, Cosme, before, the success of the healing was sixty-five percent. Now it is more like ninety-five percent and higher." She had changed. She became a better instrument for God to work through. She was able to effectively uplift peoples' frequencies with the high frequency of her singing voice. When the frequencies of our vibrations go up really high, healing occurs.

### Past Life Recall and Validation

Many years ago I took a couple through the spiritual process, one at a time. After each one went through the process, they found out that they were really meant for each other. They asked me to be the minister for their wedding. A few months later they got married and went to England for a honeymoon. When they were in the countryside, all of a sudden, they felt a strong feeling pulling them to go over the hill. They looked at each other and said, "Are you thinking what I'm thinking?" The other one said, "Yes." So they went over the hill and, there, they found a house. It felt to them that they had both lived together in that house long ago, in another life. They had remembered a pond, in the front of the house, but it wasn't there. That really puzzled them. They were able to look through the windows and were able to recognize this home as a home they had lived in before. They walked around the property and they talked to a neighbor that lived next door. After a few questions, the neighbor told them that a couple of years before there had been a pond in front of the house, but the new people who bought the house decided to fill in the old pond. My friends were really surprised that they had remembered this past life when they went through the spiritual process, and now they had been guided right to the house where they had lived together in a past life. This indeed was a real place in this real world, not just the vision they both had received independently of each other, while going through the spiritual process. So this very real experience made their love for each other grow even more. They knew they had been together before and that they had been reunited in this life.

## A Festival in Sedona, Arizona

I remember a time around 1973 when I was in Sedona, Arizona. I was one of the speakers and there was a whole bunch of people there from all over the United States. It was a festival, and I put a little statue of the Virgin Mary out in the garden and said, "God help me." So I asked the person who I knew there, if they would play Ave Maria. I get high on that. I got up and felt like I was kind of spiritually high, just kind of floaty, almost like feeling my spirit floating above me. I was elevated. As I began to talk to people, I could see through people. I could see where they were coming from, how they were feeling, and all the problems and sicknesses that they had. I could sense all of those things all at once. I saw all the differences of energies of the people in the audience. Some was negative. Some was positive. Some people were rushing and some were relaxed. It was an ocean of different people.

### God Talked Through Me

As I began to talk, I felt as if God was talking through me. I felt like I was floating up so high. I could see myself below. God was talking through me. Wow, this is pretty cool, I thought. So God sees all the vibrations. God gathered all the different vibrations into one, which he then cleansed and purified. Then God was working on one conscious, unified vibration. I was talking away and it just kept coming through and coming through. It was much better than if it was just me talking. Really nice things were coming out. That experience was very unique. After I got through it, I said, "God, that was pretty good. Keep it up." It was really nice and I really helped people that night, with God's help. I had no plan or prepared talk that night for the lecture. I just went in and said, "Okay God, you're the One. Go for it, man."

# 4

# The Elements

*Working with the Elements Is Universal*

No matter what culture or religion, there is a basic structure present in all life which is connected to the four elements. This understanding is as old as time and is a part of all cultures. So we could say the elements are universal. Fire, water, earth and air are basic elements common to all people, all life. Being able to work through the physical, emotional, mental and spiritual bodies in healing is very similar.

*How the Tree Represents Us*

The tree, to me, represents *us* ... very much so. The tree has roots. Our two feet and legs represent the roots of a tree. The trunk of the tree represents the middle part of our body, the stomach and the chest area. Our arms and hands represent the branches. Our hair represents the leaves of the trees. Now ask yourself this question: Can a tree survive without water? Of course, the answer is no. How about us? Can a tree survive without the Earth? Can a tree survive without sunlight? Can a tree survive without air? We all need water, Earth, sunlight and air. These are the four basic elements.

*Blessing with the Elements*

When I bless a person or things, I do the blessing with all the elements because each one of us has all the elements within ourselves. If we get a balance of all of them, then we will feel balanced and be able to change our vibration to a higher frequency.

*Changing the Vibration of the Sacred Metals*

For example, I change the vibration of the sacred metals. I go to each part of the body and bless each part in a certain way, so that they will heal, because on some level they feel all the elements. It's almost as if a person is missing certain minerals in the body. There is a gap that needs to be filled in with elements. I fill the gap in with water, fire, earth and air and aligning the physical, mental, emotional and spiritual bodies.

*Working with the Elements at the River*

Going to the river in the summertime is good for balancing the elements of the body. The water is there for the water element. The rock is there for the earth element. The sun is there for the fire element and the air element is the breeze. It is all there while you are swimming in the river in the summertime. That is one of the reasons why people feel so good when they swim in the Yuba River, here, in northern California. They get the balance of all four elements. We are so lucky to live ten minutes away from the sacred Yuba River. The Native American people felt it was a sacred river and it does have that feeling. Some people feel that the gold and quartz crystal, that is so abundant in the earth here, is one of the reasons for the high spiritual vibration.

*Baptism by Water*

Water is very important within our body. We are made up of a very large percentage of water. So one of the first things is for you to be blessed or baptized by water. Through this, the body becomes protected by the "Father," and it helps to heal sicknesses. King Solomon recommended that a person be baptized by water, no matter what religion they followed. Once this has been done, the body belongs to God and to no one else.

## Fire

Fire is very important, as fire is the soul light, God's light within us. Our soul and God can join together in peace and form an amazingly bright light together. It makes us one with God. Fire also works within the nervous system. We need to learn to keep calm and protected from anger. In the future the body consistently needs to be recharged, so we need to become physically strong and healthy. We need to see our body as a temple of God.

## Earth

Our earth essence must be grounded. We have electricity present in our feet and it is our ground. If we are not grounded, then our body becomes very erratic, unbalanced and out of control. We don't make good decisions when we're not grounded, and we may not be safe drivers, as it is hard to be focused when we are un-grounded. The heart goes up and down and sideways, the whole works. So it is important to be grounded to the very center of Mother Earth. When we respect nature and our Earth, we have new life. Earth energy can be very clean, because you feel closest to the Mom.

## Air

Air is important too. All extremes are important. Air keeps us free from disease. It helps to heal the body. It is the breath of God that we can't stop. If our breath stops, our body dies. It is so very important ... this breath ... this air.

## EXERCISES

### An Exercise to Align the Subtle Bodies with the Physical Body

Any woman or a man can actually sit down for a moment and do a little meditation. It is even effective if it is only for five or seven minutes. It doesn't take long. Take a deep breath and look at your physical body. Where are you? Then look at your mental body.

How is it? You can also look at your bodies this way for projecting yourself ahead of yourself, on a trip. When you send your energy to your destination ahead of time, through visualization, you will not be tired when you arrive. Jet lag and travel fatigue often happen because the energy body cannot keep up with the traveling physical body.

When you're looking at your body, as if it's in the mirror, it may look or feel scattered here and there. You will feel the tense places or the scattered energy and the imbalances, with practice. Now you need to come back. All the bodies need to be aligned in an oval shape all overlapping each other, evenly, as one egg, in balance. Sit down and bring in your physical, mental, emotional and spiritual bodies. Send white light from your heart up to your third eye and then project it forward to your destination, so as you travel, you are moving into your energy, rather than leaving it behind you.

### An Exercise to Calm the Emotional Body

The emotional body plays a very important part in our life. When we get very emotional, our solar plexus area (around our naval area) shuts down, and that causes our system to become very erratic. Our body short-circuits. The body begins to burn out if we get overly emotional very often. We need to take a deep breath and bring the light of God in to fill the chalice of our heart and lungs. We need to feel the peace as vast as the ocean in our solar plexus. Let the sunlight shine through the sky above the ocean, and let the sun shine through the solar plexus so that you can balance and heal your emotional wounds or upsets. Remember to keep breathing deeply and slowly.

### "Flame, Be Still" Exercise

Visualize a candle inside of yourself and talk to that fire. Say, "Flame, be still." Take a deep breath and be still. When you calm the stillness of the candle, you calm the fire and the energy of your body's nervous system.

*"Stilling the Ocean" Exercise*

Another exercise is to visualize yourself at the ocean. By being at the ocean you can see the water moving around, the in and the out of the waves, the swells, and the wind blowing. Imagine the sun beginning to set over the ocean. The colors of the sunset and the water begin to change. You put your hands out and take a deep breath and say, "Water, be still." You will try to get the water to look like clear, smooth silk. As you do this, you can see the sun above very brightly, and below in the water you can see the reflection of the sun. By doing this exercise you will be able to control the water essence of your body, which is so connected to the emotions.

# 5

# Spiritual Exercises

*Cosme teaches beginning, intermediate and advanced classes.*
*Each class is usually held over a three-day weekend.*
*There is instruction, spiritual information, and exercises*
*in all of them. The following exercises and information*
*come from a variety of classes*

### Yah We (Yah Way)

The next subject I would like to talk to you about is about "Yah We" (Yah Way). As you may already know, Yah We means God. It is a dance in which we dance with God. If you want, you can dance with nature, you can dance with the trees, or dance with the flowers and waterfalls. Yah We is the other end of the spectrum from Tai Chi. Tai Chi is a system of flowing movements that was created a long time ago, in the East. It is made up of very precise movements that you learn to do. It is passive energy in motion.

God's energy feels much more like an active energy. Whenever you turn to the left, you must also go to the right. His movement also uses deep breathing and brings joy and prana (life force) into the body. In Yah We we draw in energy from the sunlight. We face the East, drawing the sunlight into our body, and at the same time we are drawing energy up through our feet from Mother Earth.

You may like to do Yah We early in the morning at sunrise. You can bend your knees low sometimes, or raise your knees up high, using your steps and feet with grace. There are endless different positions and movements. God is flowing the movements through you and activating and inspiring the way your body moves. It is God's energy moving through you. You use your arms and your legs and your feet and your torso, your shoulders and head. It is pure grace and pure moving beauty, which increases your love for the Earth and for God. Your own beautiful movements are an expression of that which you give to God and what you receive from God. Every little finger is used in motion to express the exclusive and unique feeling you are receiving from God and then giving back out to the world.

Yah We sometimes moves fast and sometimes slow. Sometimes you may dance like an angel, completing a circle to the left and then completing a circle to the right. We move forward in motion and move backward in motion. After you learn how *you* dance, other people show you how *they* dance. We have to show a group of students how to do this dance at first, but then one by one, they take off and share their own inspirational dance with us.

### *Dancing with a Reflection in the Mirror*

Then, part of Yah We is having more than one person dancing together. We could all dance with the person who is sharing their dance. We or the partner follow the person's every move. It is like dancing with a reflection in the mirror.

The second day, early in the morning, around seven o'clock, we all get up, and put our hands together in a prayer position, right over our heart. We tune in to feeling the heartbeat of God within us, and then we begin to dance again. But, this time we use music. Beautiful music enhances feeling God's love.

### *Dancing with a Partner ... Like a Mirror*

After we dance, we gather together and pair up with another person and we do a dance with each other, using two forms, both Yah We and Aikido. Aikido is a martial art which, through our moves, causes no harm to ourselves or others. It helps us be in harmony with the universe. Yah We and Aikido are very complimentary movements and they blend well together.

There is a person in front of us, and we dance in their direction, and then they dance back as we move towards them. We take a deep breath and, as we exhale, our partner dances towards us or to the side of us as we continue on with the deep breathing. It's a rhythmic breathing, a dance that helps us become one with our partner. We feel that it is like dancing in heaven with God.

### Dancing as a Group, in Heaven with God

Once we are done dancing with partners, we dance all together, as a group. Intermingling, we enter each other's space, dance around, and share in that space, with love, grace and beauty, without even touching each other. It's just nice as we feel the whole universe moving in perfect order, harmony and peace. So this is Yah We dancing.

I also learned that sometimes people try to do other things, such as intuitive exercises we do in class, but sometimes they just can't get it right. Just by doing some Yah We, it draws in this prana, balance, and love to the person. It seems to increase their intuition, and afterwards they can usually really do the exercises well. It draws in a higher energy than the energy you get from your own breath alone. It goes deeper and holds energy from God, along with oxygen and light. It's like dancing with God at the holy altar, in communion and sharing. To feel every part of yourself become alive like this helps you to feel more what God is. Words can't really explain the experience and the huge feeling of love. Love evolves. It grows. When you use the word "love" and reverse it, it becomes "evol." With love you evolve your spirituality through the movement of God.

### Yah We Helps Balance Our Positive and Negative Polarities

Doing Yah We dancing helps balance our positive and negative polarities, the male and female sides, and the inhalation and exhalation of breath. It is important to be balanced in all these ways. Sometimes people use too much of the male energy in them and sometimes too much of the female energy.

*Balancing Male/Female Polarities for a More Balanced Personality*

You can even change your personality tremendously, into a much more balanced, well-rounded personality. When a person has an extreme in either direction, a person gets to be very abnormal in their expression. The body can get very off balance too and become energetically lopsided.

It's like electricity. Our positive and negative poles have to be balanced. Let's say we look at our car battery to see if our positive and negative contact is good. If the positive part is not connected correctly because of too much acid around it, it won't be able to function to its full capacity. It still works, but it can't function correctly. In time, it may stop working completely, and you won't be able to start your car. So we all need both positive and negative energies to be in balance.

## The Third Essential for Balance: The Grounding

Obviously, the body needs to be grounded to Mother Earth for the body's whole electrical system to work properly. When you have electricity running through your house, you have positive and negative poles. If you don't have a ground then you will bounce all over and you will not have a strong, focused and secure feeling in your body. So by balancing your energies and then grounding them, you become balanced.

## Physical Symptoms: From a Lack of Grounding

I can't imagine what it would be like if you didn't have a ground. You'd be getting "shocks" throughout your whole body. That is what you might feel when your body is not grounded. Your mind gets too diffuse and you might be spaced out, bump into things or feel uncoordinated. It is hard to focus when you are not grounded, and you can also get depressed and discouraged. You may also feel tired for no reason. Your head and certain muscles can all begin to have an uncomfortable, dull, heavy feeling. Sometimes, little pains show up and migrate around your whole body, moving here and there. The pain can be in one place one day and another place the next. A doctor might be so puzzled with the symptoms. Getting grounded, and being grounded every day, can make a lot of bad feelings go away and can heal many chronic health problems.

## Breath and Grounding

Another important part of getting grounded is to inhale deeply and exhale all of the breath out. Paying attention to breathing deeply and completely is very important. Shallow breathing tends to disrupt your grounding, and deep, complete breathing tends to maintain the grounding.

## Excess Male or Female Energy

At first you may use too much positive, male energy from the body. You can get very hard, rigid, and feel restrictions in your physical body. If it stays this way, it spreads into the mind and creates a rigid mind. Then the body can become crystallized and sick.

If the body tends to create excess female energy, then the body becomes very delicate, very sensitive, and very creative. I also learned that this type of imbalance can lead to hot-headedness and stubbornness. The brains get very, very hot at times.

Everything depends on how we use God's energy that comes so freely into us. We can create something bad or something good. We can create perfect balance or a serious imbalance.

## Perfect Balance Feels So Good

There's nothing better than having a perfect balance in our system. It makes us feel so good all over, and so clear and peaceful in our mind and emotions. Creativity flows best when we are in balance. It is like being in ecstasy with God all the time. With our body completely balanced and grounded it works like a charm.

*Healing Our Ancestry: The Mother's Side and the Father's Side*

Another subject that I teach in my class is working with your ancestors —your Mother, and her side of the family, and your Father, and his side of the family, and then the Grandparents on both sides of the family. We do this on the physical, emotional, mental and spiritual levels.

A lot of times we are connected through our umbilical cord with them, without even knowing it. And sometimes we are connected at the solar plexus. Things that have been done wrong, and things that have been done right with our parents, grandparents and ancestors, have to be cleared from us so that we can completely free ourselves, to be ourselves. Otherwise it is like carrying around old smelly laundry and old dirty luggage from the past. Even though we may have some scars from our family, and negative patterns that have been passed down through the generations, we need to forgive and forget in order to free ourselves and go on spiritually. Even the scars and wounds that we carry can be grown out of and healed with God's help.

It's like during the time of Moses when he came down from Mount Sinai. People had to pay their karma because they had fallen out of grace with God. We and our family need to pay karma back too, for things that were done that were not in harmony with God's laws or love. So karma, or the law of cause and effect, is connected to us through our genetics.

We have things to work out regarding our family. We are born into a certain family in order to learn certain things. So the sooner we learn the lessons that they are here to teach us, the sooner we can grow and then be in the light and grace of God, and be free of the genetic linkages.

On the physical level we can inherit certain types of physical problems from the family line, or at least be susceptible to certain conditions that run in the family. Sometimes it's high blood pressure, diabetes, heart disease, arthritis or eye problems. We all have a certain genetic make-up. These are called pre-dispositions. But it makes us wonder, if every one of the ancestors ate certain things that contributed to these problems. They may have taught the next generation to like these same unhealthy foods, such as too much starch or fats, for example. We often eat the same way that our genetic ancestors did. So how do these health problems and even emotional problems get passed on from one generation to another? What causes the heart problems that may run in a particular family? Did that family all chow down on lots of fatty, greasy food and never get much exercise? These are all things to investigate about your family. If they're alive, ask your parents, grandparents, aunties and uncles and even great-grandparents. Check out the family's favorite recipes that have been passed down. Is it a healthy diet they ate? Did they grow a garden and have fruit trees?

So how can you change things so that you can avoid your family's health problems? Were they caused by foods, or emotional problems and habits? Is it caused through the chemistry of your body? Were problems caused by enzymes or lack of enzymes, vitamin or mineral deficiencies, or having a greater need than most people for certain nutrients?

Is it something that you just don't understand yet? Was it the climate that generations of ancestors lived in? Some people's ancestors came from really cold climates in Europe. Other people, like me, came from a tropical climate, such as Hawai'i and the Philippines.

It really amazes me that my people in Hawai'i believe and expect that they will eat plenty of food and die happy. One day I was visiting my sisters. A whole group of men were playing cards together at a round table. Even the priest was there. One of them was talking about the surgery he had after a heart attack, and an ailment that caused his heart to malfunction. They were all saying how bad each one of them was. I feel that you know what your family's problems have been, and that you can do things to avoid them. Why not? We don't have to be copy-cats. For me, I liked greasy, fried food and too much pork. I loved to eat lots of the local food in Hawai'i. I liked it too much and, I thought, if I keep eating like this, things wouldn't turn out too good for me.

## Moderation

Anything that's extreme is usually not good. Things need to be in balance. We have to learn not to be greedy. We need to learn to share things, even our food. We also need to have respect for our physical body, because it's the vehicle for our spiritual body. Our soul is sacred, but so is our physical body. It is sacred, and that is very important for us to know. With our body we know that, whatever we do, it will come back to us. It's like a car. If you don't put gasoline or oil into your car, it will die out someplace. It may not be a happy time. We need to tune up our car every so many miles, so we also need to tune up our body every few thousand miles too. It's very important to remember our own tune-up.

So going back to our family—even though we might be adopted or our grandparents might have already died, we can ask God to help us understand our family background by giving us a vision or a dream. The problem may be hard to look at, but you may say, "Okay, I've done my best."

If people can't forgive us, it's okay, but we need to forgive them, and we need to forgive ourselves in order to grow more with God. We may find some negativity about a situation, but we also need to find the positive part about it. You can see the flaws, but you can also see the good things. We can use the positive expression to better ourselves in life. Basically, if your family has a tendency to get cancer, you don't have to be a copy-cat. It's just a lesson you need to learn in order to avoid the problem. You may say, "I don't need to learn that lesson. I don't smoke." My sisters and I don't smoke or do the things that our family members did in the previous generations that brought this sickness to them.

Different people have different things to learn. We need to learn to be proud of ourselves. We all definitely are trying to better ourselves and to be successful in life. We want to be content, happy and live in peace. What you create in life can be very delightful, like heaven, or we can make life here on Earth a hell. It's our choice. When you accuse someone and point your fingers and thumb at them, you say, "You did that!" But you notice that, as two bullets go out from you, three bullets come back at you, with the other three fingers. None of us are in a position to judge someone else. So use wisdom and do the right things in life. You don't even have to be smart. You just need to use some good common sense. That's the important thing.

I remember a time when I was in Hawai'i. I was with this girl I ran into in high school. We weren't really smart, but we had good common sense. We both loved to eat good food. In fact, some kids just came to school just to have good food. In Hawai'i it's yummy and delicious. Somehow it just tastes so different to me than the food on the mainland. So our homework will be to look deeply into both parents, and their families before them. If you don't have some of the information, just ask God for help in seeing and understanding.

## Express Yourself

We're often told as kids to be quiet and not to talk. If we don't express ourselves, we hold everything inside our body and we become like a time bomb of repressed emotions. So we need to learn to communicate with someone that we trust. It could be your priest, a minister, a therapist or a psychiatrist. It could even be our Father or Mother or best friend. The important thing is that it should be someone that we trust. We need to be free to let this stuffed up feeling come out of our body. It is not only bothering us in our minds, but it's in our cells and muscles and organs. Our repressed feelings and blocked expression stays in our body. We don't want to keep that heavy stuff inside of us because eventually it makes us sick.

We need to be free to enjoy our freedom. We want to smile and be happy. We want to have good health. This is one of the ways we can do it. Sometimes I say to people, "You know, if God wanted us to look into the past, God would have given us a third eye in the back of our brains. But instead, he gave us a third eye that is in front, on our forehead. So make the best of it. See from your heart, and your third eye will see from the heavens with God."

# 6

## Spiritual Healing Classes

### The Animal Nature Within Us

In my basic class I teach my students about the animal nature that is within us. This is the totem of the animal or a spirit of an animal. Sometimes we get it from our friend or from our spiritual group, but it's a totem. Sometimes it is genetically passed down from one generation to another. It can be an animal that we have created ourselves, or it can be an animal that was transferred to us by making love with a person that carried this animal. It can come into our body through sex. At times, this animal can hinder us, if it is not clean. This animal could rob the energy of our body. It can be male or female, and it can have positive qualities or the ugliness of the dark side. This animal can make us feel very uncomfortable as well as the people around us. This animal may even smell. Sometimes the smell can be detected by people around us and make them feel uneasy. It can smell like an acid, and sometimes it smells like ammonia or sulphur. Sometimes it hides, but we can still smell it. Sometimes we see it in our dreams. This animal can gradually decay and eat up our body from the inside out. If we have a negative animal, we do not want to keep it, as it can cause pain and suffering to us as well as the people around us.

This animal may have been with us since the time of our birth. It is here to teach us a lesson. Until we are aware, it controls us, rather than us controlling its energy ourselves. It is like having a little kid inside of us that is hot-headed, stubborn, and wants to get its way. This little kid will drag us every which way, getting us in trouble and giving us all kinds of headaches, nightmares and problems. So we need to learn to control our vibration and our energy rather than have this animal control us.

## The Animal Can Be Changed

This animal can be changed. We are the one that needs to take responsibility for this energy. We need to face the creature that is within us, that makes us temperamental and makes us get mad. We can call the animal good or evil. It depends on how we see it and how we use its energy.

How can we change it? I know we can go to many different kinds of people to get help with it. We can have our body prayed over. We can correct it ourselves in dreams, or visualize the animal that is within us and ask it, "What are you doing there? Why are you inside of me? What do you want? What are the causes and the consequences? What is the purpose of this animal within me? Why is it in my house? Why is it in my temple?" You can ask it all these questions. You will be surprised how it will respond to you and how tricky they can be, at times. You can also call an angel to help you. You can have a spiritualist to help you to clear up this problem. We can even use Ajax cleanser, in our visualization, to clean up this low vibration entity inside of us. There are many different ways, and we need to find a way that we can accept. Then we must release the problem.

## Using the Name of Jesus Christ

You know, sometimes we even have to say, "In the name of Jesus Christ and the blood of the Christ," to have a stubborn, negative entity leave us. We have so many different ways. So what is yours? We can bring together two or three people to pray, and then God will help us even more. Using the name of Jesus or naming "the blood of Jesus Christ" has brought miraculous help and the release of negativity countless times. These pleas and prayers have been used for hundreds of years.

## The Angels Will Help Us

The angels will be there and when you call for their help, they sincerely, honestly come. There is a little spark in our heart that flickers like a flame flickering on and off, and angels can see it from a very long distance. It's flickering in our heart like a little S.O.S. signal for help. We can call them, and they will come and comfort us. We can tell them our needs and our problems. Of course, if we don't believe in angels and their help, we won't be likely to receive it. If we believe in angelic help, then we get it. Again, it's our choice.

### Cleansing and Purifying the Animal

There are some people who cleanse and purify the animal using an iridescent white light or the violet flame, like a laser. We also need to pray for help. The answer will come to us. The world looks pretty good to us if we have someone to come and sit with us, watch over us and guide us through this cleansing process, or spiritual purification journey. When it is done right, then we experience a feeling of purity, cleanliness and peace within. Once this animal has been cleansed and purified, then our body and emotions can begin to heal at a very deep level.

### Some Animals Transform to the Positive

Sometimes the animal turns into something really good and the animal becomes our ally, charging up our body with energy. When this happens, we have succeeded in giving the animal a new job, a job of helping us keep strong, energetic and healthy. It may also accept the job of helping to protect us from harm. When the animal accepts this kind of job, then it becomes a real friend.

But it is not always possible to transform the animal, and in these cases we need to get rid of it completely. Most animals can be cleansed and purified. You can ask God to cleanse and purify it, and then take it into the heavens, so that it can be used for something good.

*Rebirth*

So once the animal is cleansed and purified from the body, there is an emptiness. At this point we can replace it or have a birth or rebirth of a new baby inside of us. Well you might think, "What do you mean by rebirth?" I do not mean it as a woman giving birth, literally. I mean it symbolically. We can all have this rebirth, whether we're male or female. If we have both male and female polarities, we can relate to rebirth.

I remember when I did this. I gave birth to a baby boy. So by having a rebirth, this inner child can grow very quickly and be happier in life. It's a new, healthier beginning in life, a second chance to be happy—or happier than we were when we were young. We are going to take excellent care of this baby, or inner child.

Being "re-born" teaches us certain things that make us a better individual. It causes our soul to grow. We can have better relationships with other people. There are so many positive things it does for our soul. Either our animal goes away, or it matures into a positive influence and teaches us more and more as we go through life. This helps us to be healed more quickly, both emotionally and physically. So just as if we were going to a birth, we ask, "Okay, God, what am I going to give birth to, a boy or a girl?" Then we have to have our assistant, or mid-wife. The baby might be a boy. It might be a girl. Who knows?—sometimes we might even have two. And in your visualization you can create a new house for the little girl or boy to grow up in—just the kind you always imagined. You can clean up the little girl or boy and have them look just how you want them to look. You have so much love for this little boy or girl. Even if you didn't have it the way you wanted—when you were growing up or in a relationship or marriage—you can make the love perfect with this little boy or girl that lives inside of you.

It is good to have a rebirth of this inner child, but it is also important to have a rebirth with God, inside of us. It is between our soul and God. That is very important, as well. So with this baby we have a new enlightenment to help us to grow in a way that we could never imagine before.

## Other People See the Difference in Us

If the animal can be used more in a positive way to create a happy, spiritual growth, it can enhance our earthly life. Once we cleanse our body, we will see people who will look at us and say, "Wow, you're so sweet. You look so good. Something has changed in you. You look so healthy."

## A Healing Technique from the Philippines Using the White Plate

I use a method using a white plate. On that plate, images and pictures will appear that tell a story, before we are done. The pictures and stories will give us information, as to what is going on with the person I am working with.

I put a white ceramic plate upside down, next to the person. We will later be throwing the plate away, so we do not use our good china. Thrift stores are a good place to get white ceramic plates. I gather the energy from the person's aura, from around the head area, especially, and from other areas of the energy field where I find blockages. I look deeply in the energy field around the body and deeply into the body and see where the dark energy lives. Then I sweep it out of the person with my hands and put it inside the plate. All this time I am praying.

I then take a match and burn the bottom of the plate with the flame from the match. I keep on burning until the angels and spirit guides tell me to stop. When it is time to stop, I turn the plate over and look at it. The burning process make images and designs appear on the plate. The dark, sooty smudges appear from having been burned with the flaming match.

This is the interesting part. When you turn the plate over, shapes and pictures appear in the black and grey soot on the white plate. You look at it and it's easy to see images in there, which are the cause of the person's problem. You can see the animal in there. Let's say, for example, you have a person that has ill health and a problem with inflammation of the hip and spinal areas. A picture of it will show up as one of the images on the plate.

Other things about the person's life can show up as symbolic or literal images on the plate. There is a spirit watching over us.

Sometimes I see Jesus watching over the person. Sometimes I see something that represents the Holy Spirit. Other times I see things that have happened to the person. I may see different angels and spiritual guides that are helpers for the person.

At times I see that there is a spirit that has a sledge-hammer hitting the head of the person that I am working with. That usually means the person has a bad headache or has problems with headaches. So in this case we find out that the problem is not internal but coming from outside, from an interfering spirit that is giving the person a headache.

When the person I am working with witnesses the images that show up on the plate, they can have something to look at that shows what is happening. It is really interesting for people. When I talk to them about the blockages, interference or story that shows up, they can see it with me. I may point it out but many times I don't need to, because they're seeing it for themselves. It's important that they are participating in it themselves. Once the person can see the blockages, interfering energies or situations that appear on the plate, they know they can participate in doing something positive to heal it. They can see that it is real, and it may even point out a danger waiting ahead to their health or well being.

The next step is taking the plate over to the big Holy Candle that I have burning. They turn the plate upside down over the candle flame and pray. They ask God to cleanse and purify the situation. They pray for forgiveness and they pray for guidance and help.

### Watching This Being Done in the Philippines

I learned this method when I was in the Philippines. In my experience with it, I have found it to be a very easy way to work out certain kinds of problems. When I was in the Philippines, I visited and learned from one of the healers there. While I was there, we heard a knocking on the door.

This young fellow was there to ask the healer for help. The healer said, "What is wrong with you?" The young fellow said, "I have very, very bad stomach pain." So the healer invited him into the house and used this plate technique that I've just described. Of course, I was watching. When the healer looked at the plate, he said, "Oh, it's a dog." This young fellow, who was in so much pain, looked at the plate and said, "That is the dog I saw at the river. I threw some rocks at the animal." So this is what happened to him—a bad belly ache. In this case this young fellow had pain because of how he mistreated the animal. We need to have respect for animals. They are important beings on our earth, and we can learn to communicate with animals on a spiritual and telepathic level.

So what happened is that the healer showed the young fellow that what he had done to the dog was causing the pain in his stomach. Then the healer said some prayers and did some special healing with his hands, which released the animal from his body. Afterwards, there was no more pain.

### Help by the White Plate Technique

A woman from Europe had trouble with her eyes. They looked like they were popping out. She was looking for help, but no doctor had been able to help her. She had gone to numerous spiritual healers but had not gotten help from them. She came to the United States to try to get help from a medical doctor, but she had not been able to solve this problem. So somehow this woman ended up in the Philippines with a healer from down in the South. He was not a psychic surgeon. He did the white plate technique with her and drew the negative energy out of her. When it was done, he turned the plate over and there was an image of a man with an inverted triangle face, long nose, beard and big ears. His hair was slicked back and you could see his eyes.

When it was shown to the woman, she said, "I know this guy. He works where I work. The man was teasing me about my eyes." When this woman finally found out the source of her problem, she knew she would be able to be free of it. She faced the situation directly. The healer prayed over her. The second time that the healer worked with her, her eyes came back down to normal, from their distorted, swollen state. Now that was pretty neat.

## Bringing Peace to Animals

Speaking of animals, one time there was dog that came up from behind a house. As I was approaching this house, which I had visited before, the dog began to bark at me. I looked directly into the eyes of the dog and said, "I'm here and I'm there. Be at Peace." The dog stopped barking right in the middle of a bark, turned and walked away. These are some examples of how we can be co-creators with God and how we can make changes in our life, for the good.

## An Exercise Demonstrating the Power of the Integrated Bodies

Another wonderful test that we do in the basic class is to use all of our bodies: the physical, mental, emotional and spiritual bodies. We bring them together, throughout our body's force field.

## The Hand Exercise with a Partner

In this exercise we have another person stand in front of us. The palms of our hands face the palms of a partner's hands. The elbows are slightly bent. We may remember the time when we were young, and we held our hands up to our Mom, or someone else, to play "patty cake, patty cake." Do you remember that hand position?

Well, this is how we hold our hands. The person in front of you holds their hands up, too, and then makes contact with your hands, palm to palm. Both of your sets of hands will be touching each other. So first, what we do is push the partner with our hands. Each person will take a turn, physically, pushing the hands of the partner. The second time we do it, we use our mind power, too, to see how far back we can push the partner. Both partners take turns doing that.

Then we come back together again. This time we try using all our bodies to push the person back: First we push with our mind. Second we push with our mind and our physical body. Third we push with our mind, our physical body and solar plexus. Fourth we push with our mind, physical body, mental body and spiritual body. With all these bodies aligned, we push with our solar plexus force. This time we find that we can push the person much farther back. This is because this alignment of the bodies increases our strength, many times over. The partner will be pushed so far back that it is shocking to discover this much strength inside.

### The Power of the Aligned Bodies

This exercise demonstrates how strong we are when we engage all of our bodies together, aligned, as one. It also gives us faith and confidence in the great things that we can do. By focusing our power and using all of our bodies, rather than just one or two of them, gives us unlimited possibilities. When we use all of our bodies together, we will be able to accomplish more of our goals in life and will know how to powerfully accomplish the tasks.

Practice makes perfect and we will have a lot more confidence in ourselves after we learn to use all of our bodies in unison.

### A Clairvoyance and Clairsentience Test

Another exercise we do entails everyone being blindfolded. I am some place in front or on the side of the group. I clap my hands and they have to swing their hand towards the sound. Then I move again and I clap my hands again. Again they have to turn to the sound and find me again. After a while I stop clapping my hands and the students have to feel and sense me in order to turn their hands towards me. In this last phase of the exercise the students have to see much more clairvoyantly and clairsentiently to find me.

We all go through these tests in order to tune up our intuitive senses. People who think they have no intuition are amazed to find that, by doing these exercises, they do have intuitive senses. And as people go along with these exercises, their intuition develops and improves quickly, in almost every case. This is really a lot of fun because sometimes I duck. Sometimes I go down to my knees. Sometimes I lie down on the ground and they have to find me. Usually they do a pretty good job of finding me too. They may be surprised that their clairvoyance and clairsentience is working better than they ever imagined.

## Seeing in a Different Dimension

In the next test, everyone forms a circle and each person is blindfolded. I go up in front of one of the students and touch their shoulder, and they are to speak their name. I say "Are you ready?" and they say, "Yes." All of a sudden I will swing my hands and arms and legs towards them, and they are actually able to block me very well, as they can "see" or "feel" me on a different dimension. This is a lot like doing martial arts blind. Other senses kick in to gear besides the eyes. We are through with this exercise when we have covered all sides. They feel good about what they have just done.

Then I go on to the next person and touch their shoulder and say, "Are you ready?" and give me their name and say, "Yes." I will push my hands towards them, almost touching them, but not quite. I will kick my legs towards them too, but I won't quite touch them. I ask them to block me. Usually they are much more dangerous to me than I am to them, because when they block me, they block hard with their arms and legs. This shows us how intuitive each person can be.

## People's Difficulty with Focus

I learned through life that many people have a hard time "focusing" because there are so many things that are happening in their life. They are distracted with too many projects. There are a lot of emotional things and situations that they can't cope with either. They can't face the overload, so when they try to focus on one subject or task, it is very difficult for them. Emotional overwhelm can mimic attention deficit disorder (A.D.D.). Often when the emotions are cleared and people have learned coping tools, their ability to focus is amazing. Sometimes clearing out the blockages and unhappy emotions in the "spiritual process" helps clear the feeling of being overwhelmed and scattered. Clearing emotions and staying clear requires constant vigilance.

## The Focus Exercise During Babble

So I give my students a focus exercise for this. One person lies down on the grass. There might be at least five people around them, in a circle. Let's say that there are five people in the circle and each one calls out their own number, one through five. The person lying down in the center will have to focus on the number that I call out. Each person that is assigned a number will be focusing on and thinking about a certain subject. I may call out number five. So the person lying down in the center has to focus on number five and listen to her "little talk" about the subject that she is thinking about.

After a few minutes I may say, "Number one." Then the person in the center will focus their energy and attention on number one and number one's little conversation. The person in the center will listen to what the person has to say, shutting off all the energy of the other people in the circle, who are now all talking at the same time. It will take a lot of focusing on number one's talk to hear what they have to say.

Then I may say, "Number three." Then the person in the center must focus on number three and listen to what number three has to say.

After all the numbers have been called and each person has given a talk about their subject, I say to the person lying down, "Explain what number one said." The person who is number one has to confirm how accurate the person is at remembering their talk. Then we go through all the different numbers and do the same thing.

The students realize, "Wow," they can really focus on one particular energy and get it clear without interference from the others' talk and energy.

Sometimes we have three or four groups going at the same time. Then, all the groups join together and we do the exercise again with the big group. Then it may be twenty people talking at the same time. The person who is focusing may just crack up laughing with all this racket going on. The person doing it may be amazed that they can still focus. So the person who's going through the test really learns that, wow, they are really surprised that they are able to focus correctly and clearly. The main reason for doing this exercise is that it can be applied in everyday life. They will be able to focus on whatever energy they need to focus on, without getting hysterical or confused by multiple distractions. This is a little lesson that I learned from God. God told me to share it with people so that they could better their life with it, too.

## Subtle Energy in Land Locations

If a person comes to the Nevada City area and they have very hyper energy, I find that it's very hard for them to be here because they need a lot of action and stimulation. People that like a lot of stimulation might have trouble being here in the woods, unless they really retire or want to relax. Otherwise, it seems very difficult. People gravitate to certain land locations where they feel their best. This can change a number of times in life. There are other considerations such as work, friends and family, besides the feeling of a place. It's great when it's all in "sync."

When I was driving through the mountains of Colorado, I could hear a lot of music. It was the music of the mountains ... nature's music. I heard a lot of tones ... high tones, low tones and tones in between.

## A Monotone Energy in Kansas

When I drove through Kansas, it was a monotone energy and sound. Then I realized why people in that part of the country love country music. They like emotional music because they have to compensate for that flat energy in parts of the Midwest.

What I do a lot of times is pick up the very high energy from high mountains and bring it down to where the energy is very low, to help raise the vibration in that area. It is a way of borrowing the frequencies of one area and bringing them to where they will benefit another area. The high mountains have a lot of good energy. I just take it with me and charge up a lower energy place, so it can come back to life again. It is like adding water to a plant that is wilting. It actually makes it come to life again.

When I go to Hawai'i, the frequencies change depending on where I am and what time of year it is. I can pick up on both high and low energies. There are some very beautiful high energy healing spots and other spots that feel heavy. There are old battlefields in Hawai'i and grave sites that must be respected too. If you are sensitive, you will pick up on these things.

## Fine-Tuning Our Energy Reading

Most people never pay attention to these subtle levels of energy. As we get more and more spiritually developed, we really get in tune with reading energy. We will notice subtle differences and sometimes not so subtle differences in different locations and especially in different homes Of course, you will really feel the energy differences in different people. As a healer you have to be able to read the energy of a person. As you progress as a healer, you get more and more detailed impressions of health conditions, emotional and family problems, relationship issues, etc. You become good at reading the chakras and the layers of the aura, or energy field. You sense or see the areas of blockage or injury. You feel, see or hear the overall inner music of that person.

## Clearing Energy with the Waterfall

In my intermediate class, I take the students to a waterfall that flows into the sacred Yuba River. The waterfall cascades down from a creek into a lovely pool and then it goes into theYuba River. It is such a beautiful place. People that I take there never forget it.

There is a special reason I take people there. It is a part of the healing process. The water and the sunshine can cleanse the bodies really fast. The students can go under the water for three minutes or for one tenth of a second and it clears the whole energy up quickly. It changes things like day and night.

*At the Waterfall*

When we go to the waterfall, this is what we do. We pray through every chakra, and we ask God to help us to cleanse and purify it. We use a little candle before going into the pool and the waterfall. The candle is for our soul, our spirit, and our physical and emotional bodies. As we pray, we prepare ourselves for this initiation in the waterfall. We let the water in the waterfall bless us, on the top of our head, while we're praying. Remember, this is not a really huge powerful waterfall. It is gentle enough not to hurt you. I don't suggest doing this in a big, powerful waterfall coming down on your head. When we come out from under the waterfall, it is that time of day between day and night ... dusk. Dusk is a good time to see the whole body illuminated. Sometimes the colors of the rainbow can be seen in the person's energy field.

*We're a Rainbow*

We speak about the rainbow that we have in Hawai'i and other places around the world. We have an expression that says that if we can get to the end of the rainbow, we will find a pot of gold.

When you are under the waterfall and you have the sun shining on you, it is like being in a rainbow, as the sun touches the water. All of the chakras are represented by the rainbow. Once all the chakra colors have opened up, we become a rainbow, and we really do become the pot of gold at the end of the rainbow.

*The Rainbow of Our Chakras*

When it rains in Hawai'i, the sun shines through it and we have the rainbow colors that appear in the sky. That's how we get a rainbow. So in our bodies, we also have a rainbow. Each chakra, or energy center, is part of our body's rainbow. In our sacrum area or root chakra, we have the color red. We have orange in the spleen center. In the solar plexus we have yellow. We have green in the heart and blue in the throat chakra. Then we get a purple or indigo color in the forehead, or third eye area. There is white at the crown chakra at the top of our head. White-gold is illumination. It is also wisdom and knowing. It is a pure energy that comes from God, as long as we don't mix it with our intellect or ego. The top of the head is like a fountain of golden white light. All we need is to be working along with God.

## The Pot of Gold, as the Holy Halo

In Hawai'i they say if you get to the end of the rainbow, you will find a pot of gold ... the great reward. But the pot of gold is really within you. It is in the aura, at the top of your head, after all the chakras have opened up and blossomed. You become very sacred. You become a holy one with God. You get the sacred white, golden light around your head. This has been called a "halo" throughout history. In paintings, the saints are shown with halos around their head. This is their pot of gold from having made the journey up the rainbow, opening all the chakras and developing all the beautiful spiritual qualities that go with each one of them. All the rainbow colors become brilliant and lit up as they open and blossom. The aura around the person becomes very beautiful. The top attainment is the pot of gold, or the halo. This is the holy man or woman. Each one of us has the potential to find our own pot of gold and wear this holy halo.

## Charging Our Bodies with Rock Energy and Yah We

After the waterfall, we always go and lie down on the big, warm rocks and pull energy into ourselves from Mother Earth. A big boulder can re-charge our body. It is rock medicine. The Native Americans knew how to heal themselves with rocks. We can learn to do it too. After this, we do the Yah We dance on the big flat rocks around the waterfall pool. We do this very quietly and gracefully, with no talking at all. We want to hold this energy inside of our bodies.

*A Cleansing and Purification Ceremony*

After we return from the river, we go through a cleansing and purifying ceremony. We cleanse and purify ourselves with fire, holy oil and frankincense. We lie on the ground and let the energy come into our bodies. It goes down our back, into our hands, and then downwards to our torso and legs. We draw in the sunlight into our bodies. It goes all through our bodies and then returns to the center of the Earth. Then it returns back up again, criss-crossing at our solar plexus area, in a figure eight pattern.

*Balancing All Our Energies*

All these exercises help to balance our positive and negative energy polarities, the yin and the yang, our Mother/Father vibrations, and the Alpha and Omega. This helps us to expand our energy and reach a higher spiritual vibration. It feels very much like dancing with God.

# 7

# Prayer and Blessing

## Let's Talk About Prayer

Let's talk about prayer. Lots of people pray but often in a way that doesn't work too well. I always say that 90% of the time prayer doesn't work. It's either that a person has confidence and heart in it, or they pray in the way they have been taught to pray, a formula prayer. Sometimes people pray this way because they feel it is the best way to pray. But does it really work? Does the message really get across? Are we really able to change the energy of the situation? Sometimes we do change the energy. Usually we can't, because we do it alone.

We need to pray with God, in order to change the vibration. If we do it by ourselves, it is difficult to get results. With God's help it's easier and faster to get results. One thing I use to convince people is to ask them to let go of their old way of thinking and try something new.

## Praying Over Our Food

I ask people, "Do you pray over your food?" Some people say "yes" and some people say "no." So then I say to them, "Try praying over your food in your own way. It gives the food a light energy and makes it easier to digest." If people pray over their food, it makes it good and healthy for them. If a person is able to bless their food with love, the prayer gives the food strength and life force. If you do it for less than a minute, I say, "Okay, it works." And then I found a way for people to be able to see if the food prayer and blessing really works or not.

## Testing Prayer Strength

I can use muscle testing in numerous ways. First I can test the strength of a person's arm over the food that is not prayed over. It's weaker. After they bless and pray for their food, I put their arm over the food and test the arm muscles for strength again. After the blessing, the arm is strong when I muscle test it. This is a really good demonstration of what good a prayer or blessing does for our food—and then for our body.

After the demonstration I tell them that I know how to do this and now they know how to do it too. This is a great surprise for most people to learn that they can actually change the vibration of their food and their body this way. By doing this they can become even stronger and healthier and much more delighted with God. This big difference is created by prayer. We human beings make life so difficult, and yet life can be so simple. Our mind and our feelings can determine how far or how little we can move ahead in life. So I'm trying to teach you an easy way of being a co-creator with God.

## The Sugar Demonstration: Muscle Testing and Prayer

I use muscle testing in this exercise. The person holds their arm out straight and resists when I put pressure on it, to push it down. I use the same strength each time, but sometimes their arm is weak and other times it holds up straight to the pressure. When the answer is yes, the arm tests strong, and when the answer is no, the arm goes down. Remember, I use the same pressure each time. I muscle test with one or both arms.

What I do is put sugar in a napkin and have the person hold the napkin with the sugar. I test the arm and the arm will go down on anybody, as sugar weakens the body. And then I test them again. The test shows that they become very weak, holding sugar in their hand. It is said that sugar short-circuits the whole electrical system of the body. It's almost like it puts a sluggish feeling into the body. It makes the body move slowly. So, after making a test with the sugar, a lot of people find out that they become very, very weak from sugar. Then after this is done, the person being tested returns to normal, because they haven't actually eaten the sugar.

Then we pray over the sugar that it would nourish us, charge up our energy, and make us healthy and strong. So the students have a little moment to pray. Then I muscle test them again, holding the sugar that they prayed over. Usually the arm goes down like it did before, with the sugar. It seems the prayer was not effective.

So the next part of the demonstration is that they pray over the sugar again, asking all the same things as before, but this time asking God to work within them. I asked them to pray for whatever they wanted but with the help, breath and light of God shining in the center of their hands, like little sunlight rays getting bigger, bigger and bigger and the sun rays shining outwardly in all directions. This gives the chance to purify the whole energy even better. So they were doing this prayer experiment with sugar and, when they could fill it with God's breath and light, their muscle test tested strong. Their arm would not go down. The energy of the sugar had been transformed with this prayer, calling on and feeling the light and breath of God.

## Blessing Water

You can bless water too. It is very easy to change the vibration of water. You can qualify what you want it to do for you, such as healing a sickness or losing weight. You can put your hands over a glass of water and pray over it and ask it to help you, in any particular way you need help. When you ask God to bless your water, you will be amazed at how much the vibration of the water changes. It helps you assimilate your food and nutrients better. When we muscle test people after they have prayed for their water and drank it, they become very strong and very powerful. It becomes a hundred times stronger than what it was before.

## Praying from Your Heart and Soul

When people realize that they are co-creators with God, their prayers get very powerful and are very effective at bringing results. This means praying from your heart and soul, not praying a formula prayer. Prayer power constantly grows in energy when you pray this way.

Once a person has actually witnessed being able to change the vibration of their food and water, to make it healthier, and more powerful and strong, it lets them know how to pray. You can pray with whatever religious background you want. It is the Holy Spirit that you pray with, that really shines through. It works! It really comes through. If you're a Native American, you can do the same thing too. You let the Great Spirit's sunlight shine through, and you will be amazed at what can happen.

### The Signal of a Prayer

In the spiritual world a sincere prayer from the heart is seen like a flame. The flame flickers on and off, on and off, making a flickering signal. This is how it looks to God's helpers and angels in the spiritual world, when people on earth pray from their heart. When there is a real emergency, the angels come down and help people. When it's a time of life and death, the angels usually come to the rescue. The more you really mean your prayer from your heart, the more the flickering flame in the heart signals the angels.

### Mixed Message Prayers

Lots of times people say something in their prayer, but do not express it as clearly and purely as it should be. They may say one thing but a different part of their body is saying "no." There is a mixed message in that prayer, and it is less likely to be answered.

### Co-Creating with God, as a Way of Life

Once this has become a way of life, you will never be the same again. Even a tree can believe it, and you believe it with all your heart, with all your being and with all your feelings. With every breath that you take, you know that you can change your vibration. You are breathing God's healing light. It can help to heal your body and heal other peoples' bodies, as well. If there is any reason why we can't help to heal a problem, we need to pray with our food and our water to change the vibration, because we all come from the same place ... God.

We want to learn to work together. We want to create together. We want to learn to heal together, not only ourselves, but the Mother Earth, as well. We need to learn to get along with each other, because all of us have a part of the truth. Working and sharing with others, we will have the whole picture of what life is about and what God is about.

## When Two or More Are Gathered

Like I say, when you have two or more gathered together to pray, God's Holy Spirit will be in your midst also. Two or three are very, very powerful when they pray together. You might like it. It might even tickle your soul. Lots of times we underestimate our abilities because we have our ego and personality in the way. We need to trust God. We need to work with God. We need to become one with God.

## You Can Use Your Own Prayers

Being able to change food, herbs or water with the power of prayer is very important. You know some prayers for your health. You may also alter your prayer to affect your destiny or your future for yourself, your mate or your loved one. You can go on and on and on in the development of your career with prayer. You can make the changes in your mind and believe it is going to happen, just as you see it in your visualization. You are a co-creator of God, so create something that is good, so that when it is time to harvest, you will have a good harvest. As you plant a seed in the ground, you are there when it is time to harvest. You eat the freshness, the goodness, the delicious taste. You can fill your chalice with this good food that you have created for yourself and the people around you.

# 8

# The Chakras or Energy Centers

## Chakras Are Spinning Wheels of Energy

*Chakra* is a Sanskrit word from India, meaning "wheel." A chakra is an energy center that spins like a wheel. It is a part of our spiritual body, not our physical anatomy. Each chakra relates to one of the endocrine glands. The root chakra relates to the reproductive system. The second chakra relates to the spleen, and the third chakra relates to the solar plexus or adrenals. The fourth chakra relates to the heart and the thymus gland. The fifth chakra relates to the thyroid gland, and the six and seventh chakras relate to the pituitary and pineal glands. A clairvoyant person can see the colors that come out of the chakras which make up the aura.

## THE ROOT CHAKRA

The root chakra is called the red chakra or the first chakra. It is about survival, sexuality, and basic issues about our grounding to the earth. It also works with the organs from the back to the front. To me, the root chakra is like a light bulb and it shines its light up to the neck area. Many times I find that there is a blockage there. This is very common. When there is a blockage there, the energy can't go up and feed the brains. Often the root chakra isn't properly grounded. When it's off, there in the throat chakra, the person will be off in their head. They may be jumping from one house to the next house, or one place to the next place, because the root chakra is not balanced. They may be scattered and inefficient in their work. It is like a hot energy that's trying to find a place to settle down inside of a person. I look into that area and I also see this heat, like red ants under someone's feet.

The root chakra is also connected to the front part of the lower abdomen area. It goes from the back to the front part of the male and female organs. So the more it is cleansed in the back part of the root chakra, the greater the healthy function of the reproductive organs. Once the cleansing and purification have taken place, there is an energetic shield that is placed on the chakra to protect it. Placing the shield on the chakra helps to hold that vibration in place.

The root chakra can have blockages, but it can also be dirty. The person can go in there and meditate and do visualizations in order to clean it out. It's like house cleaning in the basement of a building. Most of us need this cleaning and clearing.

## Grounding

Because this is the survival chakra, it is where we are rooted to Mother Earth. It is our very grounding. It is amazing how many people are walking around every day totally un-grounded. They have no idea how much this problem is messing up their life, and sometimes their health. It is hard to think straight or make decisions when you're not grounded. What I see from the root chakra is the way it sends energy into the male or female reproductive organs. They're related to each other.

## The Root Chakra at Puberty

When I look at the energy field of women, and especially girls in puberty, both the root chakra and the pubic area has energy moving back and forth and in and out. Let's say, for example, that a girl is in a store shopping and this natural, active energy is moving back and forth like a kind of magnetic radar. A guy could see this young girl, and although he may not be thinking along these lines, he may be affected by it. He senses this active, magnetic moving energy in the girl's root chakra as it can actually stimulate and arouse his male sexuality. People call this sex appeal, but it is active energy in the root chakra that is being broadcast into the environment.

## Sending out Cords and Hooks

This sex appeal is even more compelling when the person with an activated root chakra sends out a sexually charged energy cord to someone else. It feels like an invitation to the other person. It can feel like sexual stimulation if the invisible energy cord is sent from one person's first chakra right into the other person's first chakra. The expression, "I'm hooked by her" or "I'm hooked by him" is quite literal, on a subtle energy level.

This sexual energy being projected out of the sexual, root chakra is almost like a beam of radar being projected out there to stimulate another person. The girl or guy may not even be aware that they're projecting this strong energy. They may do this unconsciously, just to have the person give them an admiring look or to get some attention.

There are certain men, too, who project sexual energy out towards women. They hook into a woman's root chakra with their sexual energy. It feels like a kind of charisma or charm to a woman. The woman may explain the attraction by saying, "I don't know why I'm attracted to this guy. I really don't like or respect him very much. He really isn't my type, but I just seem to be under his spell." They may sum it up by saying there is chemistry between them. Some people call this flirting. But flirting is often done with smiles, eyes, body posture, fragrance and tone of voice.

This compelling energy, either actively spinning or being projected out of the root chakra, can be very sexually provocative to another person. It can even be sexually manipulative. A person who is not sophisticated in subtle energy dynamics may not know what's going on. As a result they may not be able to resist a seduction. It is really good to be well educated in the art of recognizing subtle energy dynamics.

## A Part of Youth

With young girls and guys, all this is part of growing up. Feeling all these energies are natural and biologically healthy, but it really helps to understand how it all works. These feelings are especially strong in the teen years and twenties. In puberty a lot of young girls don't even know the power they have over guys with this energy. They also don't understand it very well. They do know that it gets them lots of attention. When guys feel the sensation of this energy going back and forth, certain types of guys go a little crazy.

### Invisible Energy and Chemistry

The energy the female has is stimulating and there are certain pheromones that come out of a female. It is like a flower and the male energy goes hmmmm ... like a bee looking for the flower. The bees and flowers are very similar to this. An older man, even a Grandpa, may see a young woman and say, "Gosh, I want to feel young again." He may want to feel his root chakra stimulated again, but not act on his impulse. A weaker man, with no control of his impulses, may become a molester. This is really a criminal thing, and there's no excuse for it. It is so very, very damaging to the child. But we do need to understand the energies and chemistry that causes the temptation. Basically it is using the energy on the physical level rather than the spiritual level.

### Taboos and Boundaries

A healthy person would never feel tempted to molest a child. They would have built in taboos and boundaries. That feeling would not arise. Molesters or parents that incest their children are very emotionally sick individuals who need to get professional help.

The root chakra and the sexual organ actually have a power that vibrates in unison. This energy can attract unwelcome and unsavory people without really knowing it. Young girls should be trained about this. If they come to my class, they will gain an education about all of this. I have some advice for them about how to keep that energy from being projected out, and arousing men.

*Dangers of Projecting Sexual Energy*

Some girls enjoy that energy and like the men to flirt with them. Men may call them "teases." They may feel an importance or power in being able to attract men. Some young girls are totally unaware of putting out this energy. But, they may have no idea that it could lead to molestation, date rape or even rape and murder. Not every girl that has been molested and raped is projecting the first chakra energy, but sometimes it is an extra added impetus to a potential rapist. One of my ministers had a teenage daughter who did not project this energy. She had been taught to contain her energy.

*Teaching Young People About Their Energy*

I would like to take young people and instruct them about this energy. I would guide them through a visualization looking inside of themselves at the first or root chakra to see what it looks like in there—how the energy is vibrating and moving. Once they have a look at it, and realize that it is a real thing, then they can begin to take control of that energy. They would know how to use it and protect it, so it does not cause vulnerability.            •

*A Dog on the Loose, or a Dog on a Leash*

That sexual energy is like a dog. If it's on the loose, it can move around making trouble in the neighborhood ... chasing cats or dumping people's garbage cans. But when you walk the dog on a leash, you have control over the dog, so it can't make trouble. It is the same as pulling the energy back into yourself, so that it's not projecting or radiating out there and hooking up with anybody.

*Subtle Energy Dynamics Are Multi-Dimensional*

Most times people see things only in terms of the physical, material world. Their definition of "reality" comes from school, the media, marketing, family influences and TV. More materialistic people tend to see things more on a physical level and may not be able to understand subtle energy dynamics. For them, the world may only be three-dimensional. But if we look at reality like a cube, and look at it from different angles and levels, we will see more. We will see how everything and everyone is all interrelated in a multi-dimensional way. It is complex, just like our body's systems. When bad things go through our bodies, each system, like the lymphatic system, has its own pathway and flow. It may be one body, yet, each system has its own particular path and purpose. Yet, they're all interrelated and cannot function alone. Just because we may not be able to visually see something, or dissect something relating to the body, does not mean it's not there.

Subtle energies from chakras and energy cords have a very powerful influence on us, our health, and our interactions with other people. It is important to understand how the subtle energies work, so they can serve our life positively, rather than create chaos and undesirable relationships, ill health, and self-sabotage.

### Moving the Energy Upwards Rather than Outward

Mothers and fathers can teach their children to be in control of their own body and to move the energy upward rather than outward. There is a big difference. Rather than have the energy horizontal, moving out towards someone else, it would be more vertical. A person is more centered and more grounded that way. There is a more decisive and wise way of making decisions when a person is grounded and centered. When the life force energy is moving upward, vertically, it nourishes the body rather than destroying the body's energy field.

### Staying Grounded and Centered

The vertical energy has more power, and does not go under the influence of other peoples' disturbing emotions. When our energy is reaching out and hooking up horizontally, we are too connected in to somebody else's energy field, and they may have too much influence on us. We might start acting like them or picking up their emotions, habits, and way of talking. We can start to lose some of our own uniqueness. If we're too connected in, we may even pick up their sicknesses, headaches, aches and pains. It is better to know ourselves and be ourselves.

### Vertical Energy Is a Kind of Protection

For young women especially, keeping the energy pulled in and going up and down, instead of outward, is a great self-defense measure against unwanted attention or "would be" criminals. Having our children learn grounding exercises and running vertical energy gives them a gift for life. Many adults have never learned these very important things about this invisible subtle energy. But it is never too late to learn.

### An Interesting Observation

Here's an interesting thing that happened regarding homosexual energy. A couple of times I worked with gay guys. When I stood next to them, my body began to sway towards them, and I almost felt like I was being hypnotized. I never felt attracted to men or the gay life. These guys had such a strong energy towards men, that the projected sexual energy could even sway a man like me, who is not attracted to men. Someone who is not operating with as much awareness of energy might just respond to the energy, or think somehow that they are suddenly attracted to men. At the very least it would be confusing. They might even begin to wonder if they are gay.

## THE SPLEEN CHAKRA

The second chakra, or the spleen chakra, is just below the navel area. It has to do with procreation, and is orange in color. It has to do with family, sexuality, relationships and emotions. It also involves issues of trust, spiritual community and individuality. There are two parts of the spleen chakra. One has to do with reproduction and the other with creativity. The upper part has to do with the physical spleen which has to do with purification of the blood and the immune system. If it is blocked, it may indicate that there is too much difference between your will and God's will for your life. It is also an area where the person is connected with the umbilical cord to the mother, as well. A person's birth mother can still connect and sometimes control their child through this umbilical energy. Originally it is for the protection of the child. The Mother is connected to the child through this chakra and can feel if it is about to encounter danger. It is that feeling a mother gets to check the child in the next room just as they are about to get into trouble or a dangerous situation. However, when a person is an adult, that connection can sometimes cause interference.

The spleen or second chakra is also connected to creativity. Once the chakra has been cleansed and purified, the body will feel more wholesome and healthier. During the "process" we have already gone in there and looked at the colors and the blockages and the causes of the problem. It has been cleansed and purified. We have done it, but not alone. We have done it with God's help.

So the beginning of the rainbow is the root chakra, and the next one up the ladder is the second chakra, which is right below your navel and appears orange in color. People who write books about chakras go into much more detail about them, but I look from a different way. I don't really like to read people or do readings. I like to get things face-on from people and from God. I sometimes have a different interpretation which is very general and simple. For me, the spleen chakra is like a woman who gives birth to a child. The procreative energy is there, and there is a very close relationship to sex in that particular area. So this area is about re-birthing and also about creativity.

### Psychic Weight Gain

Sometimes, in both men and women, the energy slows down in this area and gets very sluggish. On a physical level it can cause people to gain weight in their abdominal area. It can also cause people to feel sluggish. If the belly is too big, it can sometimes interfere with being creative. Creativity is one of the big qualities of this chakra. So it's important that the energy in this chakra is clean and flowing well. The energy also crosses over to the other side and affects the kidneys, liver, gall bladder and the spine. Having the energy clear and flowing opens up our creative potential, and we have a better chance to live up to it.

### Big, Creative Hawai'ian Guys

In Hawai'i the big, heavy guys are very creative. Some are artists and musicians, like Brother Iz (Israel Kamakawiwo'ole). Brother Iz was over five-hundred pounds. His mana (directed life force) and charisma were immense. They come from their heart and that's the difference. So the late Brother IZ really was an inspirational man who helped many people through the healing energy in his voice and the uplifting messages in his songs. He carried the culture and Aloha of old Hawai'i.

### Stuffing Energy

But the average person stuffs all their energy in their belly area, and slowly the area dies. When it dies, they can't create things, because it is like a bud that can't open up into a flower. So it dies, as a bud. It can't open because, on an energy level, it is blocked and shut down.

### Another Umbilical Cord

There is another umbilical cord that most people don't know about. It is huge and milky white and it comes out of the back behind the belly button. This milky white cord is connected to God. What it does is cleanse your spiritual body. It comes out the back side of your second chakra and goes up to the heavens above. It helps you to be creative, but it also helps you to cleanse your spiritual body.

## Energy Cords

Most people think of the umbilical cord at the top of the head. In the Bible, they call it the silver cord. They also call it a bowl of light. Most people are familiar with the silver cord, but don't know about the white umbilical cord in the back side of their spleen chakra. If the silver cord gets thin and is ready to break, it can mean that the person is ready to go over to the other side. It is like a rope going up. It is a little like vibrating plastic. If it is not the person's time to die, the cord will not break. But sometimes people have a close call, and the cord is very thin and weak and needs to be re-strengthened. The spleen or second chakra is also connected to our sympathy for other people and their feelings.

## Are We Feeling Our Feelings, or Someone Else's?

We may feel what others feel. The solar plexus does it too. If someone is sending third chakra energy to you, it makes you feel empathetic to how they are feeling. Say, for instance, that someone is having a bad day and they are reaching out to their partner or best friend. The third chakra energy might contact their friend and make them feel empathetic towards them. They might feel sort of sad and think about "so and so" and think, "I'm feeling kind of sad." I think that the third chakra makes you feel sympathy which is also connected to the kidneys. This energy reaches out on an energy cord, and we need to learn the difference between our own energy and that which could be sent to us by someone who would like to plug into our energy.

## THE SOLAR PLEXUS

In the third chakra, which is the solar plexus chakra, there are a lot of emotions. It is yellow in color. People have a tendency to put a lot of garbage in that particular area and use it as a septic tank. When a person can't figure out a problem with their brains, they have a tendency to shove it down below to their solar plexus. When this chakra is being misused, the person has a tendency to judge and control others. It has feelings of guilt, anger, frustration, nervousness and impatience. So the area becomes very stuffed up and very blocked. It has a tendency to block up the lymphatic system, as a result. It also makes the gall bladder and the liver sluggish. After many years this kind of garbage disposal begins to weaken and fall apart. If it spins in a counter- clockwise motion, then it actually causes big problems.

You may experience very poor health and the energy inside becomes darker and darker. That is not how it was meant to spin, normally. It is meant to spin in a clockwise spin. When we learn to relax, the energy is able to open up more completely. The nervous system is centered there. So if a person gets very angry, it can possibly cause burn-out. It gets dark. It short-circuits. Then the body begins to die. The solar plexus chakra is like the equator of the mother earth. The North Pole is the top of the head. The South Pole is the bottom of the feet. When the emotional body becomes very static, in that area, it goes from physical to the spiritual like a hula hoop. It goes in and out. It can get out of balance, and then that can cause the lower back to go off balance. It can also cause the mind to become very unclear. Whatever a person says will come out the wrong way and tend to be misunderstood. This is because of the imbalance. If the person uses this third chakra in the correct way, then there is a lot more balance in mental and physical ways. When they are able to relax and breathe deeply, more energy will move through the chakra in a clockwise spin. It comes out like beautiful sunlight.

It seems that Asian people have a good way to calm the solar plexus area and they tend to use it in a positive way. We here in the United States have a tendency to use it in a negative way. If a person relaxes and breathes deeply, they would find out that more energy can move through on the physical, mental and spiritual levels. The person feels more energetic, but at the same time more peaceful and wholesome. Each person is unique and has their own color and sound associated with the peaceful movement of a chakra. Without judging but loving, people begin to heal their solar plexus. Of all the chakras, this chakra has the most instinctual and animal vibration. This is often where we get those hunches or gut feelings.

*Imbalances in Third Chakra Causes Problems in Fifth*

The imbalances of the third chakra, from emotional disturbances, can cause thyroid problems. They will cause over-activity or underactivity of the thyroid. The thyroid relates to the fifth chakra of creativity and the spoken word. The emotional disturbances in the third chakra, the solar plexus, affect the liver, gall bladder and pancreas, which are all in the mid-abdominal area. If the solar plexus is used like a garbage disposal, then the energy of it goes up to the thyroid in the fifth chakra and causes thyroid disease. Hormonal problems in women can cause the thyroid to get imbalanced, and then that problem can lead to heart disease later. The thyroid says finally, "I've had enough." The next action is on the heart. There are all kinds of creativity. We can create from the mind and the brains. Creativity comes from the right side of the brain and then it comes down like that from the head. There are all kinds of creativity. I have a brother-in-law who can talk all day and night. But he talks on the mental and emotional levels. He talks real fast and he is really good at it. He could even convince you to buy a car.

## THE HEART CHAKRA

When we go to the heart, we can see the physical heart but also a spiritual heart, which is the heart chakra. It is green in color. When you are true to yourself and to the God within, then there is a real love there. This reminds me of a story of a friend who was praying wholeheartedly. When people pray, they are asking for help from God and God's workers, either for themselves or someone else. She had a heart chakra that was reaching out in prayer.

We are often tested by family and relationship rejections. We need to let go of hatred and resentment and strive for unconditional love. Much love can also be expressed through animals, flowers and nature. That is good, but we have a tendency to get hurt feelings, caused by the thoughts, words or actions of others. So when you go inside your heart, you can more easily see the past, present and future. Filling this space, that sometimes feels heartbroken, with God's love is very important to complete soul healing. Once this chakra is cleansed and purified, we go up into the throat chakra.

### A Story from the Spiritual Process

I remember one time I was taking a man through the spiritual process. We were already up at the heart chakra in this journey through inner space. He was working on clearing things out of his heart chakra. I was going through his inner heart with him, as his guide. At that time he had put materialistic things in front of God. God was already within him, but he was trying to get to God. He called God, Jesus, the Holy Spirit, the masters and the angels to help him. He was such a strong guy, that he was able to block all that was coming through. It was about three-thirty in the morning and he couldn't get through it. So I said, "Okay, let's stop for now and sleep. We will wake up and see what the next step is that God has for us to do. So we went to sleep and we woke up at nine in the morning, and we went back to the heart chakra.

### The Mind Was Blocking the Heart

God said that the blockages were not only in the heart, but that the blockage, that was blocking the heart chakra release, was actually in the forehead. So somehow the forehead or third eye blockage was causing the heart chakra blockage.

### We Had to Ascend the Chakras out of the Usual Order

Basically, what it boiled down to was that the mind was blocking the heart. So we went to the forehead center and we found entities there. They were from one end of the temple over to the third eye all the way to the other temple.

### Entities Were Misguiding Him

The entities were misguiding him to say or do this or that, and it was not accurate guidance. It was not the real truth, as the entities were deceivers. Before this experience in the spiritual process, he did not know that he had been guided by these tricksters, who were not of God. They did not represent the real spiritual truth.

Once he knew that he had these entities, he wanted to clear all of this up. Once he was able to clear it up, in the forehead, we went up to the brains. The left side of the brain, which is analytical and logical, was the first side he cleared. Then he went to clear out the right side of the brain, which is the intuitive and spiritual side. The back side of the brain, which happens to be the emotional chakra, was the last part to be cleared up.

### A Return to the Heart Chakra

Once all these were cleared, we were able to go back to the heart chakra. This second time we could go through and clear and release the blockages very easily and quickly. It was interesting that the clearing of the heart chakra hinged on clearing out deceptive entities in the brains and third eye. We usually go up through the chakras from the bottom up. This time we had to go out of order, for a while.

Often the mind blocks the heart from opening up to its very fullness. Once a person goes into his heart chakra, he knows the physical size of the heart, which is about the size of a fist. This man went into his heart and was surprised. You know what he found in there? He found God and the whole universe inside of his heart. He also found his soul dwelling there too. They came together as one, and it was wonderful. Again, this is the kiss of God ... the union of the God within us and ourselves.

### Over-eating and Negativity Pollute the Heart

What happens here to so many people is that they have been hurt in their heart. Also, a lot of people deceive themselves. People pollute their heart by over-eating and emotional negativity. Both of these things weaken the heart area. People haven't been kind to their own heart ... their own center of love. I don't say this to be nasty; it's just that most people just do not understand what love is.

## Love and EVOLution

If you turn the word love around and read it backwards, you get the beginning of the word, evolution ... evol. To evolve or move towards evolution means to open your heart and move into a higher state of evolution. Real love does move you ahead in your evolution. Clearing negativity out of your heart and your life helps you to open your heart center more and more. If you abuse your heart by overeating, and getting too heavy, you can be kind to your physical heart by losing the excess weight and adjusting your eating patterns. From love to "evol," you grow with God. You go forward with spirit. That is evolution. The whole human species needs to evolve more. When it does, there will be no more greed or war. There will be cooperation between nations, and the open heart centers of the human race will want to see everyone happy and healthy. Cooperation and love will overcome greed and competition.

## Looking for Love Outside Ourselves

Most times people try to find love on the outside. It could be a mate. It could be nature's beauty. It could be a cat or a dog. Everything is outside of the person. That's all okay, but it's not as genuine as the love on the inside. The inside love has to come first. A lot of people hide the warmth and the love inside of themselves. They are afraid of getting hurt or rejected. This inner love is the inner God, the God within us. This inner love is connected to our soul. Instead of looking for an outside answer to love, that is not really there, we need to find love and happiness within ourselves. After that is accomplished, we may be able to attract a mate of a similar vibration.

## Each One, a Unique Gift

Some people are artists. Some people are doctors. It doesn't matter what field a person is in. The most important thing is that real love is coming through what they are doing. If there is no love coming through, the person's body will get stagnant and cold and will die. So it is a spiritual love in the heart chakra that we want to open up to, rather than just the emotions of physical love.

## Telling the Truth

When people are not telling the truth, the energy will come up from the root chakra to the heart chakra. Then it either goes around the heart chakra or goes diagonally across it. It does not make use of the heart. In lying, it detours the heart in one of these ways and it does not nourish the heart fully. Gradually, when the heart is not fed spiritually, it begins to die. People who lie do not nourish their heart chakra energetically. If you have a bonfire and you don't add wood to the fire, the fire will die out. If you don't fill and nourish you heart, it will die. So it is a very different feeling with the heart. To me, love is like the positive and negative polarity. It comes in and ignites, and you get illumination from that. This is called love.

## A Loving Couple and God ... a Pyramid

A relationship of two people, who have love and happiness within their own heart first, have a good chance of having a happy and lasting relationship. Two people who are co-creating with God, and have found the God within themselves, have a tremendous potential to be good examples. They are creating a pyramid with God. These people who find God's love to be a part of themselves have received the kiss of God. There isn't anything sweeter in life. God will teach all of us, more than we could ever imagine, about life. For each of us there is a certain lesson to learn in life or a destiny for us to fulfill. Each of us has a unique electromagnetic field or auric pattern around our bodies. Each of us has our own gifts to discover or develop to a higher level. God will help us bring everything to a higher level when we open our hearts to co-creating with God.

## More About the Heart Chakra

I was going to talk more about the heart chakra. There is a physical heart there, without any doubt. Without it we are not alive. But when you go beyond that dimension, you get into the spiritual heart. It is very, very big and has remarkable dimensions. If people don't believe in a heart chakra, it's okay with me. They may not be ready for it. Some day they will learn about it, and possibly in this lifetime. We are here, basically, to help one another. If a person sees love in other people, and they're loving without judging other people, then they are on the right track.

## The Love of God Does Not Judge or Condemn

This is how we need to feel, even if other people are going through hectic things or doing things that you wouldn't do. Even in chaotic or negative people there is a light hidden inside of them. Maybe they have not been able to uncover it yet. If our heart chakra is open, we will be able to see these people as a light that hasn't yet been uncovered. We would not hate, judge or condemn them. That does not mean that we have them living with us and spreading their hectic energy into our life. We have to help others, if we want to be helped, even if sometimes it seems like the longer route.

## There is a Timing for Being Ready to Open

Some people are not ready to open their heart in this lifetime. They may still be working on the solar plexus level. But that's okay, because there are different times that children are born in this world and different times that they go to the other side. There is a continuous rhythmic energy flowing through life. I have had people come in and say, "If I had come to you last year, I would have never believed in this stuff. But something happened, and I'm here and I'm open to it now." I've had people say, "I heard about you six years ago, but now is the time to come, not before." I've had people come back and say, "Well, I haven't come back to see you for five years." I say, "That's okay, I've enjoyed my vacation. Thank you."

*Some of the Sensations of Heart Opening*

The heart gives warmth and radiance to the whole body. A person's face will be lit up with the joy that is felt inside when the heart is open. When the heart chakra is opening up, some people feel sensations of heaviness, tightness or a little pain. They could even confuse these sensations for the beginning of heart trouble. Since real heart trouble gives pain, sometimes a person has to check out their heart with their doctor to be reassured. It is better to be safe than sorry, especially if it gets worse or doesn't pass quickly. If it is a severe pain, then a person should check out medical attention right away.

What happens here is that, when this tremendous amount of light energy comes through the physical organs, membranes, cells and blood, the body can't handle it yet. It's like being in a completely dark room and opening the door to very, very bright sunlight. It's too much to handle right away. I have actually seen people going to doctors, left and right, and the doctors couldn't figure out what was wrong with them. The light energy quickens everything so quickly that the physical body has a hard time trying to keep up with it. But the body does adjust in time.

There are several things that seem to help relieve that tightness. The first thing is a warm bath with a cup or two of Epsom salts in the water. Having someone massage the area on both sides of the spine, right behind the heart and between the shoulder blades, with deep but gentle pressure, also helps. A foot massage helps relax the whole body, especially when pure lavender oil is mixed into the oil or cream.

I've seen it take from a few days to over a year for the physical body to catch up. As the chakras, or energy centers, open up and circulate more light, a sense of God's love, peace, and beauty can be felt. When this light shines through the body, a person can feel the oneness with God.

## Feeling God's Love and the White Lotus

After you really feel the love of God within you, there is another step. When you realize what love is, a symbolic white lotus appears. Often you can see it on your inner mind screen or in a vision. Sometimes you don't see it, but you feel it. It comes with a softness which is completely without the fragmented feeling of a hurt or broken heart. It is just clear and pure.

## The Marriage Heart

Then you know what love is all about. Before that, we go through life learning about different types of love. Some is hit, some miss, some good, some bad. But I also have observed that when people live together but the heart is only half-way opened, it is like the hearts are overlapping each other, but only half merged. When they get married, I have observed the two hearts become one. That one heart is so much bigger and brighter than two individual hearts, or the half-merged hearts that I often see with people that date or live together.

## The Heartbeat and God

For me the heart is like this: You have no control over it because God controls our heart. God beats your heart. It is in the temple of your body, in which your heart beats. It's the music. If a person says he doesn't believe in God, then I say, "Well, stop your heart." A person can't do it for a very long period of time. The beat of the heart and the breathing are interlinked. It is the breath and the heartbeat that is the very life, which is God within us. A lot of people think that light is just light, but it has God's light within it. It is God's flashlight.

## THE THROAT CHAKRA

The throat chakra is a blue-colored chakra. This is the place of communication which can be used in a positive way. It can communicate love and harmony, or it can be used like a razor blade or stinger to attack people. Whatever you say comes back at you. You are the creator and you are the one who receives whatever you say, do and feel. It turns and comes back to you. A lot of people speak only from the mouth or sometimes they speak from their emotions in the solar plexus. Some people speak from their mind only. They need to have God speak with them and through them with inspiration. Sometimes in the cleansing and purification we use practical tools. We use white light, the Christ spirit, and you may use certain types of spiritual soaps, vacuum cleaners or laser beams. Whatever works for you to cleanse and purify the chakra is fine. Then it's clean and you have a new beginning. You have a new balance in your life in all of your seven chakras—your root chakra, your spleen chakra, your solar plexus chakra, the heart chakra, throat chakra and the third eye and crown chakras. After the throat has been purified and cleansed with the help of God, then when you speak, you are speaking with God. It always comes out clean and pure, and whoever talks with you is able to understand you.

The throat chakra represents power, discipline, obedience and expression. Unfortunately, most people talk from the throat area and gradually deplete the energy in the throat area. When they are not talking from the throat, they are actually talking from the brains, and the brains are cold. The energy comes down from the brains and then talks out from the mouth. People are sometimes deceitful. Lots of times people talk from their emotions and are full of confusion and delusion. I also see people who have thyroid problems because the energy is not coming through the throat chakra correctly. So they have to take pills. The thyroid may either be underactive or overactive. I've noticed that it is quite a common condition. However, the best way to speak is to speak from the heart rather than from the brains or confused emotions. Speak from the heart. Speak from God. Speak from the soul. It's warm, and at the same time the communication can make use of the logic of the brains. The spiritual activity and the emotional or intellectual activity can come out together blended as a unit. This is the best and healthiest way for the throat chakra to work.

There is warm energy from the heart coming up to the throat, and there is cool, logical energy coming from the brain down to the throat. These two streams from above and below come out as compassionate truth. In addition, when it works correctly in this way, it keeps the throat chakra and the thyroid gland healthy. It would also help to keep the neck area, the back of the neck and the cervical area a lot clearer and healthier. They always work together and are interlinked. People need to understand that, even if you are working with the throat area in the correct way, you don't know what the results are going to be. When you communicate from your throat, you are also affecting all different parts of your body, as a unit. It's like a whole choir or a whole band. It's also like a symphony with different instruments playing different parts. But they all play together as a unit. This is actually what is happening. When a person doesn't speak the truth or if they speak in confusion, then it is like a person playing the flute, in a symphony of two. The musical instrument is out of tune.

### Foul Language

In today's world a lot of teenagers and adults use a lot of cussing in their speech. They are using the "F" word, as if it is very cool or stylish. You can walk by a group of teenagers who are really nice kids. Often their language is worse than that of the old fashioned truck drivers. This foul language is becoming common language on TV and in the movies and in some of the popular music. You can hear the kids using this foul language as they talk to each other. Some kids use the "F" word every other sentence. Even if they are not angry kids, they may be using more foul words than other words. There are also a lot of adults that use this kind of foul language. What do you think happens to that throat chakra from this kind of talk? With teenagers, it's a bit like the language gives them a feeling of belonging to a group. It shows power in the profanity. It's almost like having a tattoo. It helps you to be accepted in a certain group of people who all have tattoos. In a low-life life-style cussing makes kids feel like they are "someone." But in the end the result is not good. It doesn't make someone special to be good at cussing. Someone's good actions and good words make someone special, in the end.

### A Life of Bad Talk Led to Throat Cancer

I remember, from a long time ago, a guy who was the manager of an apartment complex with eighty-four units. People would come in and he would be very, very prejudiced and he was very vocal about it. He was very judgmental. His negative words could be about a person of color or they could be about someone he didn't like. He was very verbally nasty in his prejudices about people. I was around him for a long time because my parents lived in the same apartment building for twenty-five years. I got to see and hear everything that was going on around there. The next thing you know, he got sick and had to go to the doctor. He was diagnosed with cancer of the throat. It was something that he created. His nasty and dirty words came back to him and short-circuited his system, causing this very serious illness. I'm not saying that everyone who cusses and says nasty things will get cancer. But it's just like that many times.

### Thyroid and Metabolism Disorders

People, and it is most commonly women, who overstimulate their thyroid gland (in the throat chakra area) will get out of balance. It can really affect the thyroid and the metabolism. This imbalance can create overweight, you know, because the thyroid controls the weight. Usually when the thyroid is overactive, the person is pretty thin and depleted, and when it gets sluggish or underactive, the person puts on a lot of weight.

## Smoking to Be Part of the Group

Smoking can be a habit that starts up because a young person wants to be accepted as part of a group. Everyone in the group may smoke, so smoking becomes a part of being accepted. This indulgence becomes a bad habit and is very unhealthy. It can be part of the schooling of being part of a group. But sooner or later a person has to face the consequences.

## Habits Passed From Generation to Generation

Habits like this can be passed on in the family from generation to generation. There is a lack of spiritual protection when a family lives in an energy field of negativity. They haven't worked out their problems, and they may have a lot of negative habits that get learned from the previous generation. It can be alcoholism, smoking, drugs, angry and foul-mouthed language, child or spousal abuse, sexual promiscuity, or any number of bad habits that get passed down in the family.

## Watching Dishonest Politicians on TV

When I see most politicians talking, it bugs me, because I can see right through them. They are usually playing a game, satisfying certain people by saying certain things and maneuvering the energy to win their game. It's manipulation. It is not from God. It is from their own ego and from their own personal power and the agenda that they want to achieve. It is very hard for me to handle people like this, because they are good at manipulating the energy, but the energy is not representing the truth.

## Messages We Put Out

I know people who may just play a certain kind of music or wear a certain kinds of shoes or a particular color, and then someone comes along and shoots them dead. It may be because of something they have said, but sometimes not. It comes back. It just took one person to do that. A life can be lost so easily, so carelessly. Sometimes people who do that kind of thing have a lot of money. They are going to say anything they feel like saying because they have an attitude. They have the "I'm it" attitude. This is a strong ego taking place. A careless attitude can anger other people and cause disastrous results.

## Misusing the Throat Area

The throat area develops problems if you misuse the power of the spoken word. The power is like having a car that you need to lubricate by putting oil in it. If you don't do the up-keep and the lubrication, it dries up and falls apart. So when we don't lubricate ourselves spiritually, but only lubricate ourselves on the physical level, with hatred, anger and swear words, what can we expect to happen in the future? It's the same thing when someone puts a cigarette in their mouth. What can they expect for their health down the line?

## The Truth from the Throat Chakra Is Very Powerful

Truth from the throat chakra has a lot of power in it. I can also tell you that, when a person gets older, I can see the throat chakra and how it begins to deteriorate. It also deteriorates the brains and the whole physical body. Just by looking at the throat and hearing the voice coming out, I can see these things. Some older people have a very crackly voice and some still have a strong voice. Sometimes it is a very strong sound that reflects the will power. When you have been on earth for a long time, you get a certain management power and authority. These older people get a certain power and strength from their life experience.

Some people have personalities that are very soft, sweet and very, very smooth. But if the voice is smooth and sweet, and the person is not telling the truth, I can see a black tar-like substance coming out of their mouth. So one way or the other the truth is going to come out for me to see.

*The Story of a Smoker's Teeth*

There was a really interesting case that I had. A woman came in and I looked at her and said, "When you were a very, very young kid, you had all your teeth fixed." I asked her if I was right. She said I was right. Then I told her she did it because she wanted to look good. She said, "I sure did." Then I asked her why she was destroying all those teeth that she worked so hard to get looking nice, by smoking. I told her that I could see that in the next four years her gums would begin to deteriorate and that she would lose all of her teeth. She could be walking around trying to talk, without teeth. She thought about it and said, "It doesn't make sense that I took such good care of my teeth all these years and that I'm just going to destroy them very shortly because of my desire and my pleasure from smoking." She stopped and she didn't smoke after that.

*Is It All Worth It?*

There is a lymphatic system in the throat area, and like I said, it can dry up. When it slows down, bacteria can build up. Protein in the form of cysts and tumors can build up in the lymphatic system, and then there can be a serious problem. Many smokers get cancer of the throat. Is it worth it, I ask? Marijuana can mess up the gums, too. It is true that marijuana relaxes the nervous system to release the pain of the body, but by the same token, it can become an addiction. It can be taken very lightly for spiritual growth, but it shouldn't be done for very long. I can see that it can act as a catalyst or a trigger to lead people into desiring real spiritual experience and growth. But then this desire to smoke marijuana usually drops away when true spiritual experience begins to happen. It seems that most people who use marijuana do it as a social thing.

*What They Have Done, Comes Back to Them*

I've seen older people, when their muscles begin to get hardened, stretched out and dried up. I see them having arthritis, "big time." They may be in pain for the rest of their life. I have watched people's bodies begin to deteriorate. The eyes begin to water a lot or they may be too dry. They just start to trickle away. People do things without looking ahead to what's going to happen in the future. Maybe they have such little caring for themselves that they don't even care. Many of the bad habits such as smoking, drinking, marijuana, drugs, poor nutrition and foul language pollute the system. They may get away with it for a number of years, but sooner or later it catches up to a person and their body starts to deteriorate. They may get breathing problems, lung and throat cancer, or a destroyed liver. Worse yet is when the brains are fried from drugs and they become crazy.

## Not All Sweet Singing is Healing

I have seen people who are alcoholic go to church and sing. They may sing so nicely but they may pollute the area at the same time, because of their lower astral frequency. It's really weird to see a person who takes drugs, smokes and lies go to church to sing something spiritual. I can see the energy coming out of their mouth. They are giving good energy and bad energy at the same time. They are not aware of this. They are helping people, on one level, but polluting the energy of the environment with the astral sound frequencies of their singing.

## Singing Is More than Words

I also want to say that, when we speak about singing, it's more than just words. It's more than the letters. It's more than the tone itself. It is the light energy that comes out of you. You can say the exact thing you want to say to a person, but the person may pick it up on a different level and interpret it differently, because you put it out on that particular level.

## Side-effects from Church

There is a side-effect from being in church with people who are addicted to substances and/or lying. These are both abuses of the throat or fifth chakra. An ordinary churchgoer may feel really good when they first go into church. But sometimes when they come out, they may wonder why they feel irritable. Of course, this isn't always the case when going to church. But if you feel inexplicably irritable after church, it may be that you picked up some bad energy. It could be that you picked up the mixed energy and message of sweet singing with negative astral energy propelling the voice. People can absorb negative, astral energy into their brains, muscles and emotional body. Different people pick up and absorb things differently, depending on their temperament type and their sensitivity.

### Communicating with Clear, Clean, Light Energy

The best way to have things not be misinterpreted is to have a very clean energy coming through us, like a blue light that comes through us when we talk. When I see the blue light (to me it is blue), I feel the energy is clean and clear. But in the other chakras there is a white energy in the center of the color.

When most people talk, they talk with words alone. Words can be easily misinterpreted. The real way to communicate is with the light energy and love coming from the heart. Like with my language, it's hard for me to talk clearly because I was born in Hawai'i and I speak a kind of pidgin English. So, when I talk to people, I talk with the light energy. Light energy comes from God and from my soul ... which is connected to God. I do use words, of course, but using the light energy, too, helps people to understand my words.

A person can be very intelligent. Every word can be exact. Every pronunciation can be correct; but if the inside of us is not correct, then people will misinterpret the communication. Our communication will be unclear. When our heart and light energy is engaged in our conversation, people respond well to us and understand our communication.

## Anger Looks Red

When people say angry things, the color that comes out of them is red around the mouth and the brains. Sometimes I see it in the solar plexus too. It manifests in different parts of the body. Also from there it can go up into the movement of the hands. The body can react to it. The body doesn't lie. The colors that I see don't lie.

## A Difference with Actors and Actresses

There is a difference with actors and actresses when they are acting out a part. When they do that, the energy in the body is very serene, but they may be acting out an angry scene. If they are acting out an angry part, their body and their own energy will be calm. If an angry person is chosen to be the actor for the angry scene, then the red colors will be there as the anger and red color is part of their general astral vibration. If they have a lot of anger in themselves and they activate their own anger to play the part, that is different from the more calm and emotionally detached actor, and the colors would be red.

## The Throat Center and Our Talking

So the throat center does play a very important part. When we speak, it goes out into the air. The air has molecules which go out into the air. Then wind currents take it everywhere. This air, filled with our real motivation and feelings, goes out to the person we are speaking to.

## Healing Energy in the Voice

There are people who use the fifth, throat chakra, with their voice, as a healing tool. People like this have a healing energy in their singing voice or their speaking voice. Their voice can be healing as they are also merging their soul with God. God's energy and blessing goes out from their voice, for instance, if they sing or speak in an auditorium.

*A Healer, Who Healed with Her Voice*

I once worked with a woman who sings in auditoriums. When she sings, people get healed. She really had a wonderful voice and healing ability through her singing voice. I got to meet this healer personally, and took her through the spiritual process. It showed when I read her, that she was spiritually wide open in all directions, except in one area. The part that was not open was the back of her brains. The back of the brains have to do with past lives and emotional issues that you don't want people to see. The issues can come from childhood all the way up to the present, but it can also come from past lives. I helped her to open this area and to illuminate that dark part with light.

## THE SIXTH CHAKRA ... THE THIRD EYE CHAKRA

I would like to talk a little about the sixth chakra, which is often called the third eye, or the forehead or brow chakra. It is deep blue, actually a kind of indigo, like a blue and purple color in motion. The third eye is also the all-seeing eye of God and one of the clairvoyant centers. I like to call it "the third eye."

This is the all-seeing eye of God. Yet often it gets polluted through drug use—both medical drugs and pleasure drugs can pollute the third eye. It needs to be cleansed and purified so that the person can see with and through God, both from inside the body and also from the heavens above. After cleansing and purifying the third eye, then you can go to the crown chakra which is located on the top of the head. Anytime I find people who have blockages there, I find out what is wrong, so that they can make the corrections. Then all the different parts of the brain can function better.

Ordinary people wouldn't see anything. When the third eye is clogged up or dirty, the webs inside look kind of grey. With many people the third eye is closed down, so they don't have much intuition working in their life. Actually we came in with intuition, but gradually things happen in life that cause people to shut down. When children are seeing things clairvoyantly or intuitively, parents often discourage the child by telling the child that what they're describing is just their imagination. If parents create a stressful environment, it can cause the child to shut down the third eye, or if there is too much of an ego trip, or living disconnected from spirit. Sometimes psychics who do readings on the chakras will read the third eye as being a kind of grey purple color. They will be reading the junk that is jamming up the third eye. When the third eye is clear and bright, it is more like a clear white color. White has all the colors of the rainbow. When you have your third eye open and you run into people who are looking at you with their third eye, you can see their third eye looking at you. It is a very interesting thing to see. The open third eye is for seeing the truth about things. You see both the good and the bad.

### Jesus Predicts Our Gifts with God

One aspect of Christianity is believing in Jesus. They say that Jesus is the way and to follow Jesus. But Jesus says, "These things that I have done, you can do also ... greater things than I, you can do." This means that we, too, can have the gifts of the spirit that Jesus exhibited. This predicts, from Jesus' own words, that we could do even greater things than he. This is amazing and people have a hard time believing this. But if they believe in the rest of the Bible, why do they have such a hard time believing this? These are the words of Jesus. This shows that we are co-creators with God. If you were to ask me, which is the fastest way to grow spiritually?... the Buddhist way, the Native American way, the Muslim way, the Christian way, the Jewish way, etc. I would say the Christian way. For me, Jesus is the way. This is my personal belief, yet I see all the other ways as valid spiritual paths.

### Create Your Goals with God

It is important to create your goals with God. If you don't make goals, your life will be miserable. There will be nothing to strive for. The thing here is that you are able to share with people. When you share with people, you lighten up their life with the light that you have inside of you. Then it will go like a stack of dominoes. What you shared with them, they will share with another. And that other will share with another or others, and so on. That God light shines out to many other people as well.

### The Holy Spirit

In Christianity we talk about the Holy Spirit, and this is as close as it comes to explaining spiritual light. I've thought a lot about the Holy Spirit. Is it male? Is it female? Where did it come from? How high is this spirit? Is it really from God or not? I looked into this in great detail and I've been to many Christian shrines and holy places. Christianity takes the Holy Spirit to another level. Some people may say, "I was hit by the Holy Spirit, or I was slain in the spirit." But how can a person tell if it is the Holy Spirit or some other kind of spirit—a guide or a departed loved one, or an Indian spirit guide, for example? Not that a spirit guide would give negative counsel, but how does one know where the information or blessing is coming from? How does a person know the difference between a guide, master, angel or the Holy Spirit? It may very well be a good and helpful spirit that comes from God. The energy may be of a high enough frequency that we know that it comes from God. The energy is clear, peaceful, clean and uplifting. I've seen a lot of things in my life, while I've been doing healing work with people. Sometimes knowing the difference is very subtle and takes a lot of experience and discernment. But the Holy Spirit feels holy, is highly inspiring and brings the fruits of God ... love, joy, peace and healing.

### There Are Two Ways to See Clairvoyantly

One expression of the energy that creates clairvoyance comes up from the opened up heart chakra, that is full of love and compassion. When I see clairvoyantly, I can see from the heart. The heart energy actually goes up and stimulates the energy of the third eye and that creates a high quality clairvoyance. That's how I am able to get accurate information about people's health problems, emotional issues, and life stories.

## Clairvoyance Entering the Crown Chakra

There's another way to see clairvoyantly. There can be a kind of energetic umbrella above you, which is connected to the opened seventh chakra or crown chakra. The energy of God, the Holy Spirit or the angelic guides comes down into that crown chakra or umbrella-like light funnel and gives the information or "knowing" in that way. So there are these two different directions in which to see clairvoyantly—one coming from heart energy rising up to the third eye, and the other coming down from the heavens above into the crown chakra and then into the third eye.

The energies that nourish and vitalize us come through these chakras both from the heavens above, through the crown chakra and from the earth below, into the feet, up the legs, and then up through the chakras. Our body contains a two-way highway that conducts energy. The energy should be open and flowing. But, for the energy to be open and flowing, we have to clear out the blockages and have all the chakras in balanced motion. The word "chakra" means spinning wheels. These are spinning wheels of energy that are invisible to most people, except people with clairvoyant sight.

## Dangers to Be Aware of with Third Eye Opening

I remember a woman who was seeing Mother Mary in the sky. She saw the angels and all kinds of wonderful things. But she couldn't handle it emotionally. Just as I was beginning to get into spiritual work, she lost one of her feet. She got so emotional about it that she threw off all her body's emotional energy. When a person first opens their third eye, they see the good visions and sometimes the bad. It's like learning how to walk for the very first time. It is hard to make it anywhere. It can be very dangerous. Little kids need little gates so they don't fall down the stairs. Sometimes it can be dangerous when the third eye first opens up. If a person is not guided by an experienced elder or a knowledgeable teacher, a person can do some very irrational things, or feel scared about their visions and perceptions. Finding reliable guidance is very important. Some experiences that take place with the "opening process" can be very similar to psychotic states. Being grounded, and doing things that are ordinary, help ground and stabilize the person that is going through this experience. Gardening, writing, painting, hiking, cooking and cleaning are some of the things that help ground the energy and keep the person connected to this world and everyday life.

## Mis-Guided Voices

I remember one guy from Phoenix, Arizona that had his third eye open up, all by itself. He saw all kinds of things and felt that God was talking to him and giving him directions to drop out of his business and move to Flagstaff with his family and friends. He actually did move there, but it didn't work out. That really confused him. He was convinced that he was getting direct guidance from God. In reality he was confused—his clairvoyant ability had not matured or stabilized yet, and his guidance was confused.

## The Importance of Finding Guides and Mentors

A teacher or guide that has experience is very important for someone who is just at the beginning of the journey of a third eye opening. Until there is stabilization, a person may get either good or bad images (or both) and feel that they are being told to do certain things. Sometimes psychotic episodes are actually third eye openings that have gone astray. Things can get pretty crazy sometimes if the person does not have a guide to help them. This is not always the case, but it *is* at times. There are times when the person hears voices. That experience or "symptom" can easily be confused with schizophrenia. You know, in all things, you have to look at both the positive and negative sides. There are always two parts to everything. When people pick up the wrong side, it can be so confusing. Then there are times when you may hear the right voice or voices, but your doctor may think you are psychotic. You may see visions of heaven or angels, and the doctor might still think you are having a grandiose delusion. If you are picking up negative or scary things, the doctor may think you are having paranoid delusions.

*The Third Eye Opening Can Sometimes Act Like Mental Illness*

It is a shame when a gifted person is opening up and no one is there to help them. They may end up in a mental hospital taking medications. It is very, very important to find a qualified guide. One of the biggest flaws with these experiences is when a person feels they need to figure it all out by themselves. You have to be with people who are like-minded, have good integrity, and want to help you. If you try to figure it out by yourself, it will take far too long. It may take many, many years, and sometimes it will be too late to use the gift to help people. If you take the wrong path, then you will have to double back and retrace your steps. Working with the third eye opening, and figuring out what to do with this new intuitive gift, can really be difficult. No matter what tradition or religion you come from, you need training and mentors. Truly, you are changing frequencies in your third eye and also in your whole system. When the whole process stabilizes, it becomes a gift.

*The Gifts of the Open Third Eye*

When you get good at working with the open third eye, and you have stabilized in the new higher frequency, then you can be of great service to others. You might be able to save a lot of time for someone by determining a problem or an illness. You may be able to see a problem or a potential illness ahead of time and give someone some helpful suggestions or guidance. You may have valuable insights for people, that will really help them. You may get inspirations for projects or inventions that will really benefit mankind. You may get guidance to be at a certain place, at a certain time, so that you can be of service or make a needed connection. All kinds of great things can happen once a person knows how this all works and the adjustment and stabilization have happened. When it has stabilized and your experiences have been validated over a period of time, then you begin the process of learning to trust this guidance. Part of keeping the guidance pure and true is living a clean, wholesome life and keeping your own energy clear through prayer and meditation.

*Preventing Negative Entities*

Another very important thing is to make sure you do not make any impulsive, rash decisions. Being clear of alcohol and illegal drugs is very, very important, as the system is delicate and vulnerable. Entities, or bad spirits, can hang around or attach and really cause havoc. A negative entity might start giving a person instructions about doing something negative. The person may be confused and think that the instructions are coming from God. It is terrible when this happens. Maybe some of the school shootings in the USA are related to entity possession and kids listening to dark entity voices that tell them to do terrible things.

*Healing Family Members*

When you're working as a healer with an open third eye, it is often the case that you have trouble healing your own family members. But you may do very good healing work and get results with other people who are outside of the family. This is usually because we are so tied to them and may have too much attachment. I have found a way around this. What I do is change my frequency so that it is out of the range of the family frequency. It's sort of like shifting gears on a car. I change the frequency of the third eye. I go above, below, beside or behind the energy frequency. I can go to different angles to find out the answer that I'm seeking to help a family member. Sometimes before shifting the energy it feels like fifty percent of the energy is coming one way and fifty percent of the energy is going the other way. The energy with this family member can just neutralize itself. But when I change the genetic frequency and do it with God's help, then I can be allowed to heal a family member. The object is to go above, below or around. I make everything a different frequency by shifting my third eye.

*Seeing with My Third Eye*

Sometimes when I see through the third eye, it is vibrating and tickles. Sometimes the tickle-feeling is like a slight shock. It feels real neat. I even have a really long hair that grows out of third eye area between my two eyes. Sometimes it is white, other times transparent, and sometimes red. I feel it is a spiritual antenna. At the barber shop, they always try to cut it. They did once and it was about three inches long. It was so long it could tickle my nose.

The third eye shines when people have their soul over the third eye. That combination can be used to control, manipulate and hurt people. It is not the best place for the soul to be placed. If I see the soul there, I know that I am looking at a controlling and manipulative person. It is not a warm energy like the heart chakra when the soul is located there. It is a cold energy, and a person can misuse the energy with bad intentions or anger. The same principles work either way. If you misuse it, then you are the one who has to face the consequences that come back around on you. In a way we could say that the chickens come home to roost. What goes around comes around. This is the law of karma or the law of cause and effect.

I see things opening up in front of my face, when I am seeing clairvoyantly from my third eye. The energy radiates up to the third eye from my heart, and it radiates down to the third eye from "upstairs" with a kind of umbrella-like energy at the top of my head, or the crown chakra. So the energy comes from both above and below to stimulate the third eye. It opens up pictures and movies in my third eye like a color television or movie screen, giving me all the information I need in my life as a healer.

## Clairaudience

The whole picture or story opens up in front of me. It is like a surround-sound screen bringing information to me through the clairaudient channels of the ears and the clairvoyant channels of the third eye. The pictures go back from the third eye into the pineal and pituitary glands, and then to the back of the brains. For me the third eye is like a screen on the back of the brains ... like a big screen. Then there is the clairsentient ability. That is the ability to know things by feeling them. Feelings turn into pictures for me, and then I can read them. Sometimes I just feel what the person is feeling, for a quick moment. My system filters out what's unnecessary and shows me what I need to know in order to understand and help that person. But I don't hold onto their feelings.

They don't belong to me. But for a quick second by touching into their feelings, I will get a lot of information as to how they are feeling inside. An outside smile may not match the pain inside.

Clairaudience has to do with extrasensory hearing abilities. It goes to the center of the head towards the pituitary gland and then it goes out to the ear channels. So that is like a cross. I can hear people beyond the sounds of the physical ear. It's both ways. The inner voice I hear is also from people. I can hear them talking back with information about themselves and their inner dialogue. Certain parts of people's bodies talk to me and I will hear that clairaudiently. Sometimes I hear from the outside, with a sound which is out loud, but not as much as from the inside. You have to be careful to know which voices are good and which are bad. You need to develop discernment and use common sense. The only way you can get it from the outside is to go to the inside first and then go outside. Then you will know. You will have a double way of confirming your information. The energy will match. Sometimes you can hear a voice calling out loud. It could be a spirit. It's not always a good one. If it tells you to lie down on the freeway to show your faith in God, you can be sure it is a bad spirit trying to get you killed. Common sense is very important.


## THE CROWN CHAKRA

The crown chakra is at the top of the head and is the number seven chakra on the rainbow. It's "color" is white light and lavender and it should be open, big and wide. The chakra might be a four-inch diameter circle. A lot of times, you know, it's hardly open at all. If it's shut down, it will come up looking smoky. It looks like the puffs of steamy smoke that come out of the steam engine of an old-fashioned locomotive train. If a person is too mental and has too much logical thinking, the crown chakra will not be in harmony and relaxed. Too much mental energy acts like a filter and closes up the free flow of this natural spiritual energy that comes into the top of the head from "upstairs." Your energy may get strong and then be weak, and then strong and weak. Your vitality will not be consistent if your crown chakra is partly shut down.

## The Halo of Illumination

When you get all the rainbow colors coming up together in harmony, it comes out white or white-ish on the top of the head. Your harmonized energy mixes with the energy of God. This gold white light has been seen in paintings of saints and holy people, and it is usually referred to as a halo ... a halo of light. It indicates illumination and oneness with the creator, and is created out of white gold light.

It is a mistake for people to feel that they have to be under someone's umbrella or that they have to hide their light under a bushel-basket. There is a time for a child to come out of the mother's womb, and then there's a time for the child to learn from the parents. There's a time for the child to go and get married, or go out into the world, find a career and be successful in a unique way. And this is how it is with spirit. When we co-create with God, life will be a lot more exciting and a lot more beautiful.

The silver cord is connected at our crown chakra. Some people call it the bowl of light. That is what it shows in the Bible. I have seen it spoken of both ways in the Bible. Most people don't understand what is being referred to at all. One time it was described as a silver cord, and another time it was called a bowl of light. It connects the earthly plane to the spiritual planes. The reason the silver cord is small is that many times our brains have so much stuffed inside of them. The silver cord acts like a filter to block the energy from coming through the body. See, when the energy comes into your body from the crown chakra, it goes down to the other chakras and then it comes back up again. It comes back up again, but often there is so much blockage to go through on the way down that there may not be enough energy coming up through you, from the earth's energy.

Lots of times I see people who are kind of weary and gray-looking, and they may be cold around their face area. They're vulnerable to illness because they don't have enough energy exchange going through them. They may also be angry, because too little of the energy is getting to the brain. It's like not having enough food and having low blood sugar. You get kind of irritable. So, it's like spiritual low blood sugar or hypoglycemia.

The energy can come down through the crown chakra and get stuck going down. Because of energetic blockages of energy it doesn't get close to going all the way down or all the way up, in the right way. The energy transportation system is not clear enough. The yin and the yang have to be balanced both ways.

What happens here if all the chakras are open? Then you get the white, golden light, in and around the head area, and that is your pot of gold at the end of the rainbow. That is what we see so often in Hawai'i. You see the rainbow, and at the end of the rainbow you're supposed to find a pot of gold, if you can get there. Actually, the rainbow is our way to heaven, and this secret road is found inside of us. But this rainbow only lights up when we open everything up, by clearing all the garbage and old baggage out of our chakras.

People may not believe all this, but that's okay, because they may not be ready for it yet. There are a lot of people who are ready for it now, and they will understand and make the changes. Now, people have a choice to either go for it or not. If you don't do it, it will be tough luck for your life. It is your life! We learn from this earth and from our family and community about how to live life. We learn in school and hopefully we attain wisdom from our life experiences. We learn how to do a lot of things and we get a little bit smarter. It doesn't end there.

The next level up is illumination. This is being one with God. This white gold light around the crown chakra is called a halo. The halo is always shown around the heads of Jesus, Mary, Joseph, the apostles and the saints. You will see halos around and over the heads of holy people in the religious art found in European museums and cathedrals. The Native Americans have the different feathers and colors in their traditional headdresses that stand tall above their heads. These feathers that are physically above their head represent many things. But the feather bonnet represents the aura and the halo too. The Pope, as the head of the Roman Catholic Church, wears a high ceremonial hat that could easily represent this aura and halo that is a symbolic connection to heaven. The Tibetan Lamas in their ceremonies have high hats that look similar to the Pope's ceremonial hat.

This halo represents divine illumination, which is beyond wisdom or knowledge. Illumination is the potential birthright and goal of all humans. It doesn't matter what our religion, culture or race is. Illumination is what all humans want to attain. It is being one with God here on Earth. It is unification, happiness, joy, generosity, peace, divine love and being one with God. It is the greatest fulfillment.

## More on the Silver Cord

We are born with an umbilical cord that is connected with our Mother. It nourishes us while we are in the womb. But there is also a cord that we have that connects us to God. It is the silver cord that connects to our body at the crown chakra at the top of our head. When it breaks, we die and go back to God. With many people their energy comes in through the silver cord. It connects to God's power, love and grace. Occasionally when I work with people, I see that the silver cord is ready to break, just like an old rope that is ready to fall apart. When that happens, it shows that the person has a lot of fear. They are scared that they are going to die.

## Reasons for a Weak Silver Cord

This thinning of the silver cord does not necessarily mean that the person is going to die. It does show that the person is very vulnerable. A solid connection of the silver cord is very, very important. I found out that, when people have their silver cord connected to a star or to the moon, it is not as bright. They often have suicidal feelings or intentions. Somehow they have chosen to fall out of God's grace. Also their soul doesn't get nourished enough from being connected to God. When a person is connected to God with a strong silver cord, they are connected to a very, very bright light above them. It is a bright spiritual light when you are at peace and at home with God. When a person goes against the grain of God, using their own will rather than God's will, then they face difficulty. I have seen cases of suicide, and the reason is that the individuals were not connected to God. Somehow they got disconnected. Sometimes the disconnection starts through the use of drugs. Sometimes it happens through painful relationships or going through something that causes great trauma and fear.

*Making the Silver Cord Stronger for a Longer and Healthier Life*

You can make the silver cord stronger if you want to live a longer and healthier life. I call the angels down to help reinforce the strength of the cord. People have a tendency to try to do things alone, without God and God's angelic helpers. Trying to improve the strength of the silver cord by yourself might just make the silver cord a little wilted. God and the angels bring infinite help when they are invited to help. I like to have them help me, especially when I'm doing healing work. They are the ones who are unemployed and need the job. I, myself, like doing my work here on Earth. I don't want these angels to get lazy up there. Sometimes I complain to God, "Hey, God, you guys are having parties up there, and the angels are playing harps and relaxing. We here on Earth have a job to do. Come on and give us some help. Stop goofing off up there."

We often find these things when a person is going through the journey of their inner space, under my guidance, which is called "the process." This process is also a great opportunity to correct the things that compromise a person's health and spiritual energy.

# 9

# The Spiritual Process

## The Spiritual Process

There is a spiritual process that I do with people that I have come to just call, "The Process." I do this with a person on a one-to-one level. This is an in-depth inner journey through the spiritual and physical bodies. I am the guide and I am traveling with the person, so I am able to catch the person in a flaw or blind spot very easily.

## Praying in "The Spiritual Process"

I prayed that we would find a way to cut through these stubborn problems and help people free themselves from these things. So after a few years of spiritual work, God guided us to develop a more effective way to help others. At the time we had a community of spiritual people all living together at our healing center, Cosara. We called ourselves a spiritual family. That was back in the late seventies and early eighties.

Together we developed the "Spiritual Process." My belief is that it was inspired by God so that we could have a better way to help people clear themselves and open up more spiritually. It turned out to be a really fast way of clearing out old blockages that were slowing down people's spiritual, mental and emotional growth. It also helped clear physical blockages and genetic memory blockages that caused poor health. "The Process"—which came to be our nickname for it—takes anywhere from one to three days to go through, six to eight hours a day.

The process is a journey through inner space, with a trained guide taking you through a tour of the invisible parts of your anatomy. It is a journey through the chakras and the different parts of the brain, the silver cord, the grounding, the aura and elements. The chakras ("spinning wheels") are a part of our invisible anatomy.

148

Each one has a color and a musical note associated with it. In a similar way acupuncture meridians and points are real, and have been used by Eastern physicians for thousands of years. But they are invisible to the average person. Each chakra is an energy center that spins in its own direction. It is a beautiful colored wheel of light when it is clear and healthy. There are seven points of light or seven main chakras in the body. Each one corresponds to one of our endocrine glands, and each emanates a color. When the chakras are not open and clear and spinning properly, then the corresponding endocrine glands malfunction. From the bottom up, the colors are red, orange, yellow, green, blue, purple and white/gold.

The red is the root chakra and relates to the sexual organs and survival. The root chakra is where we start. Often what they see taking place in the root chakra is seeing something like a light bulb. The person goes into that vision and focuses. More will usually appear. They will usually see blockages in what would be the neck area of the light bulb. They will see certain colors there. There are different layers of colors and vibrations. Each time a person peels away debris, the guide tells the person how to release and cleanse and purify it. The more the root chakra is purified, the better the reproductive organs will work, as the root chakra is energetically connected to the reproductive system. Each chakra is cleansed and purified in the process, starting with the root chakra and working up towards the top of our head. This is called the crown chakra and it is usually white-gold. A clairvoyant person can see the colors and shapes of the chakras. To be healthy the chakras have to be bright and clear and spinning in a clockwise spin, in an even, harmonious way. The clarity and health of these chakras determine our physical health, our mental and emotional well being, and our spiritual openness.

The "Spiritual Process" also explores the connections we have with others and it helps clear up any places of anger, trauma of lack of forgiveness. During the process we can clear off any unhealthy energy cords or connections that keep us from being fully ourselves and free. It is also an opportunity to determine where the inner God is, inside of us, and the location of our soul. Sometimes things are in the wrong places and we have to rearrange things so they are in their proper locations. We can also determine, in the process, if we are being influenced by any unwanted energies, programs from parents, or troublesome spirits.

It is all about clearing out the debris and garbage that we store in our chakras which cause them to be less than healthy and radiant. The process is set up in such a way that the person goes within themselves. I (or one of my trained ministers) will guide them with instructions and guided imagery. After a chakra is cleared, for instance, we then ask for the inspiration for a spiritual shield to cover and protect both sides of the chakra, both front and back. Sometimes it takes a little patience, but the vision or inspiration for the shield will come to us. The purpose of the shields is to keep negative or unwanted energy out.

### Where Is the Soul? and Where Is God?

During the process, I will ask them, "Where is the soul?" Usually either they don't know or, if they do know, it is in a place it shouldn't be in normally.

The second question I ask is, "Where is God within you?" Yes, it is true that God is in every muscle, every organ, every cell, but there is an anchor for us where God is very strongly within us. For instance, they may say that God is in their big toe. I learned that people usually have their soul and God in two different "rooms" within them. This is one of the biggest problems that I have found with people. Their soul and God should be unified together. Then I simply say to them, "Where is the best place for your soul to be? Where is the best place for God to be?" On the average, they will say, "in the heart." A few will say, "in the mind." Many will say, "in the solar plexus." Sometimes people see God up there on their crown chakra, on the top of their head.

When God and the soul are not linked up, people are not happy. This is why they feel filled with a kind of voidness. They feel kind of empty. I am not a bit surprised, and so what I say is, "Okay, I will give you some time with just you and God." I usually give them about ten minutes and I leave the room. Before I leave, I say, "Ask your soul to please come into your heart. Then ask God to please come into your heart and join your soul." Then they have this meeting, this divine intermingling. The person completely surrenders to the God within themselves. Then they become one with God. You can actually feel the oneness of God within you. But what is God?

### What Does God and the Soul Look Like?

To me, God is an illumination of light that is in us and which sparkles so much light. It is sometimes white, sometimes gold, and sometimes a mixture of both. I also ask people, "What does your soul look like?" Lots of times they get it wrong. The soul actually is very flexible and pliable like putty, each with different colors and a different purpose, with different things to do and learn. This is what the light is. Once the soul or spirit intermingles with God, then the person feels at peace and there is a spiritual direction in their life. Before that, there is none. The heart has been the place where the soul and God have come together for thousands of people that I have worked with in the past. It seems to be a very common denominator, and so this is what I have learned from my experience with myself and other people.

For example, you explore your heart chakra as if it was a room, inside of yourself. You look around with your inner eye and see what's in there. There may be things in the past that have hurt the heart. Your heart could have had hurt feelings or heartbreaks. Most people find wounds in their heart. There are methods that people can use to clear their wounds and heartbreaks, in order to clear the dark places and pain out of their hearts. The way to do it is with the help of God, not by yourself. You need to do it with God, in order for it to be really effective. Let's say, for instance, that there is a problem in the heart chakra. For example, maybe your Mother or Father really beat you up a lot when you were a little child. Maybe you hate your Mother or Father for abusing you. So let's say you are a woman and you really don't get along well with other females because you have been hurt so much by an important female when you were a small child. You may not be able to trust women, even if you are a woman yourself. It is important for the grown-up, who felt wronged as a child, to understand the experience. When you did something wrong, you might have gotten a spanking from a very strict Mother or Father. This may be the way your parents were trained and they did to you what they were taught to do. Another reason for abuse could be that the parent had a personality with a short fuse. A crying or whining child could cause them to be so irritable that they lost their temper and their sense of empathy. Parents who were alcoholics have even more difficulty dealing with their children. Sometimes they are just not available or responsible. They may not be home to take care of their children. Sometimes they exhibit rage and sometimes they are so altered by alcohol that they can do crazy and criminal things such as emotional, physical or sexual abuse. If they drive drunk, they can kill themselves, others, and even their own children. There can be many problems growing up. Almost everyone has some feeling of being wounded from some aspect of childhood.

### The Guide's Job

The guide's job is to help induct the person into an altered state of consciousness. The guide relaxes the person with some guided imagery and breathing exercises. Soon the person begins to have hypnagogic imagery which is like having visionary or dream images. The guide accompanies the person on the inner journey and makes a few suggestions along the way. The guide will often be seeing the same thing the person is seeing. Spirit helps the guide be able to share the vision of the person going through the process. The guide is also a protector who makes the person feel safe and reassured as the person encounters things inside, that they may not have known were there. The process is a safe space to allow unconscious or repressed material to come to the surface.

For instance, when the person is looking with their inner eye at their solar plexus chakra, the guide may ask several questions. The guide may say, "What color is it? How big is it? Does it have a smooth spin to it? Does it have a wobble? Does it have any dark places?" If the person sees a dark place or something strange, the guide will ask the person to put their attention on it and look deeper, to see what that dark place represents. Most often images begin to arise, or movies begin to roll, showing some important things from the person's past history. This reveals the meaning of the dark spot or blockage. The guide may discuss the situation with the person and offer tools or guidance to help clear it.

Sometimes spiritualized tools are used in a person's visualizations, such as vacuum cleaners, lasers, a wand of white light, or a Christian cross. One time a person used a "Roto Rooter" to clean out a really stubborn blockage. A process of forgiveness is often needed to clear away old pain. The Holy Spirit may be invited in to clear the blockage away. It is then cleansed and purified, and a shield is found to protect the chakra, when it is all clear. Many people feel physical sensations of release and clearing. This shows that this is more than a visualization exercise. Real energy blockages are being released. Often there is such a feeling of freedom, openness, and a very tangible warm glow in the solar plexus chakra, after it has been cleansed and purified.

### A Feeling of Joy and Open Heart

When the process is complete, there is such a feeling of celebration and joy. The feeling of openness and crystal clarity is fantastic. The energy in the body is open and flowing. This is actually the natural state of joy that we were meant to have in our lives. The heart is open too, and so much love is pouring out. It is just such a fantastic feeling. So many people have said that they feel clear as a bell and that they didn't know that it was even possible to feel this clear.

### The Silver Cord

Then we go to the silver cord to see where the person is connected—if it is to God or the moon or a star. Lots of times it connects the person to the stars. People like this may feel suicidal, or they may carry a lot of guilt about something that they have done. So they need to correct that. God is very loving and very forgiving. In the spiritual process I continue on to the person's personality. This deals with both parts of them that need healing. Corrections are made and then we go into the soul level, and we look at the shape and the color of the soul and especially at its location.

We then go to the left side of the brain which is logical and see what we have stored up in there from the past. Then we go to the intuitive right side of the brain where we find spiritual creativity. And then we go to the back side of the brains which contains the emotions and our memories and traumas, which we have accumulated from then right up until now.

In the lower, rear part of the brains is a secret place where people try to hide certain things that come from the past. The door that accesses that area is a very, very dark one, but once it is cleansed and purified, it becomes very illuminated with light. The person becomes one with the love and breath of God. Being in tune with our creator helps the physical, mental, emotional, and spiritual bodies come together. We are also cleansing and purifying all the bodies with water, fire, earth and air. You are the director and you have all the different instruments. Each instrument has been tuned and then all of them are tuned and harmonized with each other. Then the whole orchestra can be in harmony and play a very beautiful symphony. It is both inner and outer. Other people can see it and you can feel it.

So all kinds of people—from gurus to spiritual healers to housewives—are going through this spiritual process. Actors and actresses have been helped in reaching their creative goals and purpose in life. Once a person has gone through all the chakras and the different parts of the brain and the elements, and cleansed and purified them, they feel whole and very clear and bright. Usually I can see how accurate the person is both within themselves and with God. Sometimes there is a little more for them to learn or understand, so I show them the weak points and direct them where to work on themselves.

Once the person has completed the process, numerous things can happen. There can be a change of job, change of location, or even a change of partner or friends. The process will make you feel very close to your partner or it will pull you away completely. This spiritual process is very accurate and real because there is a communion with God at all times. We have asked for God's blessings and help with it. Once a person has been cleansed and purified in this way, then they become more open and true to others and themselves, no matter what field they are in. Before going through the process, people may have been able to help people on an average of thirteen per cent. Now, can you imagine helping ninety to one-hundred percent? Being accurate with God makes your role as a partner, friend, or co-worker more beautiful. The spiritual process really cleanses the inner part of your bodies and opens everything up. I see it as more than a "tune up." It is a most valuable spiritual overhaul. Along with a daily practice of prayer and meditation, I believe it the quickest path for accelerating your spiritual evolution.

### The Woman Who Wouldn't Complete Her Process

Once I was taking a woman through the process and she was really enjoying it. She was seeing accurately too. Then she wanted to take a little break. When she came back, she said she didn't want to continue. She wanted to stop right there, just as we were about to go into the brains. Nevertheless, she left. I asked God why she didn't want to complete the process, and God said that she would not see me for six years but then she would return for help. Originally when she decided to go through the process, her purpose was to be able to do healing work. But her real purpose was to make money. That is the wrong motivation for going into healing work.

Six years later I was down in the Bay Area in Alameda, California. Somehow she found me there. When I saw her, I realized that her mind was almost gone. She was a beautiful woman but she was kind of spaced out. She really wasn't all there. I felt that she had used a lot of pleasure drugs that has killed part of her brain. She was almost like a vegetable. I cried inside of myself because she wasn't willing to take that next step six years before, to clear out her brains. She had gone in the other direction towards self-destruction.

## Finding Animals Within

In the spiritual process people can sometimes find animals in themselves. They may be creatures that they have created or brought in genetically or through a relationship. So they need to go inside and purify it. Occasionally, you get energy that's very difficult to clean out. Sometimes it's a difficult energetic mass, like a spider. You pull off one leg at a time, until the spider can't move. Then you can get to the main part of the energy body that needs to be cleansed and purified.

## Making a Deal with God

One March, a long time ago, I was taking a few people through the process and all of a sudden there were carloads of people coming in and they all wanted to go through the process. Everything was a semi-emergency because they all needed help. I took them one at a time. The more I would say "no" to working on so many people, the more people came. So I made a deal with God. I said, "Okay God, I will make a deal with you. I'll work with all the people you want me to work with. This is fine, but I would appreciate having next month to rest." It was a learning stage for me. I worked with people who all were gifted in different ways. I was meant to learn from these gifted people.

## The Process Completed

Once you complete the spiritual process, you can renew it anytime you want to. You can go back and pass through it again to renew the cleansings. This method helps accelerate your growth and progress in life. It helps you to find ways that you may sabotage reaching your highest potential. It will help you see blind spots that keep you stuck in addictions or unhealthy habits. There will still be daily problems, but there will be a way to work at solving the problems, and with these new tools they will be much easier to deal with. The more you cleanse and purify your bodies, you will find that the company you attract will be of a higher spiritual caliber.

Like attracts like. So the cleaner and purer you are, cleaner and purer people will come and work and spend time with you.

If your energy is low, then you attract other low energy towards yourself. So if you want the best, and you want more than just an astra-emotional vibration in your life, you will not settle for anything less than God's vibration. Now you will attract in the frequency of the Christ, the masters, and the angels.

The timing of when a person comes to me for a second process is something that only the person wanting it would know. Somehow my mind is blank about what it is supposed to be, because it is only for them. It is a very personal thing. It is a sacredness and holiness that is only theirs. Once I work with a person with their earthly problems, there is a communication between our souls. We are both human beings here on earth, but we are also human beings with God.

Many times, when a person comes to me, they will get just what they need, no matter what situation they are in. God will provide for them and show them the way. The spiritual process can be done in a room or outside in nature, walking in the woods, along the side of the river or at the waterfalls. A person could even go through the process in a supermarket. That would be challenging and unique, but it could be done. Wherever you are, you can work with God and work with yourself for the rest of your life. Once you find this harmony within yourself, you will have no more inner war. When there is no more war, you can use all the freed-up energy much more effectively for yourself and the people around you. I always feel that when people work with other people, they should give the best of themselves. In the presence of your creator, with every breath and every heartbeat, and being who you really are, you will have a more beautiful life.

While taking people through the spiritual process there are times that the person may not be able to come up with an answer for something. So I will sometimes tell them some of the inner laws of a spiritual life to help them fill in some of the empty spaces or provide the answer that they are searching for. All the pieces start to come together, and they usually see the whole picture of their destiny. They can see how much illumination they have in their body and they see how open they are. They can see if they still have interference in their life or if they still have a tendency towards drugs, alcohol or other addictions. They will see if they can set themselves aside and let God's light shine through them.

## Forgiveness

There are so many different causes of these problems. So, we need to learn to forgive the person or persons who have hurt us in the past. Then we have to learn to forgive ourselves, because we are just as guilty as they are. The experience took place, and we had to come together with them to learn some kind of lesson. Whatever the case, we were in that situation and connected to it. We don't really feel God's forgiveness of us, if we don't forgive ourselves and others. We need to learn to let it go, because if we don't let it go, then what is our life all about? Is it about being resentful, bitter, angry and feeling sorry for ourselves? When we carry all this garbage from the past, it makes us miserable. It is not fair to ourselves or to our body because the hurt in the mind and emotions hurts or kills our body, after a long period of time. The body is not happy, and so when you go to a doctor and say, "Fix me. I have a health problem," what are you really saying?

## Healing Emotional Problems

It's important to know that the problem may need medical intervention but the emotional causes may go back a long way. When you do that forgiveness of yourself and the other person, you need to do it with God. You can say, "God, take me to a new place inside of myself. Teach me your love. Teach me what real life is within myself. Teach me to cope with this physical world. I want a better life than the one I have had." That is an example of having a conversation with God ... and co-creating a new life with God.

*Letting Go of Pain and Changing the Program*

People can look at the situation in two ways. One, they have been hurt in the past. They can feel resentful and hurt for their whole life. Number two is that they have learned that they got beaten up or hurt in the past, but they do not intend to do this to their own children. They make an intention to raise their own children in a different and better way. The chain of pain has to be broken, otherwise it just gets passed from one generation to another. The choice to learn from the experience instead of staying victimized allows a person to be a better parent to their own children.

*Refreshing "The Process" on One's Own*

The person is given tools, such as their shields, to go back in and refresh their process on their own. They now know how to maintain their inner anatomy and keep things clear. This is a kind of inner house cleaning. Once we know how to do it, we can keep our own inner house clean. One knows about the energy cords that can come in from other people or emotional blockages from worrying about oneself or others too much.

# 10

# The Fountain of Youth and Longevity

## The Fountain of Youth

The air can cleanse your body like the wind or the soft breezes we get in Hawai'i. Air can nourish you with the breath of God. This is what we call the fountain of youth, when your body is working together like a big, happy family. I believe that youthfulness is good for all of us to achieve, no matter how old we are. I feel we need to BE IT AND LIVE IT. We need to be the person and live the life that God wants us to have, so we can be an example for other people. This is what I try to do in every aspect of the work. But all the bodies have to be in balance—the physical, emotional, mental and spiritual bodies—in order to create that fountain of youth. We could say it could be seen like an office chair with four legs. If one of the legs is off, then it throws every part of the chair off. We need to learn to keep in balance so that our bodies work together as a unit. Each individual has its own particular job to do, but they need to be working together in harmony. This is how God designed us to be peaceful and healthy and to live a very long and healthy life.

When I talk about youth, I mean becoming young and healthy again. Sometimes I tell jokes to people like, "In the morning I wake up and take out my spiritual iron and iron my face. It takes all the wrinkles out of it." And I can say to you very truthfully that I have never had a face-lift, but I feel as youthful as a young kid. I am genuine—this is what God has given me. And also I smile and joke around with people a lot. All the cells of my body have a smile in them and God's colors flying. At times I feel like God is tickling my heart. I giggle a lot because I have learned to create a connection with God, in my mind and in my heart. I feel that God means us to be happy and joyful. We are meant to use all the senses that God has given us. And I get it across to people better this way. I'm a happy Hawai'ian. Giggling and laughing is contagious. People like a happy clown.

It is really a thrill to be happy and joyful. We spoke about changing our vibration. I really enjoy changing the vibration a lot. It uplifts and lightens everything that is done or said. The energy field, which is what we call an atmosphere, feels really good, uplifted and light for everyone to enjoy.

### Longevity Research Study

One of my doctor friends travels all around the world doing research about people who live very, very long lives. He calls this "longevity," and he feels that by finding the causes of longevity he can pass on the tips to all of us, so that we can all have longer and healthier lives. He found that people who had very long lives were very childlike and simple and didn't make things very complicated.

He asked a woman, "Is there any time in your life that you have gone through some heavy emotional stress?" The woman said, "I have no stress." She had a very long life already and she gave a clue to one of the biggest reasons for being very old and very healthy. The key is either no stress or not letting stress get to us, and having a childlike wonder and simplicity.

My doctor friend also got in touch with the tobacco companies and told them that the tobacco that they put out has a lot of chemicals in it. He said that according to his research, the people who smoke tobacco and lead long lives all live in different countries that grow tobacco as a plant and don't put it through chemical processing. Why would a person want to put chemicals into the body in the first place? It is not natural. Also the smoke is toxic for other people to breathe. This doctor friend of mine travels all around the world studying people, in many cultures, who have had very long life spans. He discovered that many of them either drank some vodka or some wine. But he said that the way we drink in the United States is different than the way people drink in many other countries. Most of these people are farmers that sweat it out through their hard work. That is a big difference from drinkers in the United States who often have desk or sedentary jobs. Now that's a big difference. Being physically active makes a difference, as the activity is purifying the body. The way Americans drink is usually sitting around in a bar or in a house in front of a TV. We don't often sweat it out.

### A Native American Grandma's Story of Longevity

There was a Native American Indian Grandma that I heard about that lived to be one hundred and eleven years old. When she was young, she used to drink a lot. During that time in her life she drank a fifth of whiskey a day.

You wonder how she could live to be one hundred and eleven years old. But in her traditional Native American life, she went to her sweat lodge every single week and that purified her body. It was a part of her spiritual practice. Not only did she work hard as a housekeeper and ironing lady, but she also did her healing and prayer work and sweat lodge ceremony every week. Now that made a great difference. She did quit drinking at one point in mid-life.

One day she just said, "This is enough" and she never had another drink again. You would think that there would be a lot of damage in her body, but the weekly sweat lodge and those prayers helped to offset what she had done to her body. If it was just for pleasure only, it would have been very detrimental, but because of her spiritual life and cleansing, it didn't do the usual damage. Like I said before, saunas and hot tubs reduce the level of damage.

### Changing the Vibration

If I were to take a glass of wine, I would actually change the vibration and make it work for me rather than just drinking it straight on, the way it is. I would re-qualify the energy. What I have found in the longevity research is that people live longer if they drink a little bit of wine or vodka, like they do in Russia, Italy and France. Of course, if they drink too much, it doesn't have a longevity effect. It ends up doing damage to the body. But I don't drink any of this myself.

Researchers found out something interesting about the healing effects of red wine. It is the purple grape skin that causes the beneficial effect. So people who don't want to drink red wine can get the same beneficial effects from purple grape juice.

You can also hold a bunch of purple grapes in your hand (or as a visualization in your mind) and pray that its medicinal effects open your veins and arteries. It will work for you this way, without even eating the grapes, because you qualified what you want them to do for you, with your intention and prayer. You are doing it with God. You are co-creating with God.

### Regulating the Body with Positive Thought

I have come to understand the energy of opening the veins and arteries and now don't need to hold or visualize grapes in my hand. I can stimulate the blood, with my mind, to open up the veins and arteries and then have the blood circulate in a healthy, open circulatory system. We have power over our body when we co-create with God. We can learn to understand our body. Then we will know what kind of adjustment it needs. Then we can set the intention and prayer with a positive statement. If our heart was beating too fast, we would not say in our prayer, "God, please help my heart to not beat too fast." That kind of prayer emphasizes "beat too fast." We would say something like, "God, please help me to regulate my heart to a healthy, natural rhythm."

It is very important to make the statement in prayer or thought in the positive. It requires that we watch our words and our thoughts. They are qualifying our energy and lives all the time. Awareness and vigilance helps us to see where we are at with our speech, both inner talk and outer talk. All this relates to the throat chakra, as our speech is located there.

### The Lymphatic System:
### The Secret of the Fountain of Youth and Our Life Contract

It is important to know about cleansing and purifying the body. Life is about giving and receiving, receiving and giving. People are looking for the fountain of youth. It is a secret fountain, but it is actually within us. It is our lymphatic system. So we must keep the lymphatic system cleansed and open, and then we will have a longer, healthier life. It's not only important to have clean blood, but it is also the water flowing through us, through our lymphatic system. It will determine the length of our life and how long we will be here on this earth.

The lymphatic system works twenty-four hours a day. You can fast and starve yourself without food for a long time. Doctors don't see it as being that important, but it's just as important. People take in food, and if it stays in the stomach and intestines too long, it becomes toxic. When they go to release, it's hard like clay.

The only difference is when God's light leaves the body. You may do all the healthy things, like taking good care of yourself and living a good life. But when your contract with God is up for your life, you usually die, one way or another.

### Making a New Contract with God

We can make a new contract with God and very likely extend our life. We can pray and make an oath with God and ask for a life extension. Sometimes when people have a fatal illness, their prayers are answered and they have a miraculous recovery. At times this could be the person making a new contract with God. There is a great mystery to the way God works. It is not always the same for everyone. God is so vast that it is beyond human understanding. We have glimpses of God, and we see evidence of God in action, but our understanding is limited.

### Another Story ... About Food

This story can relate to the throat chakra, too. My neighbor was telling me about a meditation retreat she had on her land. One person that came spent a great deal of time using my friend's stove. She was cooking up her very particular and complicated diet. There were problems that developed. Other people, who were not particular about their diets, had trouble getting their meals made.

My neighbor asked for my advice. I asked if the person that was cooking so much of the time had allergies or some life-threatening disease. She told me "No, it's just how this person likes to eat." But it seemed that the whole meditation retreat revolved around this person's diet and the almost continual preparation of her next meal. She also left the burner on, after she was finished, several times. This led to some unpleasant feelings.

## The Advice I Gave

I did have some advice for my neighbor because my wife, Cherylann, and I have groups on our land, for my classes. We usually have three-day classes. People come and stay here and eat here too. We prepare food for both vegetarians and non-vegetarians ... very healthy and delicious food. We have had a few people ask to use our stove to make something special for themselves, but we don't do that. We ask that people tell us ahead of time about any dangerous allergy or condition. But we are not short-order cooks.

If someone is just a picky eater and doesn't want to have what we are serving, I ask them, "You're going to be here eating with us for three days. Do you think that you will die from being off your regular diet and eating what we serve?" Of course, people say "no." If they were to say "yes," then I would suggest they return home to eat what they have to have, to survive.

## Praying Over and Blessing Our Food

The interesting thing is that I teach a technique about blessing food in my beginning class. I teach them to pray over their food and bless it so it becomes food that is compatible, healthy and healing for their body. This is the intention that is in the blessing and prayer. This takes care of any pickiness or even times when a person may need to eat "fast food" on the road. They can be picky at their own house if they want to, but usually they return home from class with a new attitude towards everything, including their diet.

### Nourishing Our Brains and Keeping Good Company

You need to nourish your brains with good food and nutrition, so you can use it in the future, for whatever you want to do. You need to be with the right type of people that will take you way ahead in life. Sometimes a person needs to experience the bitter stuff so that they can grow to be a better individual.

Some people take the hard way and learn the hard way, and some people take the easier way. I prefer the easier. I learn through other peoples' mistakes. That also relates to staying youthful, because you have less stress. If you clean the body and the body recovers from illness, it rejuvenates and recharges faster.

### Vitamins and Mineral Supplements

We don't have all the vitamins and minerals in our food anymore, as we once did seventy to a hundred years ago. The soils have been depleted and many of the farms have used chemicals. In addition to the vegetables themselves, I take extra high quality vitamins and minerals, amino acids, and glyconutrients. They help nourish my body so that I can be much more up to par. For many years they have worked for me.

### Muscle Tone and Working Out

I see that as people begin to get into their forties, they lose muscle tone. I don't want that for myself. I qualified and talked to my body about it, and I work on my body by working out. It works. Staying youthful is related to how you think, how you manage your emotions and your spiritual life. It's also related to your whole being and how you work with people and how you think about the earth, the birds, animals, plants and trees. I believe that all religions have a common denominator—and it is love.

*Exercise and Movement*

It is also important to exercise our physical body. Some of our exercise should be aerobic. Some should be muscle toning. Exercise keeps our heart healthy, but it also helps all the other systems. It increases the metabolism. It keeps the circulation healthy, burning up fats and cholesterol. It keeps the lymphatic flowing, which keeps the toxins moving out of our body.

Good clean water is also important to keep the lymph flowing and toxins moving out. I use a water filter in my healing center. I work out with an exercise machine and I also work out with weights. Walking is very important, as it is one of the best overall exercises besides swimming. I have my students do exercises for strengthening the abdominal muscles. In addition to toning the abdominal muscles there is an improvement on the intestinal actions when the muscles that support the intestines are strong. It brings increased circulation and energy flow to the whole abdominal area. There is also a benefit to the solar plexus chakra, which rules our emotions. When that chakra is stronger, better balanced and more harmoniously spinning, the person is more stable and steady emotionally, and less reactive. In other words they have a longer fuse and don't get angry very easily. All these emotional, physical and spiritual systems overlap each other and are interconnected. Of course I practice Yah We movement dance also, which I teach in my classes. That keeps all the energy flowing and opens up all the spirit centers. When these chakras, or spiritual centers, are open and balanced, then the entire endocrine system operates at its top level. This is one of the keys to youth and rejuvenation.

*Listening to Our Body When Exercising*

I see people running down the roadway and I see many of them really overdoing it. They feel that they have to do this to accomplish their health goals, but we need to listen to our body. It will tell us what we can handle on that particular day. We can go too far with our body, and when we overdo it, it can break down and weaken or we can be overly exhausted. It is like a person who sleeps eight hours a night, but when they sleep longer than eight hours, they may feel even more tired. If anything is overdone, the cycle begins to go in reverse. None of us have to be smart, but we just have to use common sense.

What I do at times is walk from one telephone pole to another. Gradually, after two or three weeks I might be walking past many poles. Then I might move from walking to running part of this stretch and gradually increase the running. You have to stimulate your body a bit to bring out more feeling of being alive. If you walk or run, the next day you do the same thing so that you get the body used to it. It will keep the body in balance, and after a while your body will be feeling stronger and stronger. It's a lot like a person that lifts weights. At first they can't lift very heavy weights, but little by little they will be able to lift heavier and heavier weights. That's how it is. In exercising we should use moderation. If you need help, ask someone to join you in an exercise program. You can walk and run together. You can have positive conversation together. That is important. I often see the physical body, like a car. Inside our body is the engine. You can have a beautiful car, but if you have no engine, the only way you can go is down the hill. But if you have a car, with an engine that is working, you have places to go. The inner and outer parts of your body need to be working together. We all need to treat our body correctly. A man is like a king and a woman is like a queen. The whole body is like a castle. If you treat your home right and keep it nice and clean and repaired, then the home will be there to nourish you and take care of you. It takes some discipline, but you can also laugh, giggle and enjoy yourself.

### The Fountain of Youth

Everyone is looking for the fountain of youth, as nobody wants to get old. I learned when I was very young to let things happen ... to watch ... to listen and to not force things in life, as most people do. When you force things, you get older faster. The grown-ups may be speaking like, "Gosh, you're five years old. Soon you're going to be seven." When you're seven, you want to be ten. When you're ten, you want to be thirteen. At thirteen you'd like to be able to drive and when you get to be eighteen years old, you can't wait to be twenty-one. It goes on and on like that. We want to experience all the things that life has to offer. My parents had a tendency to quicken the vibration in the physical body that makes us age. So I learned to keep my own energy in me and around me, and I learned not to merge with their vibration too much. It's like being on a boat moving with the spirit of God. It's like being guided by your father above rather than being guided by an earthly, biological father. So one of the secrets is not to force life but to just BE with life. Go within. I notice that high school kids of sixteen, seventeen and eighteen years old reach the top of the mountain of their youth. Then it can be like starting on a road downhill, and by forty years old many people are beginning to age very quickly.

We can change things in life for the best, with spiritual living, if we just let things happen instead of forcing things to happen. I read in the Bible where they speak about "Let there be light." Let us be made in the image of light. Everything is light. It is not about "force" but about "let." In the book of Genesis in the Bible it says that on the seventh day God rested. We, as human beings, have a tendency to work seven days a week. We're going beyond God. We are trying to create things ahead of God and this is where most people have trouble. People work without re-charging, tuning up, clearing or lubricating their body. People need at least one day of rest each week.

## Think Ahead, Before Taking Action

People tend to do things without thinking beforehand. If people do things without ever considering what that action will create in the future, they may get caught in a trap. It is best to think ahead and look carefully at our decisions. We can move that action forward, in front of us, in time to see how it will turn out at the end of the chapter. By doing that, we learn to be a little more careful about what we plan to do in our life. We also have a tendency to move very quickly, without hearing our own heartbeat, without hearing the heartbeat of our Mother Earth, and without listening to God speak to us. We need to listen to the God within ourselves and also to the God in the heavens above. Often we can't even listen to or hear our fellow man and woman, when they want to express themselves to us from their hearts. They may have something very real and very beautiful to say. In addition to listening to our family and friends, we need to listen to what God is saying inside of our hearts.

When I was in Junior High School, I took track. At the beginning of the race, there was "on your mark, get set and bang." We ran, and as we ran we had to learn to pace ourselves. Most people use up all their energy in the beginning and then as they get closer to the finish line they are too exhausted to win the race. Sometimes it was so discouraging that they gave up on themselves. They lost hope and let go of their goals. As a track runner you learn about pacing yourself, relaxing and making sure you have enough energy to get to cross the finish line. The last lap you give all you've got, to increase your speed, the closer you get to the finish line. This is what I call the balance of life. Balance your thinking. Balance your emotions. Balance your feelings. Balance your spirit. We have a tendency to really overwork ourselves. More energy is going out than coming in. We don't have the sense of being centered. We don't have a nucleus to balance our energy field. So when we are overworked at work or at home with chores and children, we can easily forget what life is all about. We need to be able to take in and put out an equal amount of energy; otherwise our body will be thrown off. When we do things, we must learn to feel that we are doing things right, because when we begin to feel that we are doing things wrong, we tend to slow down or lose our motivation. We begin to feel bad or guilty about ourselves. Doubts come in because we are working along with our own personality. We can always call on spiritual help for whatever we are doing, and it will tend to bring about success.

### Living in Balance with God

There are many names for God, according to the beliefs of different cultures and religions—Jehovah, the Great White Spirit,

Yahwe, Allah, Creator, the Heavenly Father, and so on. Yes, God has many different names, but we all come from the same place and we need to understand that. We have a war within ourselves. The left side of the brain is the logical, linear, analytical side. The right side of the brain is intuitive, spiritual and creative. Those parts of the brain can't agree when we shove them down into the abdominal area, but we become very stuffy and sluggish if that's what we do. So we must learn to use our energy with God. It's a lot easier for all of us. I did that for myself. How about you? Because we don't understand things, many times we backtrack over and over again before we finally "get" something. I remember someone who did something bad. God had forgiven that particular person, but the person had a difficult time forgiving themselves. So you must learn to let go and work with God, who is all forgiving . God is love. God is compassion. By being closer to God in our heart, mind, spirit and emotions, we can feel and sense God in different parts of our bodies. Many times we have so much indulgence in our life that we really need to live more moderately. We may indulge in food, recreation, cars, and so many other things. It is all about learning to live in balance.

## *To Stay Slender, Share Your Food*

Once my auntie in Hawai'i gave me a whole box that was filled with packs and packs of gum. I was too greedy with all that gum, and my lesson was a hard one. I lost one of my back teeth from chewing all that gum. Another time my sisters and I were talking and I bet them that I could eat all the ice cream in the freezer. There was a big gallon of ice cream in there. I challenged my sisters that I would be able to do it. I won the contest but afterward I had a very, very bad aching stomach. So I learned through this experience not to be a hog, but to share with others. I like to share food in Hawai'i, because if I don't share, I will end up eating all the food myself. I would then become very large in size. I don't want to get that large either, even though I love the Hawai'ian local food. Yes, I never stop loving lau lau, poi, macaroni/potato salad, lomi salmon, custard pie, saimin, poki to name a few. So, to stay slender, share your food.

## Youth and Rejuvenation

Youth is more than just being young. Youth is being able to be in harmony with yourself, your environment and the people in your life. Being in harmony with nature and having harmony with Mother Earth and God, upstairs, is a complete balance in life. I remember someone said that, when you reach your forties, you really enjoy life. Between forty-two and forty-three years old I saw myself dropping down about three energy levels and I didn't feel very good about that. I was feeling sluggish, like someone on their way to being an old man. I looked at myself and re-evaluated myself. I was able to recalculate my system again as to why my body was getting old and tired. In three and a half years I reprogrammed my whole body. I created a program of food and exercise for myself so that I could get muscular, strong and energized again. I prayed about what to do for myself and I got very precise answers. In some ways I was not too happy at that time, and in other ways I was happy. I realized that on my Mom's side of the family there was a history of cancer and strokes. My father's side had cold and lung problems. These were where the genetic flaws were and I was determined to change this probable destiny. I wanted to make sure I didn't follow the health problems of my ancestors.

## Three Amazing Changes in My Rejuvenation Program

As my program progressed, my feet grew from a size seven and a half shoe to a size nine. I was kind of annoyed, because I had to buy all new shoes. I had to buy new pants too. The second thing that happened is that I grew almost an inch taller. Being in my forties, this seemed impossible but it was true. Doctors say you can't grow at this age, but I grew from five foot six inches, to five foot seven inches. This happened in three and a half years. Now you know that if you're a little bit taller, you're just a little bit closer to heaven. The third thing I experienced was that I looked ten years younger. I traveled up to Oregon to do healing work and had not been there for about twelve years. I traveled up there again, after my rejuvenation program, and met with some old friends. Inside my heart I was just crying because I could see how much the people had aged. I saw that I was going in the other direction. I was getting younger and healthier, instead of older. This is not something that just I can do. All of us can do it. When there is a situation or a problem, first you need to go within and see what is cooking inside. You need to know if the problem is coming from within or if the problem is from the outside of you. If you try to solve the problem by yourself, it will be very difficult. If you do it with God, he will help you. If you let him help you and it doesn't seem to work out too well, God did it your way. If you do it your way and not God's way, it usually doesn't turn out too well. If you are in alignment with God's will, then it turns out great!

Many of these old friends came up to me and said, "Oh Cosme, you look younger now than you did twelve years ago." I can honestly say, I do. I see how I look. One of these friends said, "Keep up the good work, Cosme. You look really good. Don't stop doing what you are supposed to be doing. It is good." Yet that particular person never asked me how I did it.

So I am sharing with you some of the secrets and common sense things that I discovered that led to this youthfulness. For some of us it is genetics. For some of us it is not. I have had three people in my life that I worked with for an hour and fifteen minutes, who lost twenty years right in front of my eyes. It was a miracle. I believe that all things are miracles. It is a miracle to have God's love in us and to have life here on Earth. It is a miracle that our heart can beat without our doing anything to control it. It is marvelous to see that every breath we take is a breath of God. It is controlled by God more than it is controlled by us. This is the force of love and light.

If we say that we are getting old, we will get old. If we say that we are getting younger, we can get younger. But if we are getting younger, only for money, then we are missing the point. We need to have youth on every level —mentally, physically, emotionally and spiritually. That part is very, very important. We also need to see the body as a temple of God. We are the soul. Our spirit is precious and should be treated as such. It is especially blessed by God as who we are here on Earth. I believe our physical body is very important because we tend to forget about the physical body and just overwork it. We need to work on oneness and integration of all the parts of our life.

There are times when we get into a space where there is no time, no dimension and no resistance. When we get into that particular space, we don't age as quickly as other people do. Now you may wonder what I really mean by that statement. It is like a bird who goes into its nest and cuddles its baby. It is like a kangaroo that has her baby in her front pocket. We human beings are like a little baby as we walk with God. He will comfort and help us in times of need until we grow and mature. We can crawl into God's arms and find peace and refuge there, just like the little kangaroo baby. That peace and relaxation can keep us going. We feel the warmth of our Father in heaven and from our mother, the earth.

The energy goes from heaven to earth. There is a cycle of in and out. There is a cycle of yin and yang. There is a cycle of alpha and omega, the beginning and the end. So what is in the small is also in the large. And what is in the large is also in the small. We are a microcosm of God. There are many times when I ask God to send me more energy. It seems like there is more energy coming in than going out. I qualify my request and it really happens that way. So, I feel re-charged all the time. I can work with many people a day, sometimes from morning to morning without sleeping. At times I work more than eighteen hours for three or four days. I am not exhausted because I have God working with me. If I was working only with my own energy, I would be completely exhausted after three or four people. But when I am in the presence of God, with him in, through and around me, I feel such an infinite love, power and strength that I can share it with each person that I work with.

Over many years I learned that I can do the same thing with sleep. I sleep about three hours a night and the body still works the way it should. I say, "At night when the flesh becomes weak, the spirit within me becomes strong. Physical food feeds our physical body and spiritual food feeds spiritual body. I have a lot more energy and can go into many more dimensions than a person who just thinks from the brains alone. The brains are cold, but the heart is warm. The heart has the spiritual flame that can nourish the rest of the body. God is like the fire, and we are like the big pot that is warmed by the fire. When we sleep, it lights up everything and everything becomes illuminated and one.

### I Was Watched Day and Night

I remember a few occasions when three different men came to my home. They stayed for several days. They watched me the whole time they were visiting to make sure that I didn't sleep more than three hours a night. They made sure I wasn't taking any naps too. After they were there about five days, they were walking around in shock because they found out that I was telling the truth about only sleeping three hours a night. They were shaking their heads and saying, "I can't believe this guy. He not only does what he says he does, but he says that we all have this capability." I told them that it developed gradually, the way a person lifts weights builds muscles. The first time you can only lift light weights, and then as you practice lifting weights, you become stronger and have more form, tone and strength.

I do believe youth and rejuvenation is important. Eating the right type of food is important. In my classes I train people how to change the vibration of foods, so that food will heal the body instead of acting as a poison, allergy or toxin producer. This keeps the foods from polluting the physical body. We work with the elements—water, fire, earth and air. We do it with God. We co-create with God. There is that light that shines through into our world on earth, and that God-light helps us to create and manifest our dreams.

### Training our Bodies for Frequent Eliminations

I use the bathroom five times a day. If I go to a restaurant, I sit down to order my food and then I have to use the restroom. I come back and eat my food. I'm like that. I trained my body to do that. My body does it automatically. If you ask your body to do anything, your body will do it because you are the co-creator of God. People forget that. We can do things like instructing our bodies. So it is important that your body stays clean.

## Healthy Elimination Detoxes the Body

I firmly believe that our intestines must be clean. When we over-indulge in food and we don't eliminate fast enough, our body becomes toxic and poisoned. I, myself, can actually release five times a day, with ease. I take some natural minerals that help to clean out the left-over food, and at the same time the minerals nourish the body. There are all kinds of vitamins and minerals on the market. Many are good and have different qualities and purposes. I know that when God got involved in my life that there was a reason to get certain brands of vitamins that would help me be my best. The intake and outtake of food from our bodies is very, very important. I also believe that the lymphatic system should be cleaned. We have a tendency to block it up. It can get dirty, as the lymph system carries the waste products and toxins out of the body. When they are pulled out and cleansed, we feel better and become younger and healthier. The food you eat and the nutrients you take are important. We may need different amounts and types of nutrients, as we're all different. We may be different and unique, but we all come from the same creator. That is a healing thought. When I go to a restaurant in town or to a different part of the country, I try to drink my water with lemon in it, as it helps cleanse and purify me.

Many of us now don't get all the nutrients we should from our food, so I compliment good food with good vibrations and prayer, and vitamins and minerals. I like to drink orange juice every morning. It is like the positive polarity coming together with the negative polarity. It ignites like a man and woman kissing. It is like the warm energy and the spark of light between them. So we take in nutrition, absorb it, and then release the wastes through the rear end door.

## When the Castle Falls into Disrepair

When this body of yours, or your castle, isn't being kept up properly, it kind of goes on strike and doesn't work so well. It can get a little upset with you. When it goes on strike, it gets sick. This is no fun because, when you are sick, you can't work and your bills pile up. You may have to pay big bills to doctors and nurses and hospitals. If that's what you like, that's okay, but if not, make some good choices and changes and be proud of who you are. You came from God, so respect your body and keep your body healthy.

## Medical Check-ups

It is good to see your medical doctor for a check up to see how your body is functioning. Your doctor can listen to your heart and see what kind of blood pressure you have. They can do blood tests to check all your bodily functions and to see if you are anemic, or if you have diabetes and many other things. They can see how your cholesterol levels are. They can easily test to rule out TB and many other conditions. They may have some important things to tell you about your body. It's good to know where you are at medically, and to get a go-ahead from an M.D. to start an exercise program. Going to your medical doctor for regular check-ups is like taking your car in for a tune-up, to make sure that everything is working okay.

## Electromagnetic Influences

Today there are microwaves, cell phones, pagers, electrical lines, microwave towers, transformers—all influencing the space we live in and our own systems, which are electromagnetic in nature. Smoke alarms—some contain uranium—can affect a person up to fifteen feet away. So the placement of the smoke alarm is important, especially in the sleeping area, and at work. All these invisible forces really do affect our life, because our body has an aura, which is itself a magnetic field. I have done muscle-testing on people both before and during a phone call with a cell phone. I have also tested them before and after using a microwave oven. They weaken when they are on the cell phone or using the microwave oven. With most of this testing I find that people lose forty, sixty or even one hundred percent of their strength after having contact with these things. Through the use of these things the body can age very quickly.

## The Digital Watch and "Frozen" Hand Story

People also have digital watches with a little bead of mercury inside. These watches can short-circuit the electromagnetic system of the body, because of the mercury that's in the watch. Once I was in Hawai'i doing some healings and I was to do a video. A woman came who had lived across the street from me when I was a kid. She was a little bit older than I was, but it was amazing to see her show up as a grown woman. One of her hands was quite locked up. The wrist, hand and fingers were all stiff and rigid. I noticed that she was wearing one of these digital watches. I asked her how long she had had it, and she said for a long time. I muscle-tested her with the watch and then without the watch. I found out that, when she had the watch on, she lost one hundred percent of her energy. After that I decided to change the vibration of the watch for her. I focused on changing the vibration into light energy that would harmonize with her body. I made the test again and again and she became one hundred percent strong. Her wrist, hand and fingers that had been so stiff and frozen for so long softened and became normal, flexible hands. This happened instantly and it was amazing. The mercury in the digital watch had immobilized her hand and wrist. So you can see how all this technology sometimes short-circuits our bodies. This was an exquisite occasion for both of us because we had grown up in the same neighborhood and now I was able to help her.

Having good people and good things around you can charge up your body too, rather than draining the energy out of your body. Getting energy drained is like a car with an oil leak. I drink orange juice in the morning. When I was a young kid in Hawai'i, I saw an old man that drank so much coffee that his hands were shaking. I never drank coffee in my life but replaced it with orange juice, which seems to balance the positive and negative polarities, like a spark of light.

## Taming Emotions and Asking for Help

Almost all ill health starts from an emotional imbalance, which then creates a physical problem. I have seen it time and time again. That is why I teach my students how to really work with, tame, and control their emotions. What's so nice is that when I teach people, I can teach them where they are at. I also teach them what they can do to correct their problems. I call this "applied spirituality." You learn, apply it, and use it correctly. Once you are able to use it and apply it, then you see for yourself that it works and you know the truth of it. Now from my point of view I can say something and it may be right for me, but it may not be right for someone else. Then, if I tell someone to do as I do, I would be out of line with the truth.

# 11

# Substance Abuse

### Prescription and Recreational Drugs

Throughout my life I have worked with many people. They often don't quite understand that what you take into your body can greatly affect your body. See, if you take pleasure drugs or even some of the medical prescription drugs, you may feel "high." People can forget that the love energy of the "high" is just a feeling on an astral vibration, and it is not authentic and it doesn't last. There can also be a lot of side-effects. I'm not saying that all of it is bad. Some prescription drugs are very helpful or essential for such things like diabetes, seizures, or heart problems, for example.

### Illegal Substances and Addiction

People are not only taking medical drugs but illegal drugs and substances. When people use these substances, they have a lot of different experiences. They get a "high" from it. I have to tell people when they use marijuana, cocaine or speed in any plentiful amount that they cause their mind to live in an illusion. It puts them mentally and physically into a lower vibration, even if it feels to them that they are on a higher vibration. It can really be tricky that way. It ends up making the body feel dark, heavy and uncomfortable when it is not using the substances.

### How Substance Abuse Increases Depression

Substances can make people feel depressed. The only relief they get, for a short while, is to have more of the substance. The cycle just repeats itself over and over. The substance makes you feel like you're crystal clear, but you're really all muddled up. It gives false messages to the body and mind and spirit.

### Endorphin Production

Over the long run it interferes with the body's natural endorphin (pleasure-producing hormones) production, and this leads to depressive states, when the natural endorphin production lags. The body becomes used to getting the endorphins from the substances and loses its ability to make enough of its own natural chemicals. Then a person feels drawn to more substances, to relieve the irritable or depressed state. But it's just a temporary fix and before you know it, there's a cycle of addiction going. Along with it there is usually a state of denial or justification. "Oh, I don't use very much. I'm not addicted. I just do it to socialize." These are things I hear from people to justify their use of substances. You know, there's nothing better than taking things that are natural to help nourish and recharge the body. I've seen people who are thirty-five years old who look ninety because of drugs.

### Marijuana, and Grey Cells

Some parents smoke marijuana with their children. The thing that I have learned from experience is that the cells inside their body turn grey. I have learned this from working with thousands of people. When I see this grey color in the cells, it always turns out that the person smokes marijuana. The nervous system also looks shot. To me, it looks very divided and split up inside. There is a lack of focus and confusion, and often it is difficult to make decisions. There is a lack of clarity even if they feel they are clear, because their energy is in semi-darkness.

### A Gray Aura Isn't Pretty

What people who smoke marijuana don't realize is that their aura around their head is grey. It looks like a dark rain cloud or gray haze. Anyone who can see auras will be able to see this around a person who smokes marijuana. The energy around their lung area will be gray, too.

## Dying Brain Cells

Many scientists have done research that indicates that the left side of the brain loses brain cells and begins to die. The feeling of the high, that they have after they smoke, is actually the feeling of brain cells dying. They may have a "high," but it is the experience of slow death of the brain. Also, little pinholes are created in the aura which is all around and interpenetrating the body.

## A Leaky Aura or Energy Field

This leaky aura with all its holes gives easy entry to entities. They can come in anytime and take over or influence the mind or body of the person. They can cause a person to get enraged or be emotionally or physically abusive. Entities are not the only reason for rage or abuse. An emotionally disturbed person who doesn't smoke marijuana can act the same way. Then entities can show up as multiple personalities that do really weird things. I have seen young school kids put on prescription drugs, maybe for depression, maybe for hyperactivity. Sometimes they are misdiagnosed.

Many of these drugs have big side-effects which are very dangerous to the body. One dangerous side-effect is that drug use creates holes in the spiritual energy field, or aura. People begin to feel very, very uncomfortable. They may not feel like themselves anymore. They may feel irritable and have trouble sleeping, and there may be unpleasant physical side-effects. Talk to others about what is right and what is wrong. Talk to your doctor about what effect a drug will have in the long run.

## Marijuana, the Aura, and Health Considerations

When I see a person who uses marijuana, I see what it does to the brains. It messes up the brains. It irritates the throat and a gray aura surrounds the person. The lungs also look gray. Over time the skin begins to dry up and wrinkle. Sometimes I can hear the pores of the skin screaming, "Help, help, I can't breathe." The cells begin to die fast.

A healthy person has clear, light, and pretty colors in their aura. The gray of marijuana smokers is not a healthy color. Also the use of marijuana makes the mind very spaced out, fragmented or disturbed. Negative energies can enter the auric field through the holes in the aura created by marijuana use and drugs. This can lead to real serious depression and mental problems.

### Cigarette Smoking Quickens Aging

Sometimes I see a very beautiful woman outdoors smoking a cigarette. Cigarette smoking is another thing that really ages you fast. Women who smoke get wrinkles much more quickly than non-smokers. Needless to say, cigarettes increase the risk of heart disease and lung problems too.

### Instant Gratification or Looking Ahead

People don't know they'll lose something important because of these unhealthy habits. They must be willing to take responsibility when the results of bad habits happen in the future. What we create will turn around and come back to us. Sooner or later it does come back to us. So the secret is to create good things in life. They come back to us in a good way. So you can be free to do good things in life too. Because if you don't, who else is going to do it? You can't listen to your mate. You can't listen to your friends, and you can't listen to your parents. Who's going to do something good for your life? In the end result, you will be the one to do it, if you want to. When I look further and deeper into people, I can see cancer in the body of some people. I see hardening of the arteries and all kinds of sicknesses. It's no fun to see a person sick. It's no fun to see a person die, especially when they could have chosen to have good health habits. Yet they did not make the right choice. Then they suffer. Sometimes their pain is so great that they just wish that they had made better choices. They usually are thinking this way when it's already too late.

## Attracting Unwanted Astral Entities

What the doctors don't realize is that the drugs put a person on a lower astral vibration which sometimes attracts entities to come into the body and take over. This can happen with illegal recreational drugs also. This is a hidden danger that most people don't understand, because it deals with the unseen world. These negative entities could have been involved in influencing the kids that did some of these school shootings. They are surely involved in crimes, a lot of the time. Sexual or physical abuse, drug and alcohol abuse, extreme negativity and rage in the environment can also attract negative entities. When they are around, they only add to the chaos and cause bad things to happen. They feed on astral energy, negativity, fear and perversion. We do not want to provide food for these trouble-makers. We don't want them around at all. We want God and God's angels in our life. Then there are blessings, not trouble.

## Drugs and the Third Eye

Some people have taken certain kinds of drugs that have burned out the ability of the third eye to give them intuitive or clairvoyant information that is valid and true. They can become very nervous. They don't know what is going to happen. They can't see in the dark or see anything. I have seen some people that have compulsive behavior such as washing their hands in the sink all day and all night. They may not take showers for two or three months at a time. I've worked with people in the past that had these type of extreme compulsive behaviors. I have always found that in these cases the third eye is shut down. Some of them may not want to go out in public or take a shower because they are scared. They can even go beyond fear into paranoia. When this happens, I can see that the pores of the skin are pouring sweat. The person might be washing their hands all the time, imagining at times that they are washing blood off their hands. This is a delusional state of mind. Wow, I have seen this type of mental illness happen from just taking drugs one time. It doesn't happen to everyone this way, but a person never knows if he or she is going to be one of these people who go crazy from one drug experience. I don't like people who sell drugs because they hurt people. Sometimes their drugs kill people, physically and spiritually.

### A Story of Drugs and Alcohol

I knew one guy who was taking drugs and alcohol since he was nineteen years old. I felt led to get in touch with him. I asked him to come up for a healing. I tried to contact him three times and he did not call me back. Later I found out that shortly after my attempts to reach him that he totaled his van, while he was high on drugs and alcohol. His girlfriend was killed in the accident. He was in the hospital and then jail. Sadly, he went nuts and ended up in a mental hospital. This is a very sad story that never needed to happen. Someone made some bad choices and look what happened. Today the schools recommend very hyper kids to take drugs, like Ritalin. But the long-range effect is not looked at. What is going to happen to these kids down the road? They just get them to take it. Recently the news reported the results of a twenty-year study. Twenty-five children have allegedly died from this medication and it reportedly has caused some cases of hypertension and elevated pulse. For a short period of time it may not be too bad. But when its use is prolonged, I believe it can be very dangerous. Yet they don't tell the public that these drugs could possibly be the cause of violence in children. Prozac and drugs like that can create a lot of problems in certain people, in just a short period of time. There have been violent episodes and cases of suicide that are thought, by some, to be connected to the use of Prozac, with certain individuals. There is nothing better than taking natural foods and herbs. Natural things will complement the body rather than fight the body. When you take artificial stuff into your body, then you will often get side-effects. Your body is not made for chemical substances. Your body will often fight the unnatural substances. Taking a lot of prescription psychiatric drugs can make pinholes in the aura too. There is no doubt about that. I see people that take these medications and they get sluggish in the liver area. I see that they need to have more potassium in their body. Eating bananas brings more potassium into the body.

On the astral level, a lot is happening. It can be very, very dangerous. Some people stay emotionally messed up and sick for the rest of their lives. Their dependency on drugs causes problems that they can't even see or understand. They think they are all right. They may feel high, so they can't be objective about the situation. From other people's point of view, they are seen as kind of "floaty." Some people feel that smoking marijuana every day is good. They call it their medicine. They feel that they are using natural herbs. I never see these people being in any kind of balance. To me they seem to have a kind of suspended vibration. It is kind of like a limbo state. Often their life is very wasteful and often they don't live up to their potential. I look at if a person does or doesn't want to work. It's okay with me if they don't want to work, because it gives me and many other people a better chance to climb up the ladder. It is their life and their choice. But you know, at a certain time people who have taken drugs can wake up all of a sudden and say, "This is not taking me anywhere," and quit.

I work with a lot of people who take drugs. I have found out that women are much more able to wake up from this than men. I believe it is because they have children. They may say, "This is not the life-style that I want to bring my children up with." I often see these women divorce their husbands, if they refuse to give up drugs. Most women are not willing to sacrifice their children for a man. It's not worth it. It's certainly not worth losing part of your brains. It's not worth having the grey stuff in your lungs, so you can't breathe correctly after some time. It's not worth it if you smoke so much that your skin gets dry and wrinkled. It's not worth it if you smoke marijuana to have your nervous system begin to dry out. It's almost like when you have an electrical wire that's frayed. You know, how the rubber around the wire starts to get cracked after a long time. This is what happens to the nervous system. This is what I see. I have seen people who look ninety-nine when they are only thirty-five.

### How People on Drugs Can Minimize Damage

I do know that people, who are not quite ready to get off drugs yet, can minimize the damage they are doing to themselves. Besides eating really good food and nutrients they need to use a hot tub and sauna to clean out their pores and to clean out their body. This is not only for their physical body, but for the astral and emotional level too. If they can't make the change for the better, then they need to be happy with where they are at. There are so many people out there who need help in order to change. If they don't want to change, then they will stay where they are at and they will gradually trickle away. It is their own choice and their own creation. I don't really judge them at all. They look at me over many years and say, "Gosh, Cosme, you look just as young now as you did fifteen years ago." They look really old. They may be younger than I am, and they look very old. This is all because they are not willing to look ahead into the future and see the results of their actions.

### Spending Time with People Who Smoke

You know, when you are with a certain group of people who smoke and do drugs, you'll notice them playing and giggling together. This group may even dress differently and think differently. So whatever group you join, make sure it is a group of friends that you can learn and grow with. You choose your own friends.

### It Is Your Choice

You can choose to be an alcoholic, too. It is a pleasure desire that is very common in our culture. We all know how many kids have lost their lives by going to parties and getting stoned or drunk. And then when they leave and drive drunk or stoned, they often lose their lives on the way home. Other innocent people in their car, or people in other cars on the road, lose their lives too. This causes so much grief. It takes parents away from children and children away from parents. Often the families never get over the

188 • *The Mystical Kiss of God*

loss of their child lost so young in life. The sadness is huge. It is a hard lesson for kids who have done something really bad, like killing other people, by just being too free and too drunk or too stoned.

## My Father Was a Bartender

My Father was a bartender and he would say, "Wait 'til I get through with this person. He's going to be really high." I understand about drinking. I drank at the age of five and a half and I stopped at the age of nine. It was my parent's custom. Some little kids in Hawai'i drink. Well, you know, it is very available to them. I would be told, "Have a little drink." I remember those days. But I quit drinking for good, when I was nine. I was walking down the street in Hawai'i and a voice came into my left ear and said, "If you don't stop drinking, you are going to die." I got very, very sick and so after that I never drank again. Getting sick like that straightened me out. I learned to listen to spirit and a lot of people don't listen.

## How I Gave Up Drinking, At Nine

A man came along and, to tell you the truth, I don't know if he was real or an angel. But I do know he was a child of God and carried the blessing of the Holy Spirit to me. I can still remember what this man looked like: He was Caucasian, with curly hair and about six foot three. Whether he was a spiritual guide, who took physical form, or not, I know he was there to help me at the time. It actually changed my whole life. I used to drink Vodka and beer. Mom gave me some wine and premium beer from Hawai'i. I was a young kid acting silly. I know that feeling and it felt good, on a particular level. But I don't miss it.

## Seeing the Results of Alcohol, as a Kid

With my Father working in a bar, I was there too, and I saw what happened to people from all this drinking. I saw people lose their lives in car accidents due to alcohol. I saw people lose their families. I've seen their livers begin to deteriorate. They would end up dying from it. I've seen the back rooms of apartments and stinky bathrooms. I've seen people with terrible headaches and hangovers in the morning. It doesn't make sense to me.

## *Two Innocent Kids Killed*

Not long ago a couple of kids on the road were killed because someone else was feeling too free. Then the kid, who caused the accident and the deaths, lost his freedom and had to be locked up in jail for a long, long time. All this happened because he took life away from these kids and took the kids away from their family and friends. Carelessness can cause great grief to large numbers of friends and relatives. This is all because of this kid's ego, his selfishness, carelessness and desire to do whatever he wanted without thinking of others. Of course, it especially hurt his family and the families of the victims.

When people drink or take drugs, they don't think ahead of time of what could happen. They have the attitude: "This won't happen to me. I can handle it." But it does happen, and it is one of the most humbling and tragic things in life. With some people the guilt can be with them for the rest of their life.

## *A Sad Story of a Gifted Alcoholic*

One time I got a call from a spiritual man who had a serious problem with alcohol. He was the type of person that was quite open spiritually, as an open channel, when he was sober. But when he got drunk, negative entities entered him and he would swear and cuss a lot. He wouldn't even be himself. When he sobered up, he wouldn't even remember the things he did and said while he was drunk. He was experiencing black-outs. In reality he was being taken over by a kind of negative entity. It's interesting that in the old days they were called alcohol "spirits." Sometimes bad spirits enter people who drink too much. I wonder how many saloon brawls and murders have taken place under the influence of alcohol and bad spirits.

## A Dark Entity Jumps Through the Phone
### from One Person to Another

One time, many years ago, this same man called up my friend, when he was drunk. He didn't realize that he was talking to her. He had always been respectful of her before, but she had never seen him drunk before. He got really drunk and called her up and started cussing. She got a really bad feeling inside of herself from his phone call. She told him she didn't want to talk to him and she hung up.

She then realized that something bad had happened to her and she felt disoriented and scared. She felt a little crazy and her body felt painful, dark and heavy. She told me that something bad had jumped into her and that it felt like a dark demon or entity. She couldn't get it out herself, so she came down to my house as fast as she could! She said, "Cosme, thank God you're home. I need help. I have an entity in me that jumped in, over the phone lines, and I can't get it out."

Once she got here, it didn't take long to pull it out and get rid of it. It was a dark entity or spirit that was attached to this drunken guy. When he phoned her and cussed at her, it jumped into her, over the phone lines. After I pulled it out of her, with the help of God's power, she felt fine and happy again. While this entity was in her, her body was wracked with shooting pains everywhere. I told her that she had to be more careful about putting protection around herself in the future. What a demonstration of what dark entities can do, when the protective light isn't strong enough. It is also good to know that the phone lines can transfer energy, both good and bad.

## Why Strong Light Protection Is Important

This lady friend of mine was a very, very sensitive and open person. After this experience she was much more careful of putting protection and light around herself. She had gotten caught by surprise. Her God-light was too dim and she was also an ultra-sensitive person. She also did not know that something like an entity could jump from one person to another over the phone lines.

## *He Could Have Been a Spiritual Teacher*

This man always said he wanted to quit drinking so that he could do his spiritual practice and be on track with God. Many spiritual teachers had seen his gifts and told him that he had the ability to be a spiritual teacher himself. Of course they said this would never happen if he did not quit drinking, and if he didn't move up into his higher self. He had the ability to explain spiritual teachings to people, but he just couldn't seem to quit his drinking.

## *The Sad Story of "How" He Quit Drinking*

Over ten years ago, this man was in a bad accident while in Hawai'i. Sadly, he is totally paralyzed! He lives in a wheelchair, in a long-term hospital for the disabled. He is up on a mountain that has a nice view of the ocean. But, he can't use his arms or legs. In fact one leg had to be amputated recently. It took this grim accident to get him to quit drinking. This is a very sad story about cause and effect, and about how fast something like this can happen to a person. Now he meditates and prays a lot. How sad that he didn't choose the easy way. God gives us a chance to change the easy way, but if we don't, we end up choosing the hard way.

Sometimes when I work with people who have an entity attachment, I get my wife, Cherylann, to cross the bridge to the other side of the river. The reason I do this is that sometimes when any entity comes out of a person, it looks for someone else, nearby, to jump into. I light a candle and pray and make sure that God, Jesus and the angels are there, to take the entity away, so it won't jump into or harm any other people or pets. Entities can't cross over the water, in this particular place. If it is strong enough, it can go into another person quickly without the other person even knowing it. It can cause a lot of different personalities. It can cause unbelievable pain and illnesses. I want to make sure that there is nothing that will be affected by it. Even if an animal is around, I can't do it. Remember how Jesus put the bad spirit from a person he healed into a group of pigs. Then the pigs ran over the edge of a cliff and died. I can see if there is going to be a problem. There is always a way out. But a lot of times people give up hope. The person needs to work with God. When praying to God, we will get the answer as to how to proceed. It is far better than the person trying to figure it out themselves.

### Turning Down Alcohol and Cigarettes

Now I hear people ask me if I'd like a beer. I say, "No, I'm allergic to it. It makes my eyes cross. My legs automatically cross over themselves, and I fall down." That's sort of a humorous way to get them to stop offering me something that I don't like.

I was in the Air Force down at March Air Force Base in Los Angeles, California. The guys would say, "Hey, Cosme, you want a cigarette?" I would say, "No, I have enough trouble with the smog down here." And people would laugh, as I'm a clown. They didn't put me down. People have been good to me. It's hard to explain how to qualify the energy of your body and your mind. Whatever is negative, you can make positive. You can make it work for you. That is what I do.

### Say "No" with Humor

I knew somebody who used to say something funny when someone would offer her a joint. She would say, "Oh, I can't even touch that stuff, because it makes my eyes start rolling around like a bull moose in heat." It was a joke. Then people would laugh and no one was offended when she said no.

### A Natural High, with God

I want to learn the best, be the best, and be myself, but I don't have to take all the external drugs or pleasure stuff to make me high. I get high the normal, natural way, with God. It's the easy way and is a lot more fun.

Why should a person get drunk and miss the fun and then not remember what happened the next day—not to mention the hangover. There is nothing better than having full control of yourself with the help of your creator. So how does all this relate to the throat or fifth chakra? Drugs, alcohol, marijuana and cigarettes are all things that go into your mouth and that is how it is connected to the throat chakra.

### We Can Change by Dancing with God

We can change. We all have the will because we have the "Will of God Within Us." The body also needs to be nourished. So like I said before, in a flash, I become a part of God and the God within me makes me strong. This choice to become a part of God qualifies my energy.

I call the light of God to come into me. By calling, then God will come and God's work will come. God will help you find work that brings out your gifts and talents. Masters and angels will come to help guide your path. If you don't ask, then you won't receive. If you ask, you show God that you are ready to learn. "Ask and you shall receive; knock and the door shall be opened."

### Learning to Use Our Minds in a Positive Way

We need to learn to use our mind in a better way than we ever have before. We need to do this in a positive, not a negative way. Don't rush. Dance with God in life. Don't be a copy cat, but be the very unique person that you are, that is, working with God.

### Calling in the Light of God

It's true ... I call in the light ... right into my body. I feed my spirituality with light. It feeds my soul, and then from there it feeds my physical body and well-being from the inside out. So we all need our physical food and our spiritual food. You will learn to be a lot more balanced then you were before. So now you know that you can be nourished spiritually with spiritual food, by calling God's prana, or life-force energy, and God's light into your body.

There is nothing better than just being ourselves and being wholesome without having to take drugs, either prescription or other kinds of drugs. Just being real and being with God to the fullness is the best way to live.

## AA

There are a lot of people from Alcoholics Anonymous that have been guided to come to me for healing. AA is an excellent program that helps alcoholics find a spiritual path that helps them get sober. In this system they call God their higher power. They have twelve steps in this healing process. I have always thought that there is another step that they need to take—a thirteenth step.

## The Thirteenth Step

Maybe people feel that a thirteenth step could mean bad luck. They may be scared to create a thirteenth step, but I feel that the number 13 is a spiritual number. There were twelve disciples of Christ and he was the thirteenth in their group. What sometimes happens with AA people is that they get to the twelfth step and then they may backslide and go back to number six again, and then have to climb back up to number twelve again. Backsliding and climbing back up can happen over and over many times.

I have two people who just got out of AA, and they find that they now have to go through the emotion of that. So I asked one of the guys to write a book about his experience with AA and what it did to help him. He had been so helped and healed from it. He had changed so much that he can now help a lot of other people who have this kind of addiction problem.

I feel that the thirteenth step is working the program to the point of success and then going out of the program and into a new spiritual group. It is important to realize that you have learned and grown from the experience. You see the value in it and know how it helped you. In some ways it's like being with your Mom when you were a young kid. There is a time that the child leaves the Mom and goes away from home. They usually get a job, go to college or get married. Sometimes it is hard to leave and hard to let go of what is familiar, so that is the next step.

# 12

# Grief and Healing

## Healing from Grief

At different stages of life we may go through a grieving process. Our loved ones die. People have to let go, so their loved one can move more fully into heaven. This requires letting go, at some point, so the loved one will not be held back here, on the earth plane, worrying about their sad friends and family that are left behind.

## My Work Is About Re-Birth and Joy

Often I happen to be out of town when the funerals of friends occur. It always seems to be that way for me. My work is a positive vibration that makes things grow. My work is not about a dying process. It's more of a birth process, because when I work with people the body becomes more alive again.

## The Story of My Friend's Grief

With one very good friend, I saw that even though he had a support system, he had many stages of grief to go through. A big adjustment had to take place. His friends came in to help him, for a few months, but he still had to face many different adjustments. When he was home alone, the grief was so strong that he got to the point where it nearly pushed him over the edge. He came to me, so he could get some help. I knew about the steps of grief and what had to happen before the healing would happen. I went ahead in time, and I knew what was needed for his healing. As we were talking to each other, I could see his deceased wife still being half here. It looked like a split face, and it showed her happiness. It showed that they had been together for so long. He could not change his life. He was having such a hard time adapting to being without her and shifting out of the energy of grief. This is understandable and natural, of course. Most people do go through heavy grief from having very strong emotional attachments or many years of living together.

## The Grieving Process

With serious grieving, we really miss our spouse, child, parent, friend or animal companion so very much. They're not here anymore. We are in shock. The secret here is that the physical and emotional love that a person comes to expect every day is not with us anymore.

## Mending the Missing Polarity

I told my friend that what basically happens is that he was the male polarity and his wife was the female polarity. They were merged together for many years. When a man and woman live together, their hearts overlap fifty percent. When they get married, the heart overlaps and gets bigger and brighter. This is what they call becoming one spirit. So when a person loses their mate, they lose their main male or female polarity. In the case of my friend he lost his female polarity. Like others, he felt an emptiness and unbalanced feeling. The inner heart light begins to get dim. A person can lose their appetite, feel an aching in their heart chakra, and have sleep pattern changes.

What he had to do was to check his own polarity, and he needed to learn to balance his own female and male polarity within himself. Because he was so strong on the positive, male side, he wasn't working as well on the negative, female polarity side of himself. The female polarity in him had been provided in the past from the merging female polarity of his wife. All of this is within ourselves, but we have to be aware of it, and we have to nourish the missing side.

## How to Help Grief Heal

Another thing that helps is looking deep inside, to where the soul is and finding the God within us. When we feel God within us, we can get close to God and feel one with God. That fills up the holes or places that feel empty, and gradually we begin to feel whole again. So it's like a kiss from God.

It also helps to have a talk with God and say, for instance, "God, I don't have human love anymore. I feel lost and alone. I miss my loved one so deeply. I need to have my love renewed with you, God."

That is just an example of having a little talk with God. If you don't have the flow of love with God, then you have no love to give to other people. You need to re-brighten your heart and your life and go out and help other people. All this takes time and patience. It's one day at a time and one step at a time.

### The Death of a Mate

After people have been married a long time and one of the mates dies, then the heart shrinks and the little engine becomes smaller again. It is such a difficult adjustment. The emotional and physical bodies are in shock for a period of time and it takes time for them to adjust, come out of shock and regroup. Both the yin and the yang and the positive and negative poles of the body need to re-balance. It's very difficult, especially if the couple has been together since childhood. So I understand what is going on because I see the energy. On a logical, materialistic level, people don't understand this at all. They only know that they are heartbroken. Their heart actually feels broken. It literally feels that way. Grieving people talk about feeling shattered. It is understandable with what they are going through. But to know a little more about the subtle levels of it, and how our body's energy works, helps make sense of it. The merged heart energy breaks apart when one of the partners dies. Healing can be much more enhanced by having a deeper understanding, instead of being heartbroken for the rest of a life.

### The Story of a Grieving Woman

The only person who can help us is ourselves. I remember working with a woman who was married to a singer. He played different instruments and always had people coming over to play music, laugh, giggle and enjoy themselves. When he died, he fell on top of her and she fell down and hurt her hip. For two years she was in pain. Every day she cried. People tried to help and console her, but she couldn't feel the help. Then one day while she was crying, she looked up and said, "What am I crying for? My husband died two years ago. I want to help myself because no one else can help me." She got up and she dealt with life in a different way after this realization. I've seen a lot of people grieve for about two years and it is understandable. This is one of life's most difficult transitions and adjustments.

### Retreats and Workshops for Grief Recovery

I've been to different retreats for people who have lost their mate. All of them were going through the same thing. They'd lost someone, and they were dealing with that loss. Somehow like attracts like. All these people were attracted to the same retreat, which dealt with grief.

When a person has a lower back problem, the breathing can often be very shallow. There's a need to recharge the body. You need to re-center your body, soul, and your emotional and spiritual body. It is like a kind of rehabilitation that you choose for yourself and your upliftment. We are not meant to be in grief all the time. It is a natural season after a big loss of someone that is very dear to us. God has different things to teach us in life. If we are open, we can take the next step. I have seen Paul McCartney of the Beatles suffer when his wife died. I don't know how long he grieved or what the process was like for him. But eventually, he found another woman and is happy again. It is really amazing that his new wife looks very much like his previous wife. There is a sadness for a period of time. That is inevitable. When a couple is separated by death, the connection is not only on the physical and heart level, but also on the emotional level. The emotional level is very, very hard to deal with at the time. But again, it is the Alpha and the Omega. There is a beginning and there is an end. This cycle is part of nature which is part of the universe. The next step of the cycle is as a newborn. New growth is the next step in this evolution.

# 13

# Raising Children

*Learning from Experience*

Let's say we have a three-year-old daughter, and we take her to someone's home where you are going to house-sit. You light the wood stove and you tell your daughter, "This is hot. Don't touch it, or it will burn you." You put her hands close to the fire and again you say, "It's hot. Don't touch."

All of a sudden you realize that you left the water heating up on the cooking stove for hot tea and the tea kettle is whistling. You run to get it and then you hear your daughter frantically crying. So you go running to your daughter and say, "What happened?" She obviously touched the hot stove and burned herself.

You will say, "Come here, daughter, let me blow on it. Everything will be okay." Then you will do some healing on it or first aid or whatever she needs. Well, you need to ask yourself this question concerning your daughter. Number one, which taught her better, you telling her the danger of the hot stove, or her finding out for herself by touching it?

I feel that her own experience will teach her in a way she will never forget. And she will be a better equipped for life, as a result of this lesson.

When small children get near streets with traffic or steep cliffs, they cannot afford to learn for themselves as they could die from the first lesson. In many cases they need to be protected when they are young. But there are many things where they can learn for themselves more than you can teach them. You can tell your children and teach them things, but you can't tell them everything.

This is what happens when people are going through certain sickness. Sometimes the healer or the person around the sick or emotionally disturbed person has to take it on and experience it in their own system. Then they find out that they need to learn a better way. It is far more difficult to release the sickness out of your own body than learning never to take it on in the first place.

201

*Raising Children*

I remember, during my time as a kid, my parents were very, very strict. So when the people in my generation got married and had children, their tendency was to be too loose and permissive. Being too loose with children is a problem because the children get too much free will, before they have a chance to be mature. Parents that give their children too much freedom to make their own decisions, for better or worse, often have children with problems. It is important that parents do not allow their children to show disrespect. Once the children know they can be disrespectful, it just gets worse. Even if they protest, children need structure and guidelines and deep down, they want it. Trying to always please children's every desire does not benefit them. It makes them think that they can have anything they want in life. It is a handicap in life if they do not learn to deal with a little frustration. They do not learn to work for their goals. It can turn them into very demanding and unpleasant people.

Children that have too much permissiveness can get into drugs and alcohol or other trouble. Too much freedom and little or no guidance create tremendous problems. Children actually feel more secure and loved when they are given structure and guidelines. Children gain respect for parents who insist on respectful behavior and language. Of course, if the parents use cussing and yelling in their language, the children will do the same. The parents' responsibility is also to be a good example. It is especially important to do fun and wholesome things together with children, so there is shared time, enjoying life.

*Emotional Scars*

Sometimes people get scarred in relationships, or from their original family, and it can really hinder their life. Their trust level, self-esteem and confidence in themselves are low. These feelings hold a person back from being their best and most creative self. But it doesn't have to stay this way. Spiritual healers can help people who have these scars and feelings. It is wonderful to be healed of old wounds and go on to be happy and successful in life.

## Incest Scars

Once I had to work with a woman who had been raped by her own family members. She was going to a psychiatrist to work out her problems, but it was difficult to resolve. I don't like to see the way it leaves scars on women. I don't like to hear about these types of things, one bit. I feel like getting a baseball bat to spank these guys, because of the long-lasting damage it does to women. It creates deep emotional problems, and it is an invasion of a person without their permission. There's a good reason that it's against the law and that people go to prison for it. Men need to learn to control their impulses. Women are sometimes the molesters of children also, but these cases are more rare than molesters who are men.

I've heard so many stories of incest where the father will be sexually molesting the daughter or even the son. Sometimes it's done when she is eight, nine or ten years old. Sometimes Mothers molest their children too. But the most common incest is that of a Father with his children. There are terrible stories of Fathers and family relatives who have molested both their male and female children.

## Healing Self-Pity

Some people pity themselves because they feel no one loves them. They get angry and bitter about it. All this inner negativity turns other people off. If they would get out of themselves and start loving and serving others, their life would change in a positive direction.

If a person really knows God from their heart, there is a completely different feeling inside of them. There is a feeling of unconditional love. And, the love you put out attracts love back to you.

## Living in the Past

Some don't want to go and want to continue to live in the past. You can't live in the past, you know. If God wanted us to live in the past, God would have given us a third eye in the back of our brains. So being in present time and seeing what is in front of us is important.

## It Comes Back to Us

Kids can get really naughty and can get into trouble with the police. They can also have both physical and mental health problems. There is usually trouble with school too. Then the parents have to deal with all these problems. They create something, and then it comes back at them later. They may try to run away from it, but it always comes back at them.

## Seeing the Consequences

One of the flaws of human beings is that they can't see the consequences of what they are creating for the future. They don't plan ahead. When they do something, they don't bother to see what they are going to harvest from a certain action or certain words. It can be very hurtful and self-destructive. In the end, there is no one to blame but themselves. They might blame their parents. They might blame their partner, minister, priest or rabbi. They might blame a doctor. But the truth is, what they have done comes back to them. It's as simple as that.

## Unconscious Re-Creations of Childhood Abuse

When a girl's been beat up harshly by her parents, as a young kid she often re-creates the childhood abuse. When she gets into a relationship with a boyfriend or husband, she expects, sometimes unconsciously, to get beaten up, either physically or emotionally. This is all about what's habitual for us.

Unconsciously, she really wants the husband to be abusive because it is so familiar to her. It operates very similarly to a program in a computer. This same thing can happen to men too. We get addicted to what is familiar to us, even when it is very unhealthy. It is a twisted way of feeling nourished. It's an old feeling that one is used to having. This kind of unconscious craving—to re-create the old situation—can certainly lead to more abuse and a very unhappy life.

Men with angry Fathers often act out the same rage on their families, even if they hated it as a young kid. The same can go for drinking. If a parent is an alcoholic, there is a tendency to follow in the same footsteps, even if the young kid hated the alcoholic behavior of the parent. People may not even be able to figure out why they act the way they do. They may or may not provoke abuse. It is familiar even if it is negative and dysfunctional. Women or men like this can never figure out why they may have had many relationships that always ended up being abusive. This is another thing that can be healed. Nothing is hopeless.

### We All Are Unique and Gifted

You can get rocks, sand, dirt, hair and feathers, and then you can mix them all up together in water. You know the rock would probably sink first, and then the feather would go down last. We need each other on this plane of existence. Each one of us has something to give. We all have a gift, but we do need to discover it. Even if a person doesn't believe the way you believe, it's okay. It's just where they are. And in time they will grow into the next grade of earth schooling. According to temperament, gifts, and tendencies, a child needs to be nurtured and guided to fulfill his or her unique potential. Allowing the child's spiritual light to manifest helps them to be receptive to all the teachings a parent must give a child.

### Learning to Live with the Good and Bad in Life

Co-create with God and you will be amazed what will come into your life and into your inner self. We are born and learn little things from our family: right from wrong, good from bad. We learn a lot of things from school. We get a lot of knowledge from the lower grades to high school and on up to college. This amount of learning is on the mental and physical levels. But when you open the sacred light within yourself, that learning expands and goes many steps beyond. So from knowledge you learn to have the wisdom to understand what life is all about, both the good and the bad.

As you get older, you want to reach for the illumination of God, so that your whole body becomes the light of God. God really wants you to create with your mind. But the mind is only part of the truth. The mind can be cold. The mind does have intelligence and creativity and emotions and spirit. But there is also the infinite mind of God which is full of love, grace, wisdom and higher knowledge. As we integrate our love and wisdom with our intellect and creativity, we can experience joy and the radiance of illumination.

# 14

# Men and Women

### Men's Challenge with Anger and Frustration

Men's anger goes from their solar plexus to their liver and heart and then goes down to their prostate. Anger and frustration goes in the direction of the prostate. Who would ever think that so many prostate problems are related to anger and frustration. With anger and frustration, men don't get as many thyroid problems as women do.

### The Intense Focus of Men

Men have different assets. Men are like horses in some ways. They are very focused and see things in just the area where they are focused. This really is an asset in most jobs. In a way they are a lot like a horse with blinders on their eyes. So not only does the anger and frustration affect the prostate, but because of the type of work men do, the heart, too, is affected.

### The Wide Range Radar of Women

I see women as having radar. They can see 360 degrees. Women register all the different things that are happening and all the different vibrations that they sense. They have a much more emotional response and a wider response than the more narrowly focused view of a man. Women see too much, all at once, and often they don't know how to handle it.

### Men Are Strong in Focus ... Women Are Strong in Intuitive View

So in general, men are more focused and women are more diffused and see a lot more at one time. The woman is made to see a lot more, and there are advantages and disadvantages. So I tell people, for a man to be a real man he needs to listen to a woman, because a woman sees the whole scope more than he does. He can learn to listen to what the woman has to offer, and take some steps to see the more complete circle of life that she sees. He'll become more of a man because he'll open up abilities in new areas of his life. This is one important thing that women contribute to men.

## The Benefits of Male/Female Polarity

The male and female energies (positive and negative polarities) combine with the light and illuminate—like a light bulb lighting up—as the electrical current runs through it. So men and women can enhance each other's energy this way, as long as they are coming together and communicating with a positive, harmonious attitude. If they are involved in a project together, are both excited about it, and are cooperating and communicating in a positive, harmonious way, the project can be immensely creative and successful. So men and women, sharing and listening to each other, create a powerful polarity balance. Each can expand and benefit the other, as they learn from each other and contribute their own unique energy to the partnership. This can work in both a personal and a co-worker relationship. This is very important to understand. Women can learn from men too. They can learn to improve their ability to focus. In a relationship both persons can learn from the other.

## The Emotional Nature of Women

A lot of women have trouble with their more emotional nature. The answer for this is tranquility, and basically getting to know themselves. It's important to know God within themselves and know the Christ spirit. Learning to balance the physical, spiritual, mental and emotional bodies will make a difference. As an analogy, think of a chair with four legs, with each one representing one of the bodies. If one of the legs is broken, then it is very hard to stay in balance with only three legs.

## Women Trust Spiritual and Brotherly Men More

Women trust spiritual and brotherly men more. This is especially true when I work with a group of women. Women understand that my work comes from God. I don't come from the level that most guys do, so women really feel safe to open up. It's interesting that women trust spiritual men who have no designs on them. I grew up with four sisters, so I act like a brother to women. I can make them laugh by joking with them, but I am serious when I am giving the spiritual reading. When they can relax with me, by the time I do the massage they surrender to God and really experience a heavenly feeling.

Years ago when I studied photography at City College in San Francisco, once I was in the basement getting my camera. Two other guy students ran up to some girls and asked if they could photograph them for a school assignment. The girls said "no." A few minutes later I asked the girls the same question and they said "yes." Numerous little cases like that happened. I have a lot of respect for women, and they sense that. I try to treat a woman like a queen, if at all possible. Women go through a lot, and they deserve to be treated like queens.

# 15

# Healing Childhood Wounds

### A Lack of Spiritual Understanding

When people don't have spiritual understanding, they tend to judge. They see things as if they were a horse with blinders on. They see a narrow view. God works with every individual differently, as each person is unique. The path to spiritual opening and understanding is going to be different for each individual too. Everyone is working on different life lessons and people travel forward on their path at different speeds. Opening the heart center is a very important part of spiritual understanding.

### You Can't Run Away from Your Own Shadow

In the end, you can never run away from anything, because you can't run away from your own shadow. See, if you are very clean and pure, there will be a white, clear shadow. But if you did something wrong, it would be a very dark shadow, wherever you go. At home, abroad or on a ship, you are the one looking in the mirror and you are still there. You can't hide. You are the only one looking in the mirror. Still, even there, you can't hide, and the only person you hurt by hiding is yourself.

### Praying Sincerely for Help

A person can pray and ask God, "God, I have learned through this experience. I am ready to take the next step. Please guide me. Please God, help me." When you pray sincerely, like this, God will help and guide you. God will guide you to other people, who live in a higher vibration, who can also guide you. Life will be much more pleasant. This harmony with other harmonious people is like a wonderful dance. You can dance with people outside while you dance with yourself on the inside. It is nice. It may look or feel like you are dancing alone, but you are secretly dancing with God.

### Many Different Helping Professions

People can go to a minister for help, or to see a psychiatrist or therapist for help. A person can go see doctors for many different kinds of health problems. All these different people are good, but they are not putting all the pieces together. They are working individually on some aspect of the physical, mental, emotional or spiritual body. They usually only deal with one of the bodies. No one of these doctors knows how to integrate all the pieces.

### Integrative Healing

We need to work with all the bodies together simultaneously. If you only have part of the puzzle, you know, it's like having only one-third of the puzzle. Two-thirds of it are missing. The picture is not there to see. So all of the pieces have to be together to create the complete picture. "Seek and you shall find." This saying from the Bible has been very true, throughout the ages. It will all open up for you. We are talking about a level of integration where all the different healing practices are brought together as one. In this process sometimes people hit and sometimes people miss. I have worked with people who have been to a psychiatrist for over twelve years. In one or two sessions I have accomplished just as much, if not more, than the twelve years of psychiatry. When you get down to the level of the soul, things move a lot faster than working on the level of the brains. This, of course, was not me, but God working through me and inspiring me.

# 16

# Balance and Grounding

## Grounding a Person

I learned that, if a person is very "high" spiritually or got that way from a mystical experience or meditating too much, there are three basic ways to ground them. Number one, giving a person some meat to eat helps ground them. If that doesn't work, then I cut a half of lemon and let the person suck on it. If the person is very "high" and kind of spacey, the lemon will taste sweet to them. When they start to get grounded, the lemon will taste sour. This is really good. By the time they get to the second half of the lemon, they are usually well grounded.

If these things don't work, then we go to a third way which is to put our thumb over the third eye on the forehead area. Then we just bring the energy back down, grounding the person as we take our hands and sweep the energy field in a downward motion towards the feet.

## The Ultimate Grounding Cure

If these three methods don't work, then we go to the ultimate method, which is to put a small ice cube in the rear end door (the rectum). That will bring a person down and back into their body real fast. Usually I don't have to use this method to help a person get grounded.

One person had a case of a premature release of kundalini energy going through their energy centers and it was too strong for them. This ice cube cure helped this person to tame down this energy. When I tell un-grounded people about the ice cube method, they ground themselves really fast. They don't like that idea at all. Just thinking about it is a grounding experience.

212

### Polarity Balance and Grounding

It's very, very important that an individual, whether male or female, have the positive and negative, or male/female polarity inside of themselves, in balance at all times.

The male/female balance has to take place within the individual first. Then it is also very important to be grounded. You see, if a person is not grounded into Mother Earth, the electricity at the borders of the subtle energy field jumps in every different direction that you could imagine. It can cause pain in the physical body. So having yourself grounded is a prerequisite to keeping the balance of positive and negative energy within yourself.

### How Our Body Is Like Electricity

This is similar to the electricity in the wall socket. When we plug in our refrigerators and other appliances, they have a positive and negative charge and they also have a ground. Our body runs just like that. If the positive or the negative energy is missing or is too deficient, it just doesn't work correctly. The energetics of the body begin to short-circuit. Ultimately the body begins to weaken.

A lot of people don't even know what it means to be grounded. For example, we are like a light bulb and the electric generator is God. It takes both to work correctly. First we have to know where we came from. We have to know that we need to be grounded to Mother Earth. Pulling energy up through the mineral kingdom gives strength to our physical body. Invisible light energy comes from the center of the Mother Earth. At the same time we need to know that there is a God within us and that we are co-creators with God. We are made in God's image and likeness, just as it says in the book of Genesis in the Bible. Any time I want to find the truth, I go back to Genesis and I find the truth every single time.

### The Body's Electrical System

The body has a positive and negative polarity and a ground, just like all electrical systems. Positive and negative energy goes from left to right, top to bottom, front to back. It also goes through the organs and cells. Every single little bit of life has a positive and negative polarity. If two people come together with an aggressive or bossy attitude, the two energies will repel. If two people come together with a "don't care" negative attitude, the two energies will also repel. It takes two people coming together with peace, harmony and a cooperative spirit to make the energies attract.

This is how God created human beings, the plants, the animals, nature and the whole universe. Each living being has a purpose, and we all have relationships with nature's energy.

### The Sun and Earth and Figure 8 Grounding Exercises

There is an exercise that I teach people to help them learn to be grounded. Our grounding is so very, very important. I do this in my classes. I have people in my class lie down on the grass on their back, with their hands at their side, and with their legs straight—if the weather is good, of course. This can be done indoors too, but I always feel that the real ground of Mother Earth is the best. I ask the students to take a deep breath, drawing sunlight into themselves from above and letting that sunlight go all through the body in a figure eight pattern. The top part of the figure eight goes up to the heavens and it is the positive polarity. The bottom part of the figure eight goes down through the Mother Earth and is the negative polarity. Where the figure eight crosses is in the middle of the human being, standing or lying on the earth, right in the solar plexus area.

### The Spiritual Body and Being Grounded

Our spiritual body is to our physical body what a blueprint is to a house. The house represents our physical and our materialistic assets, which relate to our physical body. And so you have a house, and you have a blueprint. You build the house from the blueprint. See what would happen here if you change the house without changing the blueprint? There would be problems, especially with our bodies. We can change the physical, but if we don't correct the alignment of the spiritual body (blueprint) with it, then the body will still go out of balance.

Old patterns will manifest again in the physical body if the spiritual or emotional parts of the blueprint are not changed. For example, a person might have cancer—maybe breast cancer or prostate cancer. They may get chemotherapy and radiation for it and it may clear up. But what if they have not cleared up the deep reasons and patterns that helped to create the cancer in the first place? Their healing may be permanent. But sometimes a person will get the cancer back a few years later, and it may be worse. It might affect the bones or the lymphatic system.

Why does it come back again? It could be that the original spiritual or emotional pattern that contributed to creating it, was never corrected. Perhaps there were deep negative attitudes about love and life and trust that were never cleared up. Then the old patterns can re-surface on the physical level again. So, this shows how very important it is to balance all of these bodies and have them cleared of old negative patterns. People may feel they have to do all this work alone, but they don't. All they need to do is ask for God's light and love and healing. Often God will guide you, inside of yourself, to change certain attitudes and ways of looking at life. Many times it will involve a lot of forgiveness and letting go. This really clears the patterns inside that cause physical illness.

### The Kiss of God

When the heaven and the Earth come together in the human at their midsection, or solar plexus, this is the gift that allows a human being to be a co-creator with God. This I call the "Kiss of God." When we call in the energies from the heavens above and the energies from the mineral kingdom of the Earth below, the energy begins to spin faster and faster in our solar plexus area and heart, raising our spiritual vibration. You can see the individual blades of a jet propeller when it is standing still. When it is in motion, it is spinning so fast that you can no longer see the individual blades. With our inhalations and exhalations our spiritual energy moves up and down our spine. The energy of the inhalations and exhalations become so active they blend and become one. Our passive energy can be so relaxed that it acts as the other polarity to the active energy. When it merges, that feeling is called love. Our solar plexus chakra moves like that, as the kiss of God's light and love illuminates us.

This is a kind of spiritual circulation of energy that keeps circulating around the figure eight from the sunlight of the heavens and back into the mineral kingdom of the Mother Earth, and back up from the Mother Earth and then back up to the sunlight of the heavens. And we are right in the middle getting the blessing of God's kiss. It fills our whole body with energy and makes us feel a wonderful feeling of balance, good health and peace.

As the energy from Mother Earth comes up into our feet, it fills the body with energy from the mineral kingdom—the grounding energy of Mother Earth herself. This visualization strengthens our ability to conduct the spiritual circuit of this figure eight, and receive the "Kiss of God." This is such an important exercise that we should do it every day.

If we are not grounded, we get spacey, forgetful and scattered. We also lose our energy. This exercise just takes a few minutes a day and it is so valuable.

### Avoiding Jet Lag by Sending My Spiritual Body Ahead of Me

This is what I do when I travel a long distance like going to Hawai'i or New York, for instance. I will sit down and work with balancing my bodies. Let's say that I'm going from California to New York. You know, when you're leaving home, everything is kind of hysterical. A lot of things are going on all at once. You're thinking about what to pack and what you'll see and do on the trip. I will sit on a chair and say, "Okay, emotional body, where are you?" You know, it may be jumping all over the place. Then I say, "Come back here." You do this in order to control your body rather than have your body controlling you. It's like disciplining little kids. The emotional body can get kind of restless, just like a little kid. You've got to control it, in a good way, a nice way. After I say, "Emotional body, where are you?", I say, "Mind (or mental body) where are you? What are you thinking about? Are you thinking about the cabin? Are you thinking about the bedroom? Are you thinking about the trip? Okay, come back here. Let go for a moment. Let go and come back here into my body." Then you say, "Where is my spiritual body"?

Oh, your spiritual body may be very close by you, waiting to line up. And so the physical, emotional, mental and spiritual bodies all realign in turn. The four bodies aligned as one act as one luminous light. After they come into my body and align, I send a shaft of light from my heart up to my third eye and then project it to New York, or to wherever I am going. So when I take a plane, flying to New York, I'm flying into my own energy. You may do just the opposite. You may have too much going on when you're getting ready to leave home. You may think, "I've got to get to New York." You take off and you leave part of the essence of your bodies back home— you know, the mental, emotional or spiritual bodies. So, by the time you get to New York, you're completely exhausted because part of your subtle bodies have been left behind. With ordinary people it takes a while for them to catch up. This is part of what causes jet lag. But with this exercise you can avoid jet lag. I recommend it as a daily exercise to keep integrated. It's a really good practice on a daily level, but it is especially important for traveling.

# 17

# Judgment and Criticism

## A Criticizing Attitude

In this world I find that many people have a tendency to judge, criticize, or even condemn other people. It could be towards a minister, priest, or a spiritual teacher, but most often it is directed towards family members, friends, or ourselves. In my philosophy, unless a person reaches enlightenment, they will continue to think, feel and express themselves in a judgmental way. This attitude is surely one of the things that keeps people from reaching enlightenment, and it is a habit that is very hard to break. Attitudes of criticism and judgment do not leave room for unconditional love! These feelings actually crystallize the spiritual energy in our body and cause stuck contraction and stagnant energy. There is no way for spiritual ecstasy or bliss or an openhearted love to co-exist with this critical energy.

A criticizing nature is disaster and poison to marriages, friendships and relationships of all kinds. Critical, judgmental energy actually has an effect of closing down and slowing down the flow of the chakras (spiritual energy centers) and all the energy channels in the body. It tightens everything up and constricts the energy flow. This is the beginning of a shut-down system that can lead to poor health and depressed and angry emotional states. So a person who is critical and judgmental a lot of the time will eventually have poor health, trouble sleeping, and will be grouchy and unsatisfied.

They may feel self-righteous and direct all their negativity or criticism to someone else. This type of person may be afraid to look at their own problems or imperfections, so everything is projected onto another person or persons. Another type of person may turn all their criticism or judgment onto themselves, feeling that they are worse than anyone else and undeserving of happiness, prosperity or a good life. Self-condemnation is a way of denying the God nature that is inside of us but covering it with self-criticism. A person may feel "uptight" a lot of the time, and they may have headaches and tension throughout their body. Both of these styles cause all kinds of problems and prevent spiritual opening and blossoming.

All of us are critical and judgmental some of the time, but it is important to catch ourselves and change the energy. We can either stop the critical thoughts or find a way to start flowing love and compassion to the person we're tempted to criticize. We can pray that God will touch that soul and enlighten our own mind and lead us on the path to love and peace.

*Seeing Unpleasant Truths with Unconditional Love*

When a person first starts to search spiritually and looks deeply within themselves, they may see certain things that may not always make sense to them. It may feel strange or unclear, and it may even feel like the information and insights are not correct. But as the person gets into the energy, it becomes like a reflection, on a different vibration. Then they are able to see the truth about themselves or others. When coming from a place of love, seeing truths about ourselves or others may not always be pleasant. The important thing is to acknowledge the truths in a neutral way as insight, understanding, and information.

When we see an unpleasant truth about ourselves, we are then able to start changing it, with God's love. The mistake would be to go into criticism or judgment, as immediately the spiritual energy would start to crystallize and freeze, slowing down our heart felt energy and our physical vitality. Judgment and a critical nature can cause a kind of stiffness all through the body and can lead to arthritis. Smiles never look open and loving on a critical person's face. When we shift to unconditional love, our smiles will be open and loving, like the face of an angel.

So this critical nature is found in all of us, even priests, ministers and shamans. We may be directing it at them too, as well as politicians, neighbors, relatives and friends. Besides criticizing others, we need to check to see if we are condemning and criticizing ourselves. It is important to have love, patience and tolerance for our own imperfections, as we're changing ourselves. If we condemn ourselves, it is an insult to the God which is inside of us. It can cause us to be depressed about ourselves. We can lose our vitality and motivation in life. It is that very God-nature inside of us which will help us clear out our imperfections, so that we can reach spiritual illumination. It doesn't matter what religion we follow, as we all have the God-nature inside of us. We all have the ability to become co-creators with God.

Judgment and criticism are not good for the balance of the body and the emotions. This prevents spiritual openness and joy. This is so very important to be aware of on our spiritual path. This is also one way that we sabotage or hurt our spiritual progress without even being aware of it. The tendency to judge is sometimes so subtle that we don't even realize that we're being critical or judgmental. We are so used to ourselves and our thinking patterns that we don't realize that we live with a bad habit that hurts us. The way out of it is to observe our own mind and study the contents of our inner thoughts and feelings. We will start catching ourselves, but we must approach our change with unconditional love for ourselves and our process, rather than feeling anger and disappointment towards ourselves. It can take time to learn to change negative thoughts to positive thoughts. Our prayers can help us move forward in a positive way.

Unfortunately, people don't always go deeply enough within themselves, to understand themselves or to find the truth. They may have only scratched the surface of the truth. Once they are able to come into their own vibration and energy field, they will be able to clearly see the truth and reality about themselves and about life. Once they really see it clearly, they come to understand what real truth is. It is easier to recognize the next time. There should be nothing to be afraid of in seeing the truth. It is often said, it is the truth that sets us free, as long as we do not condemn that truth that we see. It may be a truth about ourselves that we do not like, but with God's help, our effort and prayers, we can change that truth.

When I work with a person in a healing or spiritual process, I am there as a non-judgmental guide. This helps the person not to cheat themselves of some important information or miss something which is important to them. I help them to make sure they are doing it right and that they are accurate in what they are finding. With each session or process the person starts out on their own level, not where I think they should be or could be. Once they begin to find the truth, then they can trust and believe it, instead of having a war inside of themselves.

### Lying vs. True Communication

There are many reasons why people lie to themselves or others. A lot of times people use words, but they don't even tell the truth. If they are not speaking from the heart, but speaking from the throat, the mind or the emotional level, it can be very, very deceiving. It can be very cold energy. It doesn't go too far at all. It doesn't stretch out and expand like warm, heartfelt, truthful words.

People like this hurt themselves and others, as well. It never works out well in the long run. Why settle for lying and a lower form of life, when there is a higher and happier one? Lies are never told from the heart or the higher self. People may speak with lies because this is a habit that they have. It may be a way they think they are protecting themselves from being seen. They may think the lie prevents people from knowing their bad deeds or shortcoming. Their lies may be exaggerations to make themselves feel better about themselves and look more important. This may temporarily make them feel better about themselves. But somewhere deep inside they know that they are living in deception.

Some people lie because their family lied, and they think it is normal to lie. Others lie because as a young person they learned to manipulate others to get what they wanted, with lies. Some people, like criminals, lie big lies, as they are not in touch with their conscience, and they belligerently wish to deceive people. They may just have a deliberate lying life-style. They are way off from being in touch with the God inside of themselves.

When I first got into the ministry, I was very shocked. There was so much judgment, jealousy and so many ego, power and control issues coming up within the spiritual leaders. I was shocked by all this ego stuff. In these people, especially, you would hope to find a Christian attitude. There were a lot of shoulds, like, "This is the way you should think," and all that. When a person really knows God, in their heart, it has a completely different meaning. Criticism and judgment fall away, leaving unconditional love.

It's hard for me to talk, you know, because I was raised in Hawai'i as a little boy. My language is not always clear. When I talk to people, I get around this pidgin English accent by projecting light energy which comes from God and from my heart and soul. This way my communication can be understood, in spite of my accent. A person can be very intelligent. Their every word and their pronunciation can be exact, but if their light energy is not coming out with it, then people will misinterpret their words. Misunderstanding can easily occur.

When you communicate with love and light energy, you are clear and you have better relationships at your work place and in your personal life. How can you receive love if you don't give love? Love unconditionally and you attract love to yourself. The real way to talk is to cultivate our speech with the light energy of our hearts and God's love, and to train ourselves to replace criticism and judgment with unconditional love.

# 18

# Many Religions—One God

## The Buddha

When I look at the Asian belief, I look at Buddha as one good example. He sat down in a triangular form in the lotus position. He gave up all worldly things and he sat under the Bodhi tree. When I was in Hawai'i, I saw a Bodhi tree and I saw pure white light and energy coming out of it. So what was happening there? As the sap and vital energy rose in the Bodhi tree, Buddha sat and meditated. As this was the right season for the sap to rise, Buddha's energy from his root chakra joined with the force of the rising sap and energy of the Bodhi tree. With Buddha's spiritual preparations and readiness his enlightenment came at that time. He and the tree were merged together.

The Buddha was working with all the elements too. When the Buddha sat down and crossed his legs, not too much energy was going through his legs. It was more contained in the abdominal area. I feel that Asian people are able to understand a lot more about tranquility than American people. The abdomen or solar plexus area becomes very tranquil, very relaxed and very calm in this position. The triangular shape becomes like a sunlight, an amber color. It's like the womb of God inside of you.

## The Lost Years of the Life of Jesus

Think about the three wise men who looked to the heavens and the large star in the East which led them to the Christ child. All these things are working in relationship to each other, but people tend to get caught up in the details of their own life and forget about the bigger picture. Maybe people think that it's not important to know much about the stars and what they're made of. This is because of ignorance and the way we've been conditioned and trained. The attitude is, if it isn't in this book, quite literally, then it must be wrong. This is not true. By the same token, in Christianity, people believe in the Bible and only the Bible. But what happened to Jesus from age twelve until the time when he came back again to teach? They need to think about that.

There are many missing years that are not recorded in the Bible. Before you start first grade, you go to pre-school and then you go to kindergarten. The root and foundation of Jesus Christ is a life and a truth that we can only wonder about. The gospels covered the span of time that he was preaching and performing miracles, and maybe a few years after he arose from the dead. There are some stories of the wondrous experiences and miracles of the apostles in the few years following his death and resurrection. But the books of the Bible don't talk about his life from age twelve up to thirty years old.

The Old Testament is a history book and the sacred teachings of the Jewish people, before the birth of Jesus. The Bible was compiled around the twelfth century A.D. Many things could have been left out or lost, like the books that were found in the caves, the Dead Sea scrolls. But they're not lost. That's just ignorance. They really searched to find the truth. And it shows that Jesus traveled to many countries. It shows that he went to Asia. It is written in the records of an ancient monastery in Tibet that Jesus visited there and studied with the Lamas. I have a video about this. If a person has not studied, researched and trained, they may see all of this in a narrow-minded way. To find the truth a person must seek. Then you will be guided to find the truth. As it says, "Seek and you shall find. Knock and the door shall be opened." People get too analytical about God. God is a difficult concept for people to understand. What is God? Who is God? Is God a man? Is God a Woman? Is God a person like us? Is God a man with a white beard sitting on a throne?

## The Kiss of God's Love and Light

To me, God is the light. God is all love. God is a force that is beyond our conception. But people don't understand what real divine love is. It is hard to understand it, if a person's heart has not experienced real love.

First, people need to know where they have come from. I do not mean only the physical level. They need to understand their ancestry—from the parents, grandparents, great grandparents, etc.—and they need to go even further back than that: to the beginning of time, and then, before that time. They need to trace their roots and know how the positive and negative polarities came together within them. This forms a kiss—the kiss of God. At one point, God touches the Human Being. That's the kiss, and the coming together of the positive and negative polarities—from earth and heaven—within the human's system. This kiss created the Universe itself ... the animals, plants, rocks ... everything.

Jesus showed it to us. Buddha showed it to us. Sai Baba shows it to us. But the secret here is that Jesus said, "You can do even greater things than I.' And people don't see that, or they don't really believe that because they limit themselves. But they have the potential to be so much more. They can be like Jesus and do even greater things, like he said. People think that they'll be able to do something great in their next life, or in the hereafter. Of course, the Bible can be interpreted in so many different ways. Interpretation depends on the spiritual level of the minister, priest or individual reading the Bible.

Basically, God is sending love to people and surrounding people in love all the time, but they may not be able to feel it, because they have so many blockages in their body and energy centers.

### The Potential for Miracles

There's always a possibility of a limb re-growing instantaneously. Without a doubt it can happen to a lizard. You know, the tail can be cut off and then it can grow back. But again, people limit themselves on the physical level and forget about the miracles and the spiritual potential that Jesus taught us about. Miracles are always possible. I've seen miracles in my life, to show me that they are real. But it's okay for people that don't believe the way I believe. It would be exciting for them if they would at least open their mind to the possibility of miracles.

## The Hawai'ian People

You know, everywhere you go in Hawai'i, you are aware that there is a problem about what happened to the Hawai'ians with colonization. So many Hawai'ians died from diseases that were imported. Having their land taken away has wounded the culture, but it is coming back. The elders (Kapuna) are teaching the young what they learned from their elders.

For many years it was illegal to speak the language, do the Hula, practice natural healing, or practice their own religion. Now all these things are coming back. There is a rebirth of Hawai'ian culture.

Many Hawai'ians want to have their sovereign nation given back to them. But for many Hawai'ians their Aloha and love of the land remains strong, no matter what unfair things have happened. They have dealt with the situation, inside of themselves, and have put their feelings into their music, their dancing and into their love of nature. You know, they have found a balance inside.

## The Native Americans

The Native Americans had so many killed by our government. The Native Americans lost the war and, for the most part, they lost their land, their food sources and their way of life. Today many Native Americans carry a bad feeling about what the government has done. But the native people are strong today and will prevail as a culture. They preserve their culture through their ceremonies, their way of life, and their art. They pray for and try to protect all of nature. They pass this tradition on to the young ones. There is injustice going on all over the world, and wars have been going on all through history. But the Native American religion is connected to praying for all of nature and keeping the balance with the creator and the natural world.

The only way for Hawai'ians and Native Americans and so many other peoples to heal from injustice and genocide is to connect with the healing light of God ... the Creator ... Keakua. All through history there have been wars, terrible suffering and injustice. Even though these things have happened in the past and are still happening, we need to heal. I try to learn from the mistakes of history and also from other peoples' mistakes, so I can better my life and be able to help people more as a healer. Inside ourselves ... we can create that world of peace.

### Different Outside, Same Inside

Once, one of my teachers was in a hospital in the nursery section. She saw in the nursery, lying in the bassinettes, a black baby, a white baby, a red baby and a yellow baby. As she looked through her psychic sight through her third eye into the heart of each baby, in all their hearts was the same brilliant light of God. Although we are all different on the outside, we are the same in our hearts on the inside. We all come from the one divine force I call God.

# 19

## Free Will and Choices

### Decision-Making

The problem with many people is that they make decisions in their life without looking ahead to see what is going to happen in the future from that decision. When I make a decision, I say, "God, I am going to make this decision, and let's see what happens in a few months and a few years as a result of this decision. What does it look like?"

### Indecision

People often have trouble with indecision. When I have a situation like that, this is what I do. I say, "God, I am at a fork in the road. Should I take the one to the right or the one to the left? I'm not sure which one I should take." After a while I look at the situation again and say, "God, I am asking for your help, but I do not hear you telling me which road to take." Then I wait a little while and I say, "God, look here, this is what I am going to do. I feel personally that I should take the left road, but if you have something better to show me or tell me, I'll be listening and paying attention to you." So I take the left road and, all of a sudden, God says, "Take a quick right," and so, of course, I do that. If I initiate the movement, but I am still not sure, but still listening, I am willing to be corrected. God will take you in a different way sometimes than your own choice. But God's choice will turn out for the best. I always say, "Fantastic! Thank you!"

### We Don't Want Regrets Later

What will the results of the decision be? I ask God ahead of time. I don't want to have regrets later. People don't usually look at things this way. By not asking and looking, people can get into something that can go very wrong. Sometimes it is too late to go back and change it. They will have to make very difficult decisions in their life and sometimes pay some unpleasant consequences. With God's help, you can look forward to seeing if this is the best way to do something.

## Karma: The Law of Cause and Effect

If a person comes offering trouble, it will eventually come back to them. What you sow, you also reap. It is as simple as that. It may not necessarily come back right away, but it will come back in some way. It could even come back on your family. When Moses came down from the mountain, he said, "If you worship false Gods, you will have to pay the consequences. We may be paying off karma that our ancestors created. There is family or genetic karma also, as well as individual karma. We are all born into a race and a group of people to learn certain things. There is such a thing as karma, you know. It is the universal law of cause and effect. Some people say, "What goes around, comes around."

## God May Show You a Better Way

God may show you another way that is better than what you first decided. Most people act impulsively and don't think first or consider the consequences. Sometimes they do see a glimpse of the consequences but ignore what they see, because they want to follow their own desire or impulse. When people run strictly on emotional impulses, it just becomes a guessing game and can get them into trouble ... big time!

## Be with God, But Make Your Own Decisions

There is another story about a time we were in Grass Valley by the Safeway store. We were in a motor home at the time, doing some more process work. A man was trying to make a decision where to move. He was asking God, "Is it East? Is it West? Is it North? Is it South?" God's answer seemed to be "no" to each one of the questions. He was really puzzled and said, "God is not answering my questions, and I want to do the right thing in my life." Then I said to this man, "Did it ever occur to you that there are times when God wants you to make your own decision?" I always say; "Be with God, but make your own decisions."

## The Interplay of Your Will and God's Will

So there's an interplay of God's will with your will. From one end of the spectrum to the other, both of them are right. But you have to use both correctly. If you don't heal yourself, who is going to heal you? If you don't take the first step, who is going to do it for you? You have to take the first step. Once you take the first step, you ignite the energy of spirit. It's like a propane heater. You push the button and you get the little spark. You turn it on and the bigger flame comes on. So you have to start off. You say, "God, this is what I want." You have to create the initial illumination inside of yourself. Once you do that, a bigger illuminated light will emanate from you.

## Looking Ahead into the Future When Choosing

If I was going to make a choice, I would look ahead to see what is going to happen in the future. That is what I do. I plant the seed of what I want to harvest. There are a lot of people who plant a seed and they water it for a little period of time, and then they don't water it anymore. They don't nourish or water the seed, and then it dies. When this happens, it is because of a lack of focus and perseverance.

There are times when people make a decision without looking ahead to consider the possible outcomes or consequences of that decision. When we are making important decisions, we need to reflect on them and look into the future and see some of the possible outcomes that the decision may have. We need to consider whether it will have a negative effect on our lives or if it could hurt other people. After we have reflected on these considerations, it is easier for us to focus on setting our goals.

When a decision is made impulsively or blindly, it can often lead to consequences that have to be paid in the future. Many times when things turn out badly, the person is upset and doesn't think back to the moment the decision was made. Chances are they didn't take time to reflect on it and look ahead, in their reflective state, to see what is going to happen in the future.

It is also very important to be in a neutral state of mind when you look ahead into the future. If you are emotional or desire something or someone too strongly, you will not be able to see the results. You will be making a decision based on emotion or desire, not wisdom and clarity.

Life is partly predetermined and partly free will. It is about fifty/fifty. People have to be in tune with the God within, in order to follow out their destiny. They need to listen to the music that is within them. If they let themselves get influenced from outside of themselves, they might get it right, but they might get it wrong. If you get it from the inside, it becomes real. It manifests. Then there will be no false prophesies and no "make-believe" stuff. It is all real.

We have to ask God for help. We have to ask the angels to help cleanse our bodies. We will do better if we do this first, before making important decisions. Then we will be able to see more clearly.

# 20

## Material or Spiritual

### The Story of the Greedy Man

I remember a story about a man who had a lot of money in his bank account. He lived very far away and it was late at night. It took the man hours to get home. He became very greedy and decided he wanted to take his money out of the bank and take it home. He had a big bag of money from his bank, but there was a hole in the bag. He traveled a long distance and he could feel the heaviness of the bag. After walking all night, he got home at daylight a. People began to walk the streets and, as he looked behind him he noticed a trail of coins; and then to his shock and dismay he discovered that the coins had been dropping out of his bag all night, as he walked. There was hardly any money left in his bag. This was a lesson to him about getting overly attached to his money.

### The Psychic Smells of the Materialistic Wealthy vs. the Generous Wealthy

People say, "I need this. I need that." They want something, yet they are not willing to give. The secret of everything is to give and receive. I do work with people who are very, very wealthy. When I see them, I smell the physical luxury of desire and not God. It is not sweet. Some wealthy people are living with God and use part of their wealth to help people. That is a whole different smell. When I smell the materialistic and love-of-luxury smell, it is amazing. Most people do not have this spiritual gift of smelling the energy. It is not old age. It is not the skin or the body dying. It is not lack of cleanliness. It is a psychic smell that reflects the inner attitude of the person.

### We Can't Take It with Us

The amazing thing about life, for all of us, is that when we actually do die, we go alone, to the afterlife, without any of our material things. We lose all of that. But if the soul and the spirit are illuminated, then there is a sweet fragrance. There is a beauty. Our inner attitude surely does make a great difference.

### Personal Desire vs. a Spiritual Life

God is inside of us too, as we are a part of God. We should never put a lot of garbage between us and God. It may be a car, money, family or career. We have many desires for ourselves and we have obstacles too. People often have the misconception that life is for fulfilling all our personal desires. Sometimes that happens, but we are here to learn and grow spiritually and be in full connection to a spiritual life. If our desires are fulfilled, then they may be part of God's plan for our life. When we move against that plan, everything goes wrong.

When it comes to working with a person, it is important to know where they at so you know what they are capable of receiving. I have a VW bug and I have to stay under 70 mph or else I would blow the engine. So I have to work within the parameters of what the person's capacity is at the time. If you're driving a race car, you can go over 150 mph. When you deal with people, you need to respect them for who they are. Everyone has something special to offer to you. You can learn from everyone.

### Wealth and Luxury Cannot Satisfy Your Soul

This emptiness and yearning often happens to very famous people, who seem to have every happiness and success in life. I have seen this with movie stars and other famous people. They have all this love coming at them from the outside, from fans and admirers. When they go home, are alone, or are out of work, they can slump into a deep, dark depression. That's because they have nothing inside of them in the first place. If you have the true light of God in your soul, you have a real life. So, this is my own experience. To me it's like the word "love" is like the word "evolve" backwards, or pretty nearly.

Love on the human level does not satisfy any of us on a permanent level, the way the love of God does. We have to ask ourselves if the love we feel is true or fickle. How about the other person? Is it artificial love, need, or lust? We need to ask ourselves what real love is. But whether we are experiencing human love or the love of God, love does give us the opportunity to learn and grow.

## Choices Between Right and Wrong

We always have choices in life between right and wrong. If we make wrong choices, then we have the opportunity to learn from the wrong choices. Hopefully some day a person will choose to make right choices. I have met people who have self-destructive behavior. Hopefully, as they mature and suffer too much, they will grow out of it. Some people are seduced by outer appearances and don't look deeper. They may see beauty, wealth and luxury and think this is the real thing in life. Beauty fades, wealth can be frittered away, and luxury gives only temporary satisfaction. Time will change all these things. The physical eye may only look for beauty or handsomeness. But when we look at someone with our third eye, or spiritual sight, we see with greater wisdom, because the third eye is connected to the heart. Whatever we choose in life, we have to take responsibility for it, whatever it is. Sooner or later, the choices or actions will come back to us. Life is all about cause and effect.

## Having Patience with God's Timing

A lot of people try to force things. They want to move ahead and don't want to wait. There is a rhythm and timing with God. When they want to get ahead of God's plan, they age fast, because the ego says, "I want to do this. I want to be young again." It is really weird. It's like a young man saying, "I want to get this car. It's fast, fancy and good looking." So the guy spends thousands of dollars buying a car. After a little while he grows up and gets married and has children. Then he thinks, "I wish I hadn't spent all my savings buying that fancy car because now I really could use the money to take care of my growing family." All this was a learning experience.

# 21

## Journeys and Travels

### Mount Shasta

This is a story about our pilgrimage to Mount Shasta. Once in the 1970s I had a dream that I was walking up a mountain, on a paved road. There were lots of trees along the side of the road, but as I got to a higher part of the mountain, there seemed to be no trees at all. I could see a wonderful view of the mountain as I was looking down the valleys.

### Purple Crosses Appeared on My Sleeping Bag

So one day I spoke to my friend about this particular mountain that I saw in my dream. I started to describe it as having a big mountain peak and then a smaller mountain peak next to it. He said that it just had to be Mount Shasta. Little did I know that I would be climbing Mount Shasta when I was thirty years old. There was another woman that came with us. The three of us headed up to Mount Shasta and signed in, as mountain climbers, at the local police station. We told them that we were going to climb up the next day and expected to be back the following evening. We drove up as far as the road would take us and settled down in our sleeping bags for the night at a campground. At four in the morning we woke up. As I looked at my sleeping bag, I noticed that there were perfect purple crosses on both sides of the sleeping bag. It was really interesting to see these images as they had not been there before. They were light images that were lit up on the sleeping bag ... as if in a vision.

### A Symbolic Release of Past Pain

My woman friend was wearing a white outfit with a black sweater as we took off to climb the mountain that cool morning. I had seen my friend wearing this same outfit in the previous dream. There was a quality of deja vu to this expedition up the mountain. Our guide was wearing all white too. We started climbing up the mountain, in our rubber-soled shoes, using cut-off broom sticks for walking sticks. At one point during the climb I told my friend to throw away her black sweater. As she did this, she was also able to release a lot from her past. She felt a big release and afterward she felt very clear and light.

### Blessings that Appeared as Spiritual Signs

Once while we were resting, we began to notice a large boulder which was almost at the top of the mountain. Super-imposed on the boulder was an image of Jesus. We held hands and enjoyed the fresh clear air of the mountain, knowing that we were given many spiritual signs and symbols. There was an abundance of blessings in the air. All of a sudden our guide said, "Let there be light!" It had been cloudy but instantaneously sunlight appeared. For approximately twenty minutes we held hands as our bodies vibrated with strong spiritual energy. There was such a powerful mystical energy that it has remained a peak experience in our memories.

### An Energy Lift from the Pebbles

As we continued on our journey, we wanted to take the easy way to the red rock at the top of the mountain. We didn't have snow gear with us, but we had to go through some snow anyway. As we climbed higher, it became more difficult to breathe. As I climbed quickly, I noticed little pebbles would fall on and across my chest and belly. Each one had a different shape and color and they seemed very alive. As they touched me, by falling on me, they put a certain vibration into my body and made it come fully alive and energized again. All the tiredness was taken away. The guide told us that he was going on up ahead of us to check the path.

### A Message from the Bees, a Spiral Bird ...
### and a Treacherous Crossing

All of a sudden my friend and I saw two bees, a male and a female, that seemed to have an urgent message for us. They made it apparent that they needed to communicate telepathically to us. They very clearly told us not to stop, but to just keep on going. After we understood their communication, they disappeared. Our guide returned and we began to climb again. We stopped to rest briefly and the bees showed up again and urgently said, "Don't stop. Keep on climbing. Keep on climbing." We set off again, heeding the bees' message. The higher we climbed, the harder it was for us. Then all of a sudden our guide decided to go ahead again and find the next path. While he was gone, a brown spiral bird flew down the mountain from the snow level. My friend asked me why the spiral bird would be coming down to us from the snow level. They are usually at a much lower elevation.

### The Falling Walking Stick and a Prayer

Our guide returned again and we continued to climb up the mountain. We reached a part where we had to cross over a steep passage to another part of the mountain. Our guide accidentally dropped his walking stick. It fell and fell ... for such a long, long time, and then we heard it hit bottom ... a long, long way down. I put my head against the snow and prayed, "God help us. If we make one mistake, we may fall down too, and we may not come out of this experience alive. We need your help with every step. God, if I fall down and die, I will not be able to help people in this world, so please save our lives."

### The Bees' Message Revealed

Our guide had very high boots that were good for the snow. He made a little pathway for us to follow through the snow. We crossed over this very treacherous area, horizontally, heading to the other side of the mountain. We carefully followed our guide's footsteps, and finally we were safely on the other side. Just as got there, we looked back and saw a big land slide of falling rock coming down, like an avalanche, right on the path that we had just walked across. I will always thank the bees for telling us so persistently to continue on ... continue on. They told us not to stop, because they knew that our lives were in danger. What a wonderful experience to be guided by the bees.

### An Apparition of Jesus and Other Wondrous Signs

As we continued on, our guide said, "Let me continue on ahead, to find the next path for us." So he left again, and we felt drawn to look upward. We saw a vision of Jesus Christ, up on a huge rock waving his hands to us. Then we saw him lift his hands up towards the heavens. As we gazed upon his radiant image, we were struck with wonder and awe. There were beautiful pastel rainbow colors throughout and surrounding him. Truly, we had been blessed! As his image faded away, we went a little bit further and we saw another rock that had a pyramid on it. There was a spacecraft inside the pyramid and there was an image of the baby Jesus inside of the spacecraft.

### Other People Had Seen a Similar Vision

Upon returning we met a couple from Yucca Valley and we told them our Mount Shasta story and described the visions and symbols that we had seen. This man knew about that symbol. He had heard about the pyramid, spaceship, and baby Jesus. Apparently, it had been seen by other people too. Not too long ago, my friend Charles visited Hawai'i and there was a big meeting of all the major Kahunas of the Island. Charles helped to facilitate this gathering. The Kahunas seemed to know about the vision of the pyramid, spacecraft and baby Jesus too. The Hawai'ian kahunas said that there is a similar vision that they see in Hawai'i, and they consider it very sacred.

*Sliding Down the Mountain ... After Signing in, Spiritually*

As we got to the top of the mountain, we found out we were not on the highest peak of Mount Shasta after all, but on the top of the lower peak. Our guide said we couldn't continue on because we would have to descend into the valley and then climb up all over again, if we were going to go to the tallest peak of Mount Shasta. There just wouldn't be time. I sat down and felt a little disappointed.

So then I decided to send my spirit to the top of the mountain and "sign in spiritually." I could smell the sulphur coming out from the top of the mountain. As we came down from the top of the lower peak, it was very, very steep. There was a lot of snow too. Our guide showed us how to zigzag back and forth down the side of the mountain. As we did this, I yelled out, "How do you stop?" I found myself head down with my bottom end up and both legs in the air, like I was a human sled. Someone else yelled back, "This is how you stop." This method was face up but sliding on the butt. I was face down, head first and moving fast!

### Fasting Had Opened Us up to Visions

Climbing up the mountain was difficult because we had fasted beforehand. Because of the fasting, we had a fantastic visionary experience. The energy was so much higher and more illuminated. As we were coming back down, our bodies got tired and we got lost. Finally we saw a little light down below, so our guide decided to go down ahead of us and find the path to get down. We wrapped ourselves in an aluminum blanket to keep warm. I had cramps in my thigh, so I decided to pray and massage my leg.

### The Sign Said, "Avalanche, Keep Out"

The guide didn't return. It felt as if we'd better head down on our own. I remembered that at the police station the guide had said that if we got lost, to go down. When we finally got down to the parking lot, we got into the car to rest and wait for our guide to find us. When we finally got back to the police station to check out, we saw a warning sign next to the picture of Mount Shasta that read, "Avalanche Warning—Keep Out." I said, "Oh my God, that is where we just were. So it seems we were really protected by these spiritual masters.

### Life Is Like Climbing a Mountain

So many people that climb Mt. Shasta think that the highest vibration is at top of the highest peak. But we had a beautiful experience just partially up the mountain and over on the lower peak ... little Shastina. I definitely don't recommend climbing this mountain unless a person is very strongly guided by spirit. I am not really much of a mountain climber myself, as I don't like heights, but I climbed this mountain for my spiritual growth and to feel even closer to God. In addition to that, it was a great pleasure to enjoy nature's beauty and be closer to Mother Earth. This experience enriched my life tremendously.

It is very important for all of us to go to the mountains to fast, pray, to hear our own breath and heartbeat, and to receive energy back from nature and spirit. Jesus climbed mountains to pray. Also spiritual masters, mystics, Native Americans and Gurus from all parts of the world go into nature to commune with spirit or God. Whenever there are difficulties in life, I know that I must keep on striving until I get there. Life and its challenges are like climbing a mountain.

### Wolfgang ...Who Saw Us in Spirit, on the Mountain

After our pilgrimage to the mystical mountain of Mount Shasta we went on to Montague. There we encountered a spiritual man named Wolfgang Cross from Germany. He looked at us and said, "You said you would be up at the top of the mountain at twelve o'clock, but you were not there. By the way, I meditated before going up the mountain, in my spiritual body, to meet you there. I had this little bird that was in the bush and it was pestering me in my meditation, so I decided to send it to you. Reverend Cosme, did you see the little brown spiral bird that I sent to you?" We remembered the little spiral bird. He also said that he saw the guide leading the way on the path, my female companion in the middle and me in the rear. He described everything exactly. He even mentioned that my companion was wearing a tennis hat, was a little older, and got tired more easily.

This man—many, many miles away—was able to describe all of this to us and more. He also saw that there were three masters, dressed in white, that came out from the center of the mountain. He saw a master guiding me and another master guiding my companion and another master guiding our guide.

### My Friend's Experience with Violet Lights and a Master in White Robes

The masters in white robes, who were guiding us on Mount Shasta, are a part of the White Brotherhood. My female companion and healing partner went up to Mount Shasta another time with one of her friends. They drove as far up the mountain as the road went, and then they sat in the car and began to talk. Towards evening time, they decided to start back down the mountain, but the car wouldn't start. They tried again and again. Then as they sat there, they began to see lights ... bright, violet, iridescent lights. The lights were so bright that they came through the car. A short distance away they could see a spiritual man dressed in a white robe. He opened a door, that appeared in front of him, for them to enter. They instantly fell into a sleep or trance state. Only the spiritual body knows what happened, because the physical body was asleep. They followed this master through the door and that's all they remembered. Later on they woke up, but didn't remember what had happened. They did know that something happened, as their bodies were vibrating with a strong spiritual energy. Then my friend opened the hood of her car to shake the cable of the battery, to see if that was the problem. After she did this, the car started immediately. After coming down from Mount Shasta, they headed up towards Oregon.

### Had They Become Invisible?

On the way to Oregon, the two women needed to get gas. One of the women went to the restroom. The other woman waited in the car for service, but even though there were several attendants standing around, they didn't even seem to see her. She got out and went up to the men and asked them for some service. They totally ignored her words. They didn't even seem to see her. They acted as if she wasn't there at all. Then she spoke again, and the man jumped as if he had seen a ghost. She then decided to check on her girlfriend who hadn't come out of the restroom for quite a long time. She found her friend in the corner of the restroom crying. She asked, "Why are you crying?" Her friend said, "Another woman was in here and I spoke to her and the woman couldn't see or hear me. I must be invisible. So here I am sitting on the floor crying. I thought I was dead, but now that I see you, I know I can't be dead." So these are some of many extraordinary experiences that came about from visiting the sacred mountain.

### A Gathering of Healers at Mount Shasta

Another time I was a part of a gathering of healers who went to Lake Siskiyou, which is close to the base of Mount Shasta. I packed my PA system as we were all going to give talks and share our work with each other. After our talks and sharing names and addresses with each other, I went to change clothes as I was looking forward to a swim in the lake. When I got to my motorhome, there was a long line of people waiting for a healing. We had a massage table set up in the motorhome and we worked, with one person after another, from ten o'clock that morning until three-thirty the next morning. So much for the idea of a swim.

### When You Need Help, You Will Be Guided to Help

Several of the people that had lined up at our motorhome had already been up to the mountain and had meditated there. One person said that they were told by their guidance in meditation that they should go to Lake Siskiyou, that they would encounter a healer there, who could help them. So the lesson in this is that if you ever need help, listen to your inner guidance and you will be led to the help that you need, just as this person was. God, the master, the Holy Spirit and all the angels want to help us. When you want help, they will guide you to the help that you need. If your heart is sincere, God will guide your path. Once you recognize that the guidance is from God, then give thanks and God will never leave you. I have not been to Lake Siskiyou for a long, long time because I remembered that I could not have a vacation there. I could not rest. When your light shines and God works through you, that light shining through you will magnetize people who need help. People from far away who are in the dark and cold will find their way to the fireplace of God's warmth and light and love. They will come for comfort, guidance, understanding, compassion and healing. They will have love and peace in their hearts, as a result ... not conflict or war.

## Spiritual Initiations in the Philippines

During the nineteen-eighties I made six pilgrimages to the Philippines with Clara, my late wife and healing partner. This was part of the discovery of my spiritual roots. I was going to the land where my family's healing tradition came from originally. I knew that the healers in the Philippines had become famous for psychic surgery, but I also knew that there were many kinds of healers there that specialized in different things. I felt that going there would help me to rediscover the healing gifts of my family. Our motivation and wish in visiting the healers was that we could expand and deepen our knowledge of healing. We wanted to pass this blessing on to the people who came to us.

There are really basically two sets of healers. One set does psychic surgery in and around the Manila area. There are also healers that specialize in many other types of healing in the mountain area to the South. Some of the Philippine healers specialize in healing bones, while others specialize in teeth or performing exorcisms, for example. There are many specialists.

Many of the healers do psychic surgery, which is shocking and dramatic the first time you see it. I was really lucky to be able to watch a number of operations. You can really feel the Holy Spirit in the room when these operations are being performed. The healer prays and scans the body with his or her spiritual gifts and then makes an incision with the hand or fingers. There is no pain for the patient and no anesthetics. Usually, in just a few seconds, blockages and some kind of tissue is removed. You can see the blood and flesh and organs. It is so amazing! Quickly the operation is over and the incision is closed up with the healer's hands. There is no sign of the incision and there is no scar. At the most there may be a pink line that fades in a few days. The patient may be tired for a few hours or a few days because they have really had surgery! Very often there is great improvement or a total cure in their health condition.

For some people it is too late. Often cancer patients, who have had chemotherapy and radiation, do not get healed. The healers always lecture the patients about the spiritual laws of cause and effect. Whether a person gets healed or not also depends on how soon or how late the person comes to them after getting sick. It also depends on the causes of the problem. There are so many very sincere people coming to the Philippines from all over the world to find healing.

We visited a female psychic surgeon who let us watch her operations. While she was doing the surgery, she sang Hail Marys, Our Fathers, and Ave Maria. Once while I was watching her, she wanted me to pull the blockage out, while she had the body opened up.

I asked the healers if I was going to do this type of work. The healers told me to come back another time at Easter. They said they needed to go to the sacred mountain and pray about it, before giving me an answer.

Soon after we got to the Philippines, we went to a very special healer. We knocked on the door, introduced ourselves, and told him that we were from the United States. The healer said to me, "Oh, your family came from the Philippines. You've come back to connect with your healing tradition! We've been expecting you. We knew you were coming!" I sat down and he looked at me.

Instantaneously he said, "You are a good spirit and sincere. I will tell you everything I know, because of who you are and because you have not charged for your healing work."

He decided one morning that he was going to take us to meet a special healer. We planned to leave the next morning, but the healer seemed to operate on a different kind of time-frame. At eight-thirty in the morning he had one shoe on. At noon he put the other shoe on. People came by, and finally at four-thirty in the afternoon, he was ready to take off with us.

So when we got to the place we were going, I found out that a one-hundred-and-six year-old man was in charge of deciding if we were going to go through initiation or not. We waited ten days to get this permission. We had to be checked out by the old man before we were allowed to go to the holiest part of the sacred mountain. There is another more public part of the mountain. At Easter time there are about twenty-thousand people that go to the shrine there.

Finally, after getting the permission, we were taken to two special waterfalls. One had red water and the other had cream white water. It was like male and female waterfalls. They emptied into a river, down below.

One day we went out to the mountain in a group of about twenty people. Our healer lit a candle and said a little prayer. It was so foggy that we couldn't see anything. He blew on the fog three times, with his breath. Instantaneously, the fog cleared up. Two minutes later it fogged up again and he did the same thing. Again it cleared up. Then it happened a third time. After blowing on it the third time, the fog disappeared for good and it stayed clear. Someone in the group had a bad spirit in them. That one person could not go with us.

We got to an area where there were symbolic Stations of the Cross. The people here believe that the energy of the original Stations of the Cross, in Jerusalem, was energetically transferred to this place on the mountain. There is a flat rock representing the place where Jesus hung on the cross. The healer told us that one time there were two teenagers who disrespected this holy place. They were dancing around with a transistor radio. All of a sudden lightning struck out of a blue sky. They both died of the lightning strike. Another holy place was misused by a man who was yelling and screaming there. It was another clear day. Out of nowhere a dust-devil came through, spun him around, and threw him to the ground.

There is another place where there is a waterfall that represents Archangel Michael. We went there to pray for protection. The assistant to the healer put me under the water for fifteen seconds. I could hardly breathe. It was a strong current and cold.

A few days later I went to the same waterfall with the healer. He had me recite certain sacred words as I was stepping beneath the waterfall. As I did this, the experience was completely different. I could tolerate the strength of the current and the cold to the point that I could stay there all day.

Another Easter six of us, out of twenty-thousand people, were taken into the mountain by the old man, who was one-hundred-and-six years old. He was the spiritual keeper of the place. He could put his hand in the rock and pull things out of it. He opened the rock the same way the psychic surgeons can open the body, with spiritual laser-like energy. Part of the initiation was for us to light a candle, pray, and request being gifted with something sacred. The old man put his hands into his mouth and pulled out a sacred relic.

There is another sacred site that has a big boulder that looks like a head. There is a face with eyes, ears and mouth. Water comes out of the mouth and it is considered holy water.

Another time we went to the mountain with a different healer and his porter. He took us to a beautiful place called the Windows of Heaven, which was a big overlook, with a beautiful vista. We were shocked when we heard a huge booming sound. It sounded like a cannonball being shot off. We were told that the sound came from a spirit. The healer said, "We have permission to go into this holy place to pray. We lit a candle and prayed. Just before we came to the second Window of Heaven, we heard two large bangs, which gave us permission to go to the second window. Right before we got to the third window, we heard three large bangs, giving us permission again.

The next sacred encounter was with three trees, that shimmered with a white glow, all around them. Our healer tried to hit the tree with a machete, but he couldn't. The machete bounced right off the strong energy field around the tree. He tried three different times. Then he lit a small candle and prayed for permission to get a small relic from the tree. He said it was a gift from God. He said that when worn on the body, it would strengthen the energy field and make one more in tune with God.

When we were first taken to some of the healers, they checked us out in various ways to see if we were sincere. At that time in my healing career I did not charge for my services, but worked on a donation basis. This made them happy, as in their tradition they do not charge. Instead they are allowed to receive food and donations from the community. Traditionally the community made sure that the healers had houses, food and clothing. It is a really old tradition in the Philippines.

The next part of this long initiation took us to the Cave of Jacob. We had to take off all of our jewelry, including our watches. We were told if we didn't take these things off, the spirits would pull them off. This was a place of purification.

All of the prayers and rituals are based on a mystical form of Christianity. It is a very powerful force in the Philippines. The local people have a lot of faith in their prayers and believe in miracles and so-called supernatural things. We had to crawl in this cave. Then we came to an area that was like a slide and we had to slide down to a flat area of the cave. It was cold! We were told to light a candle and pray. Next to this flat area was a crevasse that was filled with water, with a ladder that went down into this water. Here we did a ceremony, immersing ourselves in the water three times. Each time we prayed for cleansing and purification, in the name of the Father and the Son and the Holy Spirit. It was frigidly cold like the North Pole.

After this we went to some holy waterfalls and drank the water. There were special herbs in the pool, at the foot of the waterfall. As I drank the herbal water, it felt like a powerful purple vibration gave my body a complete physical and spiritual cleansing.

Things that would ordinarily be considered supernatural were natural to the healers here. For instance, as we went deeper and deeper into the mountain's secret areas, the healer had to ask the spirits for permission to enter. So many unusual things happened on these journeys. After a while these so-called supernatural things just seemed natural to us. Everything was alive in a different way here. The veil between the physical and spiritual worlds was very thin.

One of the things that happened in our spiritual initiation was going into the Cave of Judgment. We went inside and the healer sat on the outside and prayed for about forty-five minutes. As a result of these prayers he found out that our energy was clean and clear and that we could go in. We had been praying with a lit candle. While going through it, we came to a very narrow part, where you have to squeeze and wiggle yourself through like a worm. It seemed that it would be so easy to get stuck. But the strange thing was, that it had nothing to do with whether you were big or small. You could get stuck if you had done something really bad, like killing someone. If you did get stuck, you could sincerely pray and ask for forgiveness for different things from your past. Sometimes it could take two or three days for a person like this to get out. Then after your purification you could just slip right through. The tightness of the space seemed to magically open up, to let you pass through. Fortunately we didn't have to go through this problem.

The next part of this initiation was going to another cave. This all took place on the same holy mountain, but in another area. When we went inside the cave, just inside, was a round pool of water. This was an oracle cave. If the spirits that are the guardians of this cave allow it, you will be able to look into the water and see your past, present, and future. We gazed into this pool and saw images.

The next cave that we went into was a Grandfather cave. It was huge, with really high rock ceilings. As usual we had to light a candle and pray as we went in. To our amazement there were fireflies making little specks of moving light in this cave. This was truly a kind of miraculous phenomena, that I have never seen before. If you are meant to know something, the fireflies will go into certain specific formations to make a word or a series of words. This phenomenal formation would be the message the spirits have for you. The messages would be written either in Aramaic, Latin, English or Togalog (the local language of the Philippines). If there was a message made up of firefly letters, the healer would intuitively know who the message is for. If a word or words are given to you, it is like a mantra or sacred words, especially for your spiritual use. When you use these words, it feels like the breath of God is in them. They don't have an ordinary feeling, as they are instilled with sacredness. They are usually used for healing, blessing or protection.

In the Catholic Church many of these ritual beliefs and understandings still exist. There are mysteries contained in the rituals that can be very powerful if one understands the full mystical teaching contained within them. In the old days the priests sang the whole mass in Latin. There are still those in the Catholic Church today that have that old mystical knowledge, but they keep it secret. Many of the really adept and pure-hearted healers in the Philippines have this knowledge too. Much of it has to do with the power of certain words or mystical objects that are empowered by rituals, ceremonies and prayers. Many of the healers have regular days of fasting and prayer. They do this to develop or maintain humility and spiritual purification. The ritual objects that are in their possession are especially empowered and energetically charged up, on these days.

We discovered that many of the healers had tiny, tiny little black books that contained their spiritual words and mystical mantras. They feel that certain words of power or phrases of power or healing were once in the Bible ... but were taken out of the Bible, on purpose, because of a very real danger that existed. If someone had the wrong intention or motivation, these words of invocation and power could be misused. The words have been preserved by the healers in the Philippines. The words are sometimes abbreviated or are written in such a way that you have to hold them up to a mirror to read. Sometimes they are written into a kind of code in order to protect the sacred. These words are to be used out of love for God and for wanting to help and heal people. It is very selective. Only certain people are allowed to know about these things, and they have to be coming from a pure and Godly place, not a place of ego or selfishness.

Sometimes the secret words are written on things made of metal, cloth, or on a picture. Certain mystical words and phrases of power and healing are passed on in families. For instance there are holy metals and other things that you can buy in the market place, but unless they have been empowered by continuous ceremony and prayer they remain ordinary. When these objects are included in prayer and ceremony, they can become a source of great mystical power and protection.

At Easter time all the healers get together, young and old, for target-shooting contests. They shoot coconuts out of the trees with their rifles. If they can hit the stem of the coconut, then they are sure that their aim is good and their sight is correctly set. I was invited to one of these get-togethers. An old man put one of his sacred objects up in the tree ... an object included in many prayers and ceremonies. It had a very powerful vibration! The best sharp-shooter aimed at it. He was a really good shot, but the bullet just went right around it. Then a young kid, a healer who was in training, put his own sacred object up in the tree. The sharp-shooter aimed and shot at it. It broke in pieces and fell to the ground. It did not have the build-up of spiritual energy in it that the old man's had. It usually takes about five years of working with these types of objects with prayer, fasting and ceremonies, before the power is built up in them. It is said that if you are wearing it on your body, it will protect you from harm and make you bulletproof! When you touch or come near one of these sacred objects, you feel it. The energy is very light and it vibrates very strongly! The old healer kept putting his object up in the tree. Again and again different people shot at it, but the bullets always went around it! These objects can be bought at a marketplace, but before being worked with they are just like other material objects. Once they are worked with for a long time, there is very, very pure energy in them that vibrates like a sun or pure gold. The objects can remain dormant until they're empowered with sacred prayer and ritual. I experienced this for myself.

While I was in the Philippines, I felt like I was walking between Heaven and Earth. It was so mystical and powerful on the mountain that I didn't know if I would walk out of this place alive, or not. I had to completely surrender myself to God. It was a very, very mystical experience for me. I knew it would change and bless my own work as a healer forever!

When the healers take someone to the holy mountain to visit the sacred caves, the person supplies all the healer's needs, such as propane for the cook stove, food, a tent and mosquito nets. There is one part of the mountain that we were on where the birds actually talk back to you. We were with a healer named Jimmy and his helpers. As you go deeper into more sacred parts of the mountain, the healer who is the guide has to get permission from the spirits of the place to take someone there.

The healer would ask permission, and the answer would come back out of the mouths of birds. It seems unbelievable, but the birds would call out in English with the answer to the request. Some of the birds were parrots, but some of them weren't. The birds said quite clearly at one point, "Stop! Go back! Go back!" The healer clairvoyantly got the message that there was a large snake going through the area and may be crossing our path. Then after a while the birds said, "You can go now! You can go now!" Boy, he wasn't "b-s-ing." He was telling the truth, as amazing as this was! These parrots were high up in the trees of this rain forest type of terrain. You really didn't get to see them that often, but you could hear them talking.

On another part of the mountain there is no water and the area is more like a desert. It's quite high up. We were low on water and a bit thirsty. The healer took us to a special little hole in the ground and asked us to light a candle and pray to God. We were told to put a little plastic baggie by the hole. If you are not pure in your prayer, nothing will happen. If you are, water will miraculously come up out of the hole and fill up the plastic bag. Well, this is how we drank water up on that dry part of the mountain.

Our healer had two old men along with us, who were carrying seventy-pound packs on their backs. They were trained in the ways of this mountain since they were young. They were like spiritual hermits who climbed the mountain like goats. One of the old men was seventy-six years old. Since we were up so high, we could see a long way away. There was a hurricane coming towards the island.

We could all see it in the distance. It was hard to keep up with these guides. We needed to pick up speed so we were shown how to put wings on our feet. First we would blow on our hands and then bend down to touch our feet, while visualizing wings on them. Boy, did we pick up speed after doing that, and we had no more trouble keeping up with them.

They also told us things about invisibility. Since we were going to be carrying home some sacred items and herbs, it was important that we not have any trouble in customs when we traveled home. We were given a piece of paper with certain words written on it. When we were leaving the hotel and on the way to the airport, we were to say the words. After saying the words we were not to look or walk back. We had to be silent and move forward. We had to go through a lot of inspections and customs, and the whole time I was not supposed to talk at all. Clara could talk, if something had to be said. We showed our passports and our tickets. We held them up, but the officers just seemed to stare into space as if they were in a trance. It seemed that we were invisible to them. Not only did they not seem to see us but our luggage was passed right over, as if it wasn't even there in front of them.

When the Japanese invaded the Philippines, some of the healers were taken prisoners of war. They would wait for an opportunity to escape, using their invisibility techniques. For instance, if a supply truck arrived and the gate was opened, they would say their sacred words and just walk out of the prison, invisible. Then they took off for the sacred mountain, as the Japanese didn't know it. After we traveled safely back to California, the piece of paper with the sacred words dematerialized right out of my pocket, and was gone.

On an earlier trip I asked the healers if I was going to be doing psychic surgery in the future. After they prayed about it at Easter time, they came back to me and said "No." So I let go of any ideas I had about becoming a psychic surgeon. They told me that my own form of healing would keep developing and that I would be guided spiritually. I had been blessed and initiated by the healers in the caves and waterfalls of the sacred mountain. Now after several journeys to the land of my ancestors, I would take all that I had learned there to help and bless others.

## Cosme's Trip to the North Pole

I was always curious about the North Pole. I had an idea of bringing some crystals up there, as I thought it would help anchor spiritual energy. Back in the eighties one time I was talking to a healer named Maestro Pauli from Mexico. He was a "curendero" and a gifted psychic surgeon. I told him about my idea of taking the crystals to the North Pole. He said, "You'll melt the snow and ice too fast, if you do that. It would act like a laser." He thought that taking rubies to the South and North Pole would be the correct stones to anchor the spiritual energy in those places. So that was one of my plans. I also felt that I should bring back some male and female rocks from the North Pole to live here on my property in Nevada City, California.

As it turned out, it was not too much longer before I was actually invited to go to the North Pole, by a psychiatrist who had a private plane. My doctor friend had gone up there the year before, and he thought I would really enjoy it. So we went on a propeller plane from San Francisco to Washington State. There was a lot of turbulence and we were praying. There was a husband and wife who were both sick. I was praying, "Please help us, God!" The Holy Spirit touched me on the shoulder and comforted me silently with the message that everything was going to be okay.

We continued our trip, landing in Canada and then on to Yellow Knife in the Yukon. Here in the Northwest Territory everyone just relaxed and went fishing. Everything was so expensive up there. A small dinner salad was $12.00 and in three days I was broke.

We hired a water plane and it dropped us off at a lake. From the air the lakes just looked like a bunch of rain puddles beneath us. Later I found out that they were all connected by waterfalls. The plan was for the pilot to pick us up five days later at another lake. We had three aluminum boats with motors that we used on the lakes. We ate canned goods that we packed in as well as the fresh fish that we caught.

The mosquitoes up there were huge and they were everywhere. Their main desire was to bite us! I used a product called Basic H which usually works to repel mosquitoes. But up there it didn't work. In fact nothing worked! I had a hat with a mosquito net and they bit right through that. We were all afraid to use the bathroom, as exposing our butts would be a sure invitation to lots of mosquito bites. It was really a problem. I slept in my snowsuit overnight in my tent, so they didn't eat me up. When the wind would blow, the mosquitoes would disappear for a short time. That was your big chance to run outside and quickly use the bathroom (which was the bathroom of the great outdoors). We also learned that they followed our fishing boats out onto the lake for awhile, but at some point they would go back and we had some relief.

So at the North Pole it was the same thing with the mosquitoes. They were out at night too. We found ourselves getting constipated because getting unzipped to go to the bathroom invited a big swarm. If we could unzip and go in thirty seconds, we would barely survive the swarm of mosquitoes. I didn't expect this kind of challenge. Other than this the whole experience of this trip was just wonderful! There were five of us that went together and then two more from the East coast joined us, making a group of seven. My friend Peter took his father up there. We saw bears, and we saw the biggest rabbits that you could ever imagine. They were the size of sheep! We saw moose in the water.

When we were flying up in the air, in the plane, we saw the strangest sight looking down. We saw such beautiful round rainbows! This, too, was a sight I had never seen before. We finally approached the town of Resolute, which was the little village at the Magnetic North Pole. The way we could recognize it was that the motel was painted a bright red. As we flew over the Magnetic North Pole, we felt such a very, very powerful vibration. It was actually a feeling that made us feel that we were up in heaven!

After we landed in Resolute, we got two motel rooms for the seven of us to share. Everyone went to bed early because they were all tired. I wasn't tired, so I stayed up and just enjoyed the peace and quiet.

All of a sudden I was amazed to see an Indian man standing in front of me. He came to me from the spirit world! I saw him manifested just like a real person, but only from the waist up. He began to talk to me and had a very important message that he wanted me to carry back to the world. He had waited a long time to find someone who could be able to see and hear him so that his message would be shared with the world.

He started by saying that his Native North Pole was being terribly polluted. He said actually the whole world was being polluted, but his native area was the North Pole. He said that it was an area that people would think of as remote and clean, but that it was no longer true. He said that industrial pollution migrated there from other places, but that surprisingly enough it was negative things like anger, war, and hatred that really polluted the energy and the atmosphere of the place. He said that it affected humans, animals and plant life. It was important for humans to stop thinking only about their own desires. Everyone needed to start thinking about family, community, the whole Earth, and all the life on it: humans, animals and plants, as well as the air, the water and the Earth herself. He emphasized that all the beings and all the elements are connected to each other. For one to be healthy, all had to be healthy. He also communicated telepathically with me about the true North Pole. He said it represented the top of the head, which I call the crown chakra. Apparently the true North Pole and the Magnetic North Pole used to coincide but now there is a shifting that is continuously moving the Magnetic North Pole. He said that the Magnetic North Pole now coincided with our forehead (third eye) instead of our crown chakra.

Then he said to me, "You need to tell the whole world that when spiritual people see things in the world, they have to look through the veil of all these pollutions and can't always see accurately, because of it. A spiritual person needs to correct their alignment by shifting their inner Magnetic North Pole to the True North Pole. This basically means to shift it from the forehead to the crown chakra. This would help them to see clearly and accurately. The way to do this is simply to make the intention, and that is how it is done. Back in the eighties the Magnetic North Pole was moving towards Russia. As it approached Russia, the effect that it would have would be to amplify the energy that was already there, both on top of the ground and under the ground. After he delivered this message with complete seriousness, he faded away. He gave me a lot to think about that night.

For good or for bad Russia changed about this time in the eighties by opening itself up to the world. The way I understand this movement of the Magnetic North Pole is that the focal point of it goes over a certain country, but that there is a triangulation of energy that radiates out from it, much like the rays of light fanning out from a flashlight. Where the bottom part of the energy pattern of the "fan of light" goes over different countries, there can be an amplification of energy in those locations too. This can turn out either for good or for bad. Now the top part of the Magnetic North Pole is heading for China, and the bottom part of the fan has gone over India and Pakistan and Iraq and the Middle East. We all know what kind of things have been going on in the Middle East recently. When this triangle of energy goes over a particular location, you can be sure that the energy, that already exists there, will be amplified. It can act as a catalyst for some kind of drama or big change! As the Magnetic North Pole is moving towards China, I wonder what will be catalyzed there.

# 22

# Sacred Journey to Brazil

*Sacred Journey to Brazil*

My wife, Cherylann, and I have been on frequent pilgrimages to Brazil to see the great healer at the Casa de Dom Inacio, John of God. He is a very special man who has many of God's saints, angels and spiritual surgeons work through him from the heavens. In his regular life he works as a ranch owner and an emerald mine. This is how he makes a living. He does not make his living from the healing work. He is a very nice and quiet man. People from all over the world come to this little village of Abadiania in Brazil where he has the Casa for healing. Poor people from Brazil and other close-by countries come there on the bus to find miraculous healings. The Casa always has a large kettle of soup for anyone who needs nourishment, which is blessed by the entities.

Many of the poor who make the pilgrimage do not have any food or any money. The Casa has a group of volunteers who help make the soup and help orient the people to this sacred place. For people coming for the first time it is helpful to have a guide and a group that helps and supports one another. Cherylann and I are now organizing and taking groups to the Casa of John of God and the sacred entities.

People stand in a long line to go up before John of God, to be seen by the "entities," as they call them. Often we think of entities as bad spirits, but in this case the meaning of entity is the saints and angelic spirits and spirit doctors that work through him. When he has the entities in him, he is not really John of God, but a host of ever-changing, highly spiritual helpers. He is the mouthpiece and the instrument that they can work through. He has been doing this work three days a week for quite a long time now. There is a kind of physical, psychic or spiritual surgery that is performed on some individuals. Others will receive what they call "invisible surgery," when they are sleeping or relaxing in their rooms. Either type of surgery has a great impact on the body and people are encouraged not to go out dancing or dining after either kind of surgery, but to rest quietly in their rooms for at least two days. The body needs recovery and integration time from these surgeries, just as people who have hospital surgery.

There have been lines and lines of people with wheelchairs and crutches and people on stretchers too. It reminds a person of the days of Jesus when the multitudes would come from all directions to be healed. Many miracles have occurred for people here. There are crutches and wheelchairs that have been left behind when people are healed. At the very least people go home feeling a spiritual upliftment, new inspiration or a feeling of such deep blessing and heart-opening that their lives change forever.

When I went through the line and went before the entity, as they call it, John of God stopped me and asked who I was. Usually each person just stops in front of him briefly, and then people are told what they need: physical surgery, invisible surgery, or perhaps several sessions in the crystal light bed or trips to the waterfall. In my case I was stopped and questioned. I shared that I was a healer, and I was asked to sit down next to him in a chair. Then for six to eight hours a day my job was to sit there with my eyes closed in meditation and prayer. The first day I had a sore butt, as I am not used to sitting still on a wooden chair all day. I felt more comfortable after that by doing a Hawai'ian hula movement with my rear end. The second day I started having the experience of sitting there but also, at the same time, moving around in my spiritual body doing healings on people. At times John of God called me up to watch him perform the physical surgeries. They were amazing, as the scars would heal up in no time, and there was usually no scar at all ... or perhaps just a faint red line. When I was asked to watch, of course, I had my eyes open. At one point he grabbed my hand in his and put my hands on the patient's body. His hands were holding mine. There was so much passion and divine love that I felt coming through my hands, and actually my whole being. At the same time it was very peaceful and very gentle. The temperature was neither hot nor cold but rather neutral. My head and body felt very, very light. I felt like I was filled with light. There was a feeling of great holiness. My right hand felt like the white light of the Holy Spirit was coming out of it. I could hear the sounds of wings, like the wings of angels.

Then I returned to my chair besides him and closed my eyes and meditated. I then started traveling—out of my body—to work on various people who were sitting on the benches in the casa. I felt like an entity, myself, moving around in spirit ... being guided totally by the Holy Spirit. I had my eyes closed, and suddenly I found myself, in spirit, working on a woman who had been on kidney dialysis. I found out about that later. In spirit I merged into her body and started cleaning out the kidneys with my hands. Two days later I got the feedback that she had been healed and her kidneys were healthy and normal again. I was very relaxed. As I said before, the more relaxed you are, the better spirit can work through you. Another thing that happened was finding myself going to someone I knew in the U.S. who had an inflamed spine and problem disc. I moved back and forth and loosened the area behind the heart and put my hands right into the spine. I found out later that the person's problem cleared up. Sometimes I could smell the spiritual smell of frankincense. To me, when I smell that spiritual smell, it means that there is a saint around, in spirit.

As I spent more days there, I got more and more filled with light. I really felt illuminated, big time. I was spending a lot of time meditating with my eyes closed and flying around doing invisible healings on people, just like the entities that visit people in their motel rooms, doing invisible healings. The energy felt like it was glowing and radiant, both in the atmosphere and inside of me. Everyone there felt the blessing of the holy atmosphere. People would have healings, emotional releases, deep understandings and realizations. With each visit to Brazil I have left feeling spiritually and physically stronger than the time before. Before leaving for home last time I had a personal interview with John of God. While we were alone, he gave me some very inspiring personal advice about my healing work and my future.

It was like being in heaven. There were other people in the current room too. The current room is a room full of people who already are spiritually open, meditating and helping to charge up the energy. The current room is like a large battery charger or generator. Sometimes there are close to sixty people in there. We also had to sit with our arms and legs uncrossed and in prayer, so that we didn't short-circuit the energy. This charged energy helped John of God and the entities to be able to do their healing work to the greatest potential. People were there from all different countries, and most of them were there to heal themselves.

This is a very busy place. There is one long line of people getting ready to go into surgery. There is another line of "first time" people who are going up before the entity to be viewed and get instructions about their treatment. Then there is another line of people that are going into the current room. Current room number two is the entity room. Current room number one is where the meditators are in prayer and meditation, charging up the energy. This is where Cherylann and I sat in prayer and meditation for two-and-a-half hours before John of God came in. There are also interpreters present who speak Portuguese, and they ask questions for the people who have come and interpret instructions for them from the entities. They also help show people where to go.

The inner current room held sixty people, but recently it was remodeled and it now holds over one hundred people. The operation room is next to it. John of God says prayers when he first arrives, and the entities come down and enter his body. They also circulate through the casa doing invisible surgeries for the people who are sitting in there for healing and invisible surgery. All this time the most beautiful and heavenly music is playing. Before John of God comes in, there is usually a sermon or inspirational spiritual talk given to uplift everyone. About twenty minutes later, people who are having invisible surgery leave to go to their motel rooms for twenty-four hours to rest. Spirit will work with them the whole time they're resting. Some people feel it and others don't. Some people see slight pink scars on their body when they wake up. The scars fade fast. They're not supposed to go out of their rooms, as they are still so open and vulnerable. Physical surgeries are only done in special cases and only on those who are between the ages of eighteen and fifty-two. There are very few exceptions to this rule. Nobody that has had radiation or chemotherapy gets physical surgery either.

Sometimes in the medium room bad spirits will come out of people. If they feel sick, they raise their hands and someone will come over to comfort and help them. Surgery can be done on an outdoor patio, on a covered stage, or in the surgery room. In the entity room John of God gives prescriptions of herbs. The entities infuse and potentize the herbs (which are in capsules) with a unique healing energy that is just for that individual. John of God is not doing any of this healing himself, as he is just the vehicle or medium for the holy entities.

Medical doctors are usually invited to watch the spiritual surgeries. There is no anesthesia, and most people don't feel anything. Some people feel a tiny bit of pain or pressure. After physical surgery people go into a recovery room, where there are special people to help them. Some people feel a little sick afterwards or feel a little pain, and these helpers assist their recovery, mainly with prayers and holy water. There are often two to three thousand people a day that come through the casa. The healings that happen here are amazing and inspiring! It is truly miraculous!

Healing is done Wednesday, Thursday and Friday. On Saturday and Sunday John of God often travels to see poor people in Brazil. He has at least three different centers. He never charges any money and sleeps one-and-a-half hours a night. This natural power spot sits on top of an earth full of emeralds and crystals. There is a waterfall nearby. At times people are told to go and bathe and purify in the waterfall. There is also a color therapy treatment that was channeled by the entities which is called a crystal light bed, or crystal light bath. There is a table that you recline on, and above you are crystals with the colors of the rainbow to balance each chakra. There is a frequency that comes out … and music, light and healing energy. The entities work through these natural crystals. The people are often told to have one or more of these treatments before they have their surgery. It is cleansing, healing and balancing.

My wife, Cherylann, was honored by the entities who gave her one of these instruments to take back to California, to our healing center, Cosara, for helping people. John of God's entities now come through our crystal light bed to bless and heal people. Cherylann had a vast background in both crystal healing and light therapy, as well as iridology and nutrition. She never mentioned it but, when she went before John of God, the entities must have seen these talents in her, because they wanted her to have a crystal light bed, and they wanted her to work with it. Now both of us put our healing clients in this bed or bath, and they feel fantastic from it. It is a great honor and blessing to be able to add this dimension of healing for the people who come to us for healing. There is a little bit of the holiness of Brazil that has come home with us.

When people leave Cosara, they have bright, happy faces. They have hope and direction for the future. Their health and their spirituality have been enhanced and they have tools to help them to take responsibility for themselves. They have learned that they are co-creators with God and most of them have received the mystical kiss of God.

# *Endorsements*

## 1. Endorsement from Christine Fischer

It has taken me a year to understand, integrate and only partially comprehend my healing encounter with Cosme. It was Holy Wednesday 2004 when I had the privilege of meeting this very humble yet humorous man. I arrived at his home on crutches with a seriously fractured ankle as well as a myriad of physical, emotional, and spiritual issues. He welcomed me warmheartedly into his beautiful California home and then proceeded to listen with an enormously open heart to the list of my travails. I had had cancer ... a stage four lymphoma, a bone marrow transplant, shingles, post-traumatic stress disorder, anxiety and depression. These were only the surface disorders, on top of more deeply hidden issues.

I was also suffering from post-traumatic stress disorder from being so close to the 9/11 tragedy ... which claimed the lives of some of my closest friends and colleagues. I had been a flight attendant for American Airlines for thirty years. The same terrorist faces that we saw in the newspapers shortly after 9/11 were already familiar to me, as these same terrorists were flying around on our planes in the weeks before 9/11. I had to serve them as a flight attendant, and I could feel their tangible hatred, directed at me, each time I passed them or served them on the plane. To make matters worse I reported their presence to the authorities before the 9/11 incident, but no one heeded my message. My intuitive instinct told me that these men were preparing to implement a sinister plan.

Cosme never flinched or seemed the least bit put off by the daunting array of difficulties I presented to him. I was inspired by his youthful appearance, his positive attitude and cheerful countenance. We spoke for some time. He was extraordinarily articulate about his work and anchored in his mission of healing here upon planet earth.

We then proceeded to his meditation garden and healing temple. What transpired there within the walls of his beautifully decorated yurt was beyond belief. I hesitate to share in detail this deeply spiritual and transformative experience except to say that through Cosme and the healing work that he did with me that I had a direct encounter with the Kiss of God.

One of the most difficult challenges of my healing was the post-traumatic stress disorder. I believe that the traumas of my childhood set the stage for the full-blown effect of this disorder that exploded during and after my bone marrow transplant. I did not become aware of how really serious it was until the tragic day of September 11, 2001.

In June of 2001, I miraculously was able to return to my job at American Airlines, after a five-year medical leave of absence, as a result of my stage four lymphoma. As soon as I stepped foot on the A.A. property at the Dulles International Airport in Washington DC, I knew that something was terribly amiss. For many years I lived on the threshold between life and death where the veil is the thinnest. I lost my Mother to ovarian cancer only two months after I was diagnosed with cancer. These experiences allowed my heightened perceptions to literally smell death in the air. As I went through security in both Dulles and Los Angeles, I became more and more uneasy. A frightening incident occurred on my plane just five days before September 11th, involving a knife and nine Middle Eastern men. This prompted me to report the incident and my intuitions of imminent danger to the chief of security in Los Angeles International Airport.

On the 10th of September I worked the 767 flight from L.A. to Dulles. I spent time in the cockpit with Captain Charles Burlingame, who had been a colleague and friend for many years. "Chick" and I had a touching conversation about the fragility, preciousness and fleeting nature of life. "All that matters is love" I told him emphatically, as I related my cancer revelation to him. He agreed and proceeded to list all the things that he loved in and about his life.

Captain Burlingame ... or "Chick" as he was lovingly called by his friends, was dead the next morning after his airplane careened and then crashed into the Pentagon.

My life, like everyone else's, was dramatically impacted by the event. My post traumatic stress disorder and post-transplant symptoms worsened until finally in January of 2004 I muttered to God, under my breath, "I need a break from this job." Two hours later I got that "break." I slipped and fell on black ice, which resulted in a badly fractured ankle. Since I had a bone marrow transplant, the fracture was not healing normally. Since this incident I have not returned to my job with the airline, as I have recognized that my flying days are over.

I know that Cosme's healing work was instrumental in accelerating the healing of my ankle, the post-traumatic stress disorder and the myriad of post-transplant symptoms. But more importantly the vision I had in Cosme's yurt has put me on the path to my true mission and purpose in life. I am eternally grateful to Cosme for this very deep healing and inspiration.

In the year that has passed since this experience, I realize that it has sustained me, healed me, brought peace into my soul, and restored what I thought was an absolute loss of hope. I am so grateful to Cosme for sharing the gift of his healing hands and his love with me. In the thirty years that I have navigated through the world of alternative healing, I can honestly say that nothing has stayed with me the way that this experience has. I feel truly blessed.

## 2. Comments from Mary and John

My boyfriend John started using cocaine in the eighties, as so many young people did. Fast forward twenty years and his cocaine use had become a coping mechanism. He was an addict. By the time we met Cosme, he was paranoid, agitated, depressed and very unhealthy. I found myself living for him, instead of with him.

I'd heard of Cosme from my boyfriend's younger brother and Mom. I confided to him that his big brother was in real trouble, and I couldn't handle the situation any more. I asked him to call their Mom for help. Over the course of two weeks everything was set in motion. I told John about Cosme, but he didn't want to listen. He flat out refused the help once again. I packed a bag and told John that I was leaving. I was shocked to hear what his Mom said next. She told me to go to Cosme's anyway, to get away from John, and get some healing done for myself. I couldn't believe my ears and jumped at the chance. I called John to tell him that I was going to Cosme's without him. The next thing I knew he was changing his mind and decided to go with me. So we were off from Hollywood, California to the mountains of the Sierra Nevada. I didn't know who we were about to meet. I had a preconceived notion that we were about to meet a mysterious man sitting in a yoga position, with a turban on his head, sitting high atop a mountain. I imagined an unapproachable man who would stare at us and then tell us we must find our own way. At the very least I expected to be judged harshly for who we were and for living and working in Hollywood.

Instead, we pulled into a driveway, parked our car, and walked past a most beautifully landscaped garden. We made our way into the living room of a quaint house. Immediately, I felt something that felt so familiar and comforting. I looked around and saw a giant fish tank with a colorful sticker of HAWAII on it. I looked over at my boyfriend and said, "Oh, my gosh, I think this guy is Hawai'ian!" Hawai'i was one of my favorite places! I have at least a dozen Hawai'ian friends.

Before I could speak further, there he was, standing before us ... a complexion of dark caramel, bright yellow shirt, running shorts and a smile that glowed so much the room felt brighter. "Hi, I'm Cosme," he said. We made our introductions, sat on his normal couch, in his normal house and talked. I felt lighter and lighter as we talked. In part I was relieved. Here was this loving environment and I sensed help. Finally I could throw my hands up, give it all up to the universe, and let the mysterious man deal with John. I was exhausted and done being the co-dependent girlfriend. After all, before we met Cosme, the closest we'd been to alternative healing was reading our horoscopes in the Sunday paper.

Cosme was honest. He told us that it would be a miracle if John could survive without his cocaine. I believe Cosme's opinion was that John had less than a ten percent chance of getting over his addiction. Here was this forty-something-year-old man with a twenty-year addiction to a very powerful drug. John had rejected the twelve step program and refused to seek treatment. Three years earlier I had met and fell in love with this man, in spite of his addiction.

We spent the next several hours watching each other as Cosme did readings on us. He looked at us like we were transparent! He gave us a "low down" on our bodies, chakras, state of mind and male/female imbalances. Next we walked through his property to a giant yurt. This is where the real journey began. I was excited but a bit freaked out wondering what was next. We walked into the yurt, and I found myself staring at the walls. There were paintings of angels and bright vivid colors. There was a picture of Jesus right there on the wall and a bible sitting open on the massage table. At this point I was so confused. What in the world is this healer doing with all this religious stuff? Not knowing what to make of any of it, I just watched and listened. John was lying on the massage table. Cosme opened the bible and read a passage, almost like he was praying. After a few minutes I realized who Cosme was. I felt so comforted that I wanted to cry in relief. I grew up pretty agnostic but always respected and envied anyone with an organized faith. I also was warned time and time again of "wanna be" self-helpers who spent their lives giving lectures and peddling books on how to live a better life. I was warned of cults and met many hippies in college who believed that "love is all you need to survive."

Here was a man who has a solid faith in Christianity, yet he was a healer giving a massage, set to music, all the while explaining the chakras. Could it be true ... a man with a solid religious foundation, who also embraced the universe and all of its mysteries? In my opinion I had just found the best of all worlds ... the comfort of knowing that Cosme, himself, answered to God, believed in Jesus, yet incorporated alternative healing techniques, perhaps with powers bestowed on him from God.

I watched in awe, over the next two days, as Cosme massaged us, sent us to the crystal light bed, and lectured John and I about how the years of cocaine abuse had crystallized in John's brain. Cosme was using massage and high-frequency healing energy to break it up and get it out of John's system, so that the healing could take place. When Cosme massaged me, I started crying. Tears flowed for almost the entire two hours of the massage. I realize now that he was releasing years of pain and guilt built up inside of me. He saw the six-inch scar on my belly, and I told him that I had my gallbladder removed when I was only seventeen. He looked again and asked me what was going on in my life when the surgery occurred. At first I was confused, but then it hit me. It was like, "Oh my gosh, my mother had just admitted to being an alcoholic." My parents had also just let the family know that they had to sell the house I grew up in, because of money issues. I was devastated that summer and before long I was rushed to the hospital for emergency surgery. Cosme told me that the surgery was emotional and he was right! Never in my wildest dreams did I think I would get an explanation as to why I needed my gallbladder out. My cholesterol was low and I was only seventeen. It all made sense now! Cosme spent the next thirty minutes pushing and prodding at my stomach. He let me know that there was still a hole where the gallbladder once was and that he needed to move things around, that were frozen in place from the shock of the surgery. My insides still had not recovered. When he was finished, I stood up, looked at my stomach and saw that it had changed. My belly had shrunk by at least one inch. I had my gallbladder out some fifteen years earlier, suffered IBS, and after this massage it was gone. Two years later there is still no sign of discomfort or pain in my belly. I've never felt better!

We spent two nights with Cosme at his home. We laughed, cried and even went into town together for meals, like old friends. John and I went home and two months later our world came crashing down on us. John was unable to give up his habit and this time he became very agitated and paranoid. I knew what I had to do. I asked him to leave and never come back. I never felt so alone in my life. I didn't know if John would drive off a cliff or drive to Cosme's. I only knew that I needed to let him go. So I did. John made a beeline to Cosme. He broke down and stayed with Cosme. I hear that Cosme had a man to man talk with John. Then Cosme enrolled John in his beginning workshop and they got to work.

The entire process was about John. Cosme made it clear to him that John had to be a man, grow up and stop using the "candy." Cosme empowered him with his own sense of power.

To this day John opens his third eye, asks the universe for guidance, and asks for what he wants out of life, anytime he has an important meeting or is feeling down. He gets it every time. He's been off the "candy" for over two years now! Cosme recently came to Malibu to marry us. Now John has the career that he's always wanted. We have the foundation, trust, understanding and self-awareness that will allow us to grow old together. We have been back to Cosme's home several times since we first met. We've gone for tune-ups, workshops, and just to visit our new friend, for life.

Cosme did not "save" anyone, but he did help John to save himself. Cosme helped John to get over a twenty-year addiction to a very powerful and readily available drug. John and I work in Hollywood and "anything goes" in Hollywood! Now we have the energy, self-awareness and power to realize that even in Hollywood, with all its party atmosphere, and "go, go, go at any cost," we have the ability to live our own lives in our own way. We are blessed to have Cosme in our lives! Hollywood needs and deserves to have Cosme, and it is my dream to let the world know about this wonderful man.

Mary and John (names changed)
Los Angeles, California

### 3. March 1996 Personal Insights / Ava Goldman

When I first saw the rainbow-colored flier announcing and introducing Cosme Castanieto's healing work, I was skeptical. What exactly could this cherubic-looking man do for me? I knew Filipino healers were world-renowned, but how was this "spiritual tune-up" accomplished, and what could Cosme offer that I hadn't already experienced at the hands of other counselors and healers?

From the first moment I saw Cosme, my doubts were relieved. Here was a little "teddy bear" whose presence was gentle and calming, whose wisdom was both frank and disarming as it resonated with my own intuitive self-awareness, and whose willingness to serve others and joyful sense of humor was a delight to behold. His healing work empowered him physically and spiritually, as opposed to draining him.

He talked to me and got to know me, before proceeding to the actual healing. On the massage table, he was able to "see" and report energy imbalances, to analyze specific health problems, and to give me specific remedies to correct everything that was "out of alignment," in all realms. He "read" my hands, my feet, and my body with prophetic insight and accuracy.

THEN, and only then, did we proceed to removing the physical and mental blocks to healing. Cosme performed a unique massage, done so that my body was actually "dancing" to the music played, as he worked on me. I felt energized, relaxed and invigorated at the end of this experience, which I estimate lasted at least an hour and a half.

I now feel more focused and encouraged to achieve the goals which I have set for myself, in many areas. I feel confident I have the keys to pursuing and maintaining glowing, radiant health and to resolving the conflicts which have plagued me in the past. I believe an encounter with Cosme will truly be profound and life-changing, where you will feel the truth of God's love for us human beings.

My experience has been echoed by others following me, who include a clairvoyant, a teacher of Tai Chi and a rancher. Cosme was able to explain to the "medium" a block she had had since 1978! The rancher said it was the first time he had experienced God's love in many years, and that his seriously ill wife was much improved after Cosme worked on her. He said he would pay Cosme every week if he would continue working on her. Such accolades are typical for this unique and unconventional healer.

I am immensely grateful for the awareness Cosme has brought to me and into my life. I would urge anyone to raise their joy, their health and their Being a quantum leap forward, by bringing Cosme's healing into their lives. If you are so inclined, I believe the basic healing class would attune one to a high mental, emotional and spiritual level.

Words can never do justice to an indescribably powerful experience. I can promise that your life will be deeply and positively charged and changed, by even one session with Cosme. I saw into my past, present and future with clarity. Cosme gave me the tools to direct my life with less pain, more bliss and increased awareness of my potential and purposes in life. I believe continued time with Cosme will radically increase healing and joy in your life, as it has mine.

At one point, I could sense energy flowing from his hand to mine as a strong, continual golden light spreading its essence up my arm and into my head and upper torso. All the twisted and torqued areas in my body and soul began to be straightened and cleared, through Cosme's presence. Thank you so much, Cosme! I am so thrilled to have brought you into my life. We are blessed to have you with us. You encourage and strengthen those of us fortunate enough to know you, even a little.

## 4. Personal Insights / Toni Lynd

I had never been to a healer; in fact, it sort of scared me. I did not know if it would be some voodoo thing or what. Some of my fears were gone though when I saw your picture on the rainbow flyer. Since both my husband and I were in pain, I decided to send him first. If you helped John, then I would go too. I did not tell John anything other than I really thought it would help him. When he came home, he looked wonderful. There was a bounce to his step, a smile on his face, and he really felt so much better. He claimed he was ten years younger.

I asked him to explain all that happened and what you had done and he tried to explain, but the best he could do was say it was a cross between body alignment, massage and just cradling him. "Wow, I am going," I said. It was as if I had a talking mirror of my life and my pain. Your beauty in the simplicity of your words and the true love and caring in your face and hands, put me at ease and in a safe place where you could do your work.

Thank you. I feel better than I have for years, physically, and I am filled with resolution, confidence, and I am so close to my spiritual self again, at last. I know I am the person I am supposed to be. I will gladly share any and all of this with anyone who is thinking of seeing you. They couldn't be in better hands. Thank you! You have a wonderful gift and I'm so glad you shared it with me.

### 5. *Personal Insights / Jane Steinberg*

I first learned of Cosme through a friend, who recommended him to me for my younger daughter who has suffered from acute asthma since birth. Nicole's first healing from Cosme brought excellent results, and an ensuing healing thirty days later cured her completely. As to this date, approximately one year later, Nicole has had freedom from asthma for the first time in her life.

I find Cosme to be an endearing and wonderfully spiritual man with whom I felt instant respect, love and rapport.

I have brought my seventy-six year old mother-in-law to him for healing. My own mother, who was suffering from hip pain, had her pain virtually taken away. Of course, I myself, have come to enjoy and reap the benefits of his wonderful touch and uplifting words and humor.

Cosme is a wonderful man, and I feel honored to know him and share his time and knowledge whenever I can.

### 6. *Testimonial / Theresa Ciafardoni, No. San Juan, CA*

I really can't remember how I first heard of Cosme. Somehow I heard that there was a man in Nevada City who did a special kind of healing and holistic health work. He worked out of a small house in downtown Nevada City, at that time. I was interested in seeing him because I wanted to have a baby and I was having difficulty getting pregnant. I had already seen a few traditional Obstetricians. Each of them had advised me that my chances of conceiving a child were very minimal, because as a teenager I had a serious pelvic infection, and I also had a tipped uterus. It had been recommended to me that I have my left fallopian tube surgically removed. This tube was scarred and blocked, and my current doctor was concerned that I had a significant chance of a tubal pregnancy. So I began looking for an alternative answer to my dilemma.

I was twenty years old when I came to see Cosme. My general health condition was fairly positive. I was young. I took good care of myself. I felt responsible for my own health. I definitely had a serious health issue to overcome. Still, I think my belief that I am responsible for my body was very helpful.

When I met Cosme, the first thing I noticed was his incredibly joyful nature. He is a man able to deal with the most serious issues and problems that we face in life, and still maintains a sense of playfulness. This is not to say that he doesn't take his work seriously, as he does. But as he works, he maintains a sense of wonder and gratitude for the world around him. He has a deep-seated belief in God and is assured by the fact that God's will is done. He rejoices in each moment, living life to its fullest. The sense of happiness that he exudes quickly overflows from his being to those who are around him. His presence is enlivening. My first response to his healing came in the form of hope and possibility.

After Cosme finished working on me, he said, "Okay, now you will be able to get pregnant. Everything will work out fine." I left there feeling calm and sure. My body felt a sense of total and complete balance. The world around me had not changed. My perception of it, had. Three months later I was pregnant with my first son. He is now eighteen years old. I also have a beautiful daughter who is fifteen years old. I don't know exactly how Cosme does what he does. I do know that he has a special gift, and I am grateful that he shared it with me and my family!

## 7. My Testimonial / Daniel Grimes, Student

Being a high school and now a college athlete, I have amassed many athletic injuries over the years. They have ranged from simple sore muscles, to more severe sprains and even major muscle pulls. Thankfully, I had Cosme to put my battered body back together again. Without Cosme, I surely would have missed many games and other athletic competitions.

One memorable visit with Cosme occurred when I was in my senior year of high school. There was a key track meet coming up and I had pulled a hamstring muscle. It was a bad injury and it looked like I probably would not be able to run. Out of desperation, I came over to see Cosme the morning of the meet. After nearly a week of constant pain and stiffness, he was able to loosen up the muscles in my leg enough for me to consider running in the meet. He also shared with me a way to send light energy from my heart to the finish line, so that my speed could actually increase, as I ran.

Later that evening, to the amazement of my teammates, my coach and myself, I ran two of my best times, one actually tying the high school record in the 100 meter! Our team placed first in both events. The fact that I had been able to run at all was surprising, but my new record was simply shocking to me.

There is absolutely no doubt in my mind that without Cosme's help and guidance I would not have been able to run that day. He worked nothing less than a miracle on me. I am very thankful to have him in my life, not only as a healer and teacher, but as a friend, as well.

### 8. My Experiences with Cosme / Nathan Schwartz

When I was first told of Cosme's work, I knew I was going to try to see him, with the hope that he could help me. At the time I was in an extremely low state of health, having been diagnosed with leukemia, some time before. This had progressed through several stages, including the need for medication, then chemotherapy, which had proven unsuccessful. It had gotten to the point where blood transfusions were needed every one to two weeks, due to an extremely low red blood cell count. In other words, the situation was extremely serious, and the options were closing down.

When I arrived at Cosme's studio, I had difficulty walking from the car to the house, due to weakness, lack of balance and shortness of breath. Cosme received me with a warm smile and hug and was also quietly observing the situation closely, as I walked in. He discussed his belief in the body's own healing powers, and while he was very frank and honest about what he found in the maladies of my body, he also gave me hope that he could help me. He starts every session with reading the body's condition. This is done using visual observation and what he finds and senses with his hands.

Cosme's physical massage on my body was like a joyful dance. It felt as if every muscle and organ was being re-activated. One of his goals was to remove blockages and restore flow and balance in the body. It gave me hope that my body still had energy which could be reclaimed. Some of the work is very active and strenuous, but he has the sense of how far he can go at a given time. I had also decided not to resist but to trust him to do what my body needed. I have been to see Cosme regularly and hope to continue doing so. The difference in my condition now is remarkable. The sessions with him make my body feel supple, more resilient and more alive. The energy and balance is restored. Most of all, I now have a sense of Hope.

On that first visit I also started working with Cosme's wife, Cherylann, who is a nutritionist and iridologist. She planned a program of nutritional supplements to rebuild my depleted body. Both Cosme and Cherylann gave me the hope that, in fact, they could help me. They gave me the sense of how important it is to improve the quality of each day of my life. Those first sessions were over six months ago now, and I have not had to have a transfusion since that time. My red blood cell count is normal now. While I continue to work with my medical doctors on the disease as well, I feel that Cosme's and Cherylann's work has been very much responsible for my present condition, which is so very much improved! In all the sessions Cosme has been working to unblock the internal organs affected by the disease, so they can gain energy flow and natural healing can continue to occur.

I am a concert pianist and had not been able to perform publicly for a year and a half. Frankly, I felt that it was something that I would never be able to do again. Recently I performed two concerts and am making plans for future performances. I am also able to do some teaching again. Naturally, the leukemia affects my energy levels at times, but I do have a life again. I know that it is very much due to the work and spirit of Cosme and Cherylann. It is an ongoing and living process, and most of all there is once again—Hope!

The spiritual element of Cosme's work has a real sense of life and light about it. There is a universal feeling there, which one can relate to, in a very human way.

*9. Michelle's Story / Michelle and Shane Shafer / March 15, 2005*

In June of 2004, my friend and therapist, Mandy, recommended that I seek the counsel of a "healer" named Cosme who was from Hawai'i and who worked in marvelous and gifted ways, to bring about strong healings in the body, mind and soul. I was instantly attracted to the idea of meeting this person named Cosme, but I also felt some concern about my husband, Shane, who is the ultimate skeptic and tends to harshly criticize people who claim to have supernatural gifts. So, I decided to make the appointment confidentially and go from there.

About a month later, I received a call from Mandy, and she said that Cosme would be in our area and I would be able to have a session with him. I was elated and nervous simultaneously, but I thought that I would just allow divine providence to manage my decision and go for it. I was hoping for some direction in my life, in caring for myself and getting an evaluation on my body and how to better care for it and prepare for the next few decades.

When I first met Cosme, I was instantly drawn to his gentle and open demeanor. He is a very compact individual, well built, strong, very happy, calm and deeply spiritual. I was immediately in tune with this amazing person, much to my delight! It was as if we had been friends for many years and suddenly came upon one another for a visit. I felt very energized in his presence and just wanted to ask a thousand questions at once!

Anyway, he told me a little about myself and he then proceeded to do a full body "scan" which gave him the insight to my physical, mental and spiritual needs, which he sees clearly and works on balancing. During the evaluation he spoke to me about what he was seeing and how he could correct the problem. I felt relieved and totally at peace at all times. There's a sweet essence when Cosme is taking care of you. It's like being totally in the moment and anticipating something wonderful. And it was, as I was getting healed. This experience has launched me on a journey that I am taking with Cosme to this day. Cosme is like a master gardener and you are the garden. He evaluates you and then cultivates and plants special items in your life for you to harvest. Essentially, he helps you garden your life.

After our session, I was totally convinced that this person was the real McCoy and I wanted to have my husband see him. He has been suffering for years with a bad back and his disposition was being affected by the constant pain. I was hoping that Cosme could correct this problem which consequently would relieve me of his harsh attitude.

When I walked out to my car with Cosme, I asked him about how I could see him again, and I told him that I greatly benefited from my session and I wanted more time, more knowledge and more help. He said that he was offering a workshop at his Sanctuary and that I could come for the weekend course. I asked him if he could do a session with Shane. I felt that it would be critical to do it before the workshop because I thought that Shane would be totally negative unless he was able to experience what I had experienced. Cosme agreed to see him, and I headed home to negotiate this idea with my husband. Now, keep in mind that Shane is a farmer from Cody, Wyoming. These people are hard-working, salt-of-the-earth types, who are usually standoffish until you prove yourself. He particularly does not care to associate with liberals, tree huggers and hippies, let alone someone who is a "healer." So what I was facing was hugely difficult and not at all a pleasant task.

I said a huge prayer and asked for guidance and jumped into the idea of a weekend in Nevada City at this place with a bunch of people who came together to learn about the healing arts etc. Shane was absolutely shocked! To think that we would spend our time together doing something so outlandish, especially with a bunch of strangers who didn't even fish. I was on pins during this, and then suddenly he shifted his thoughts and said, "Okay, I'll do this for you, but I'm not going to like it." Oh my gosh, I was stunned and I immediately booked our workshop.

We went early to see Cosme because of his promise to work on Shane before the workshop. When Shane met Cosme, I could tell that he was not impressed. My husband is six foot four inches tall and weighs in the range of 280-300 pounds. Cosme is the opposite. Shane was shaking his head wondering what this half-sized man could do for him. I told Shane not to assume anything because Cosme has great strength and powers. I asked him to just let Cosme proceed and, if he didn't like what Cosme told him or did for him, that we would leave immediately. Well, needless to say, Shane was mush in Cosme's hands. He did a very informative evaluation which Shane agreed was completely accurate, which established a sense of respect and confidence for the rest of the session. After a couple of hours, Shane was in such a state of comfort, and his pain was so relieved, that he was like a little puppy with Cosme. He couldn't believe that he felt so good and he agreed that the trip was well worth our time. It was wonderful to see this transformation, especially with a man that is such a guy's guy and didn't want any "other man" touching him. What a riot!

Anyway, Shane spent the next two days completely in a state of sleep. He would wake up periodically and then slip immediately into a deeper sleep. At first I was very disturbed and thought that something terrible was happening to Shane. When I went back to Cosme at the workshop, he just nodded his head very calmly and said that he needed the sleep and that he was going through a deep purification. He said that everything would be all right and just be happy and stay at the workshop and learn for both of us. That is exactly what I did. On the last day of the workshop, Shane was able to join us for the afternoon session and he was elated with his experience. We now see Cosme often for "tune-ups" and my husband is a staunch advocate of his work and ability. We welcome anyone who would like to email us for more information on our experiences with Cosme and his beautiful wife Cherylann, who is also a gifted scientist. We can be reached at BaseCampReno@ msm.com anytime.

I need to close this little story with thanks to Cosme for his kindness, generosity, friendship, healing, wisdom and peace that he has bestowed upon us. We thank you, a thousand lifetimes... Shalom

## 10. BettyKay Basso

I first met Cosme Castanieto while living in Chico, CA. He was introduced to me by mutual friends who held him in high regard.

In the summer of 1982 I was diagnosed with a large (grapefruit-sized) ovarian cyst. My doctor confirmed this with a sonogram and called me at my work to request exploratory surgery. He told me to check into the local hospital some time that afternoon. My shock and hesitation to have my female reproductive parts "explored" led me to investigate alternative action to surgery. I recalled that Cosme had a reputation for facilitating an individual's own healing potential. This spiritual healing was performed out of love and respect for a person's ability to learn the lessons associated with illness and disease and take an active part in the healing process. I called Cosme immediately and made an appointment to see him.

To make a long story short, with a combination of Cosme's healing work, fasting and prayer, my cyst shrank dramatically. After seven days I called my doctor (who had been worried about my condition) and requested another sonogram. I told him I thought the cyst was gone, but if medical evidence showed otherwise, I would go ahead with the exploratory surgery. The sonogram showed the cyst had literally disappeared. The doctor was amazed and I was convinced that I could take part in my health and healing in a more active manner.

Shortly after this event, I moved to Nevada City and over the years have maintained a friendship with Cosme. I have attended classes that addressed healing and spiritual work, and have had the privilege of being worked with for various conditions. Cosme's healings always leave me feeling more in tune with myself. I feel clearer and stronger physically, mentally, emotionally and spiritually. I believe that, due to Cosme's work with me, I have avoided serious disease and illness.

I count Cosme as one of my dearest friends. He is like a part of my family. His caring and deep commitment to be of service, and facilitate the highest good in each individual who seeks help, is inspiring. And, he does this without judgment or criticism. Many times I have asked for help with problems or issues that he has addressed before. Never do I feel that I am less of a person, or deficient in any way. Cosme's love and non-judgmental attitude allow me to do my best. With his help I continue to quest to keep my body/mind/spirit in good health and in total acceptance.

I feel immensely blessed to know Cosme is a part of my life.

# About the Author

**Cosme Castanieto** was born in Hawai'i of Filipino descent and comes from a family line of spiritual healers. He had extensive training with, and was initiated by, Filipino healers. For more than forty years Cosme has traveled widely, doing extensive healing work and teaching throughout the United States. He is deemed a "Son of the Casa" with the healer John of God in Brazil.

He was ordained after study at Anchor College of Truth in San Bernadino, California and is co-founder and director of Universal Cosara Temples. The purpose of this church is to promote education, well-being, and spiritual development of the individual in relationship to the family, community, and the earth. Cosme is a certified massage therapist and was trained by, and is a member of, the Institute of Integral Health.

Cosme and his wife, Cherylann, live at Cosara, their healing retreat center in Nevada City, which is located in the beautiful Sierra foothills of northern California. Cosme teaches basic, intermediate, and advanced healing classes, does spiritual body attunements, acts as a guide for the "spiritual process," and is also, in his "spare time," a professional photographer.

Cosme works on the physical body with spiritual energies that come through his hands and senses. He scans the whole body, identifies the imbalances and blockages, and looks at how the energy flows through the person. Using a combination of music, massage, and body alignment, Cosme is able to bring a person back into balance. He creates an even flow of energy which begins to circulate in a person's energy field to accelerate the healing process.

The results of this process can be seen on all levels. One's mind becomes more clear and focused. On the emotional level Cosme is able to tap into and remove old patterns, replacing them with a feeling of renewal and peace. An attunement to a higher vibration creates the opportunity to move towards one's highest spiritual potential. On a physical level, profound healing can occur.

Cherylann, Cosme's wife, is a gifted healer and intuitive in her own right. She studied closely with Dr. Bernard Jensen for many years and works with color and crystal therapy, and is a professional nutritionist. She complements Cosme's work with nutritional counseling, iridology, hypnotherapy, and sessions with the "crystal light bed" which was sent home with her by John of God to use in her healing practice.

Cosme's work opens the doorway for experiencing the ecstasy of God's love. This process can be compared to a spiritual infusion, a god-like energy that flows through the spiritual body, enlivening the entire being. As a gifted healer, Cosme has the ability to bring in a higher light and vibration that can change the course of a person's life.

To invite Cosme to teach and do healings in your area, or for further information about Cosme's and Cherylann's healing work, Cosme's teaching and travel schedule, and trips to Brazil to the Casa of John of God —please write, call, or visit their web site.

Cosme Castanieto
17490 Lazy Dog Road
Nevada City, CA 95959 USA
Phone: 530 265-5486
Fax: 530 470-0529
Website: www.cosaracosme.com

## To order more books

Contact Cosme Castanieto as above or
Email: mysticalkissofgod@hotmail.com

Made in the USA
Middletown, DE
09 December 2023

45109987R00169